CULTS

AND

THE

OCCULT

CULTS
AND
THE
OCCULT

FOURTH EDITION

EDMOND C. GRUSS

P&R
PUBLISHING
P.O. BOX 817 • PHILLIPSBURG • NEW JERSEY 08865-0817

Page design by Tobias Design
Typesetting by Michelle Feaster

Printed in the United States of America

Library of Congress Cataloging-in-Publication Data

Gruss, Edmond C.
    Cults and the occult / Edmond C. Gruss.—4th ed., rev. and expanded.
        p. cm.
    Includes bibliographical references.
    ISBN-10: 0-87552-001-4 (pbk.)
    ISBN-13: 978-0-87552-001-8 (pbk.)
    1. Christian sects. 2. Cults. 3. Occultism. 4. Parapsychology. I. Title.

BR157 .G74 2002
239'.9—dc21

                                2001052310

CONTENTS

1

AN INTRODUCTION TO CULTS

Well-known pastor and author Charles R. Swindoll tells the true story of a friend who went to an elegant student reception at a doctor's home. The hostess, who had just finished a gourmet cooking course, had decided to test her newly acquired skills. She prepared hors d'oeuvres that, unknown to her guests, featured dog food on crackers, decorated with a wedge of cheese, bacon bits, an olive, and a slice of pimento, served on silver trays. Swindoll's friend viewed the attractive morsels, sampled them, thought they were delicious, and went back a number of times for more. A short time later, he was told what he was eating. "He certainly must have gagged a little," Swindoll remarks. And then he comments:

> I've thought about how perfectly it illustrates something that transpires *daily* in another realm. I'm referring to religious fakes . . . professional charlatans . . . frauds . . . counterfeit Christians who market their wares on shiny platters decorated with tasty persuasion and impressive appearance. Being masters of deceit, they serve up delectable dishes camouflaged by logical sounding phrases.

As Swindoll notes, counterfeits do not advertise what they are really doing, and people by the millions are deceived. "Deception comes in *convincing* fashion, wearing the garb of authenticity, supported by the credentials of intelligence, popularity, and even a touch of class."

The apostle Paul warns us, "For such are false apostles, deceitful workers, transforming themselves into the apostles of Christ. And no wonder! For Satan himself transforms himself into an angel of light. Therefore it is no great thing if his ministers also transform themselves into ministers of righteousness" (2 Cor. 11:13–15).

What is offered on the silver platters looks delicious, being served up by "apostles of Christ . . . an angel of light . . . ministers of right-eousness." There is also great variety for every taste: you can live forever in an earthly paradise; you are a god in embryo; you will reincarnate; there is no sin, sickness, or death; health and prosperity can be yours; the Lord of the second advent is here; we have a living prophet; there is no future judgment or punishment; you are God— and the promises and claims go on. Swindoll observes that they might "have a 'new' look—feel and taste like the real thing—but they are not. . . . 'Old error in new dress is ever error nonetheless.' Which is another way of saying, 'dog food is dog food, no matter how you decorate it.'" Or, in the words of Paul, "For such are false . . . deceitful . . . transforming themselves into the apostles of Christ." Swindoll concludes with a serious reminder:

> Unfortunately, as long as there are hands to pick from the platter, there will be good-looking, sweet-smelling tidbits available. But some day, some dreadful day, the final Judge will determine and declare truth from error. There will be a lot of gagging and choking . . . and it will no longer taste good. Nothing tastes good in hell.[1]

THE CHALLENGE

In the Epistle to the Galatians (1:6–9), the apostle Paul speaks of the propagation of "a different gospel"—a departure from the true gospel. The church directory in the typical metropolitan newspaper and the listings under "Churches" in the yellow pages of the phone book demonstrate the variety of religious ideas and movements in existence. An examination of the teachings of these groups reveals that a number of them proclaim "a different gospel." A growing number of American religions are commonly identified as cults or sects. While many of these had their beginnings in the nineteenth century, their greatest growth has taken place since 1900, and, in many cases, especially during the last two generations.

Commenting on the growth of the cults, Gordon Lewis writes, "At the dawn of the twentieth century the cults were indistinguishable as a tiny atom, but exploding like atomic bombs the cults have mushroomed upon the American religious horizon."[2] Also, with such organizations as the Jehovah's Witnesses, the Church of Jesus Christ of Latter-day Saints (Mormons), and the Unity School of Christianity numbering membership or a following in the millions, increasing contact between evangelical Christianity and the cults is inevitable. This alone makes an understanding of the history and theological tenets of these groups imperative for an effective Christian witness.

The Exposure of Error

Those who expose doctrinal error are often branded as being negative and as not displaying Christian love. But an examination of the New Testament and the statements of Jesus Christ reveals that the negative is often rightly expressed. In his Sermon on the Mount, for example, Jesus warned: "Beware of false prophets, who come to you in sheep's clothing, but inwardly they are ravenous wolves. You will know them by their fruits" (Matt. 7:15–16). It should be noted that the Christian does not judge whether one is or is not a false prophet. Rather, judgment is accomplished by what an individual does and teaches: "You will know them by their fruits."

In 1 John 4:1, believers are instructed to "test the spirits, whether they are of God; because many false prophets have gone out into the world." Peter warns against "false teachers . . . who . . . bring in destructive heresies, even denying the Lord who bought them" (2 Peter 2:1). In Galatians, Paul said of one who preached "a different gospel," "Let him be accursed" ("May he be damned!"—Phillips). And Jude 3–4 teaches four important truths:

1. There is only one faith—"the faith."
2. This faith is immutable—"once for all delivered."
3. Christians are to "contend earnestly" for that faith.
4. There are enemies of that faith.

Indicating the seriousness of the departure from "the faith," Paul writes: "Now the Spirit expressly says that in latter times some will depart from the faith, giving heed to deceiving spirits and doctrines of demons" (1 Tim. 4:1). That this passage is being fulfilled is evident as one observes the contemporary scene.

Many other references could be cited, but it is apparent that to expose error, to stand for the truths of the Bible, and to insist on a narrowness of doctrine is scriptural. The final authority as to what is doctrinal truth or error must be the Bible.

CULTISM DEFINED

To help understand what a cult is, it must be realized that although there are many religious movements in the world, there are just two religious systems. In one, salvation is viewed as a work of man or as man's cooperation with God. In the other—true Christianity—salvation is attributed to God alone, as that which has been accomplished by God for man (Eph. 2:8–9; 2 Tim. 1:9; Titus 3:5).

What is a cult? Walter R. Martin, who was one of the most productive evangelical writers on the subject of the cults, defined cultism as

*the adherence to major doctrines which are pointedly contra-
dictory to orthodox Christianity*, yet which claim the distinction of either tracing their origin to orthodox sources or of
being in essential harmony with those sources. Cultism, in
short, is *any major deviation from orthodox Christianity relative to the cardinal doctrines of the Christian faith.*[3]

Lewis similarly concludes,

A cult, then, is any religious movement which claims the
backing of Christ or the Bible, but distorts the central message
of Christianity by (1) an additional revelation, and (2) by dis-
placing a fundamental tenet of faith with a secondary matter.[4]

Some writers prefer to designate these deviations from orthodoxy
as sects. For example, John H. Gerstner, in *The Theology of the Major Sects*, explains that "evangelicals generally use 'sect' when refer-
ring to those Christian denominations not regarded as evangelical."[5]
A denomination is "evangelical" if it adheres to the fundamental doctrines of biblical orthodoxy, especially pertaining to the person and
work of Christ. While the terms *cult* and *sect* are almost synonymous,
the latter word has a wider application.

Anthony Hoekema's treatment of "The Distinctive Traits of the
Cult" is helpful:

In setting forth what I believe to be the distinctive traits of the
cult, I do not wish to give the impression that not the slightest
trace of these characteristics is to be found in the churches. If
we are honest with ourselves, we shall find vestiges of these
characteristics in the churches too. I venture to affirm, however, that the traits which will now be described are so
uniquely characteristic of the cult that any group in which
they play a leading role can no longer be recognized as be-
longing to the true church of Jesus Christ.[6]

The distinctive traits of a cult are then discussed under these headings: (1) "An Extra-Scriptural Source of Authority," (2) "The Denial of Justification by Grace Alone," (3) "The Devaluation of Christ," (4) "The Group as the Exclusive Community of the Saved," and (5) "The Group's Central Role in Eschatology."[7] These characteristics are specifically applied by Hoekema to Christian Science, Jehovah's Witnesses, Mormonism, and Seventh-day Adventism.

An important question (developed more fully in chapter 8) is whether the Seventh-day Adventists should be considered a cult. The Adventists have contended that they should be viewed as an evangelical church, but evangelical scholars have split in their acceptance of this claim. For example, of the authors already cited, Martin concludes that the Seventh-day Adventists should not be viewed as a cult,[8] while Lewis, Gerstner, and Hoekema identify them as nonevangelical.[9] It should be added that I agree with the latter conclusion, but, along with these men, I would not place Adventism in the same class as the Jehovah's Witnesses, Mormons, or Christian Scientists. Writing in the late 1950s, cult expert J. K. Van Baalen concluded,

> The writer regrets to state that a renewed study of the tenets and the methods of S.D.A. has accentuated rather than lessened his conviction that S.D.A. — although its adherents are clearly sincere, and many Christians are among them — as a movement is dangerous.[10]

And in 1992 Josh McDowell and Don Stewart wrote:

> There are too many false doctrines mingled with the doctrines of the Trinity and grace to recommend the Seventh-day Adventists as an evangelical church. Their isolation from other Protestants is troubling as well. It was taught by Ellen G. White that they are the "remnant" of God's true church. While we recognize that there are some born again believers in their midst, this separation attitude prevents us from rec-

ommending the Seventh-day Adventist Church as a place of true Christian fellowship.[11]

And more recently, former SDA pastor Dale Ratzlaff concluded: "The Historic SDA church, meets many cult characteristics. To their credit, however, they do not meet them all."[12]

THE CURRENT SCENE

It is impossible to accurately state how many new cults have appeared in recent years, but informed observers have estimated "anywhere from 2,500 to as high as 5,000."[13] The term *cult* has been defined from several different perspectives, which has resulted in confusion. As Keith F.. Tolbert of the American Religions Center says, "Its use ranges from a neutral descriptive term to a pejorative one bent on condemning a particular lifestyle."[14] Different writers have different ways of identifying these perspectives. Tolbert states that within the "religious frame of reference, we find that the word 'cult' has taken on three distinct denotations in 20th century North American culture," which are a *sociological* sense, a *philosophical/religious* sense, and, most recently, a *media* definition, which usually describes "the lifestyle or external rites of that religion" in a negative way.[15] "The popular definition of a cult usually reflects what the media portrays — sensationalism, weird, bizarre, and criminal."[16]

Because of this portrayal in the media, when one uses the term in the philosophical/religious sense, as evangelicals have historically done, they are usually misunderstood. Craig Branch succinctly explains this use: "Historically . . . , Christians have defined a cult, or more precisely, *pseudo-Christian religion*, or *non-Christian religion*, from a doctrinal perspective. The Bible is a Christian descriptive and prescriptive source of authority."[17] While this definition will be the primary focus of this book, a survey of the current religious scene makes it obvious that an expanded definition of what constitutes a cult must be employed.

Brooks Alexander presents a helpful approach to the problem. Thirty or forty years ago, he says, it would have been easy to explain what a cult is. But today the guidelines have become somewhat muddled:

> The problem is that neither a definition based on a standard of Christian orthodoxy, nor one based on techniques of behavioral manipulation and conditioning, is comprehensive enough to cover all the ground. . . . Perhaps the best approach is one which combines the two different standards without confusing them.[18]

Alexander includes in the theological designation of what constitutes a cult such characteristics as "a false or inadequate basis of salvation" and "a false basis of authority." Most of the nontheological standards for identifying a cult pertain to the techniques used in gaining and training converts, including "isolation or 'involvement' of the recruit to the point that the group controls all of the incoming information," "economic exploitation or an enslaving organizational structure," and "esotericism"—by which he means "a deliberately created gap between the truth about the cult which is given to the 'inner circle' and a misleading image which is projected to the public at large."[19] David Breese, in *Know the Marks of Cults*, presents a good survey and expansion of the approach taken by Alexander.[20]

THE EXISTENCE AND GROWTH OF CULTS

How does one account for the existence of cults? Why do they thrive? It must be recognized that there are two spiritual forces (powers) in the universe, which oppose each other. They are led by God, on the one side, and the opposer of heaven, Satan, on the other. Satan's goal is to blind people to the gospel of Christ, to deceive the world, and to receive worship for himself (Matt. 4:9; 2 Cor. 4:4; Rev. 12:9). One of Satan's most effective tools is the propagation of false doctrine. Second Corinthians 11:13–15 warns that Satan disguises himself as "an angel of light" and his human representatives as "apostles of Christ" and "ministers of righteousness."

Why do cults thrive? Many answers have been suggested: the enlisting of large numbers of laymen; the use of home doctrinal studies; skillful methods of making converts; the use of the mass media; the publication and distribution of large quantities of attractive literature; strong financial support; the efforts made to meet human needs; the exploitation of the uncertainty of the times. All of these suggestions help to explain the growth of cults, but there is yet another important point, which relates to the church. Martin succinctly states the problem:

> It is vitally essential that we understand one of the basic causes of cultism. *the unfortunate failure of the church to institute and emphasize a definite, systematic plan of cult evangelism and apologetics.* The average Christian is, sad to say, terribly unprepared to defend his faith thoroughly. In a word, he knows what he believes, but too often he does not know why.[21]

CONCLUSION

The proliferation and activity of the cults present a real challenge to those who are true believers in Christ and the Word of God. For years the cults have confronted the church. It is now time that the cults were confronted as never before by the evangelical church!

SELECT BIBLIOGRAPHY

Abanes, Richard. *Defending the Faith: A Beginner's Guide to Cults and New Religions.* Grand Rapids: Baker, 1997.

———. *Cults, New Religious Movements and Your Family.* Wheaton, Ill.: Crossway, 1998.

Ankerberg, John, and John Weldon. *Encyclopedia of Cults and New Religions.* Eugene, Ore.: Harvest House, 1999.

Branch, Craig. "Cult or Cultic?" *Watchman Expositor* 10, 4 (1993), 21–22.

Breese, Dave. *Know the Marks of Cults.* Wheaton, Ill.: Victor, 1975.

Bussell, Harold L. *By Hook or by Crook: How Cults Lure Christians.* New York: McCracken, 1993.

Enroth, Ronald M. *The Lure of the Cults and New Religions.* Downers Grove, Ill.: InterVarsity Press, 1987.

Enroth, Ronald M., et al. *A Guide to Cults and New Religions.* Downers Grove, Ill.: InterVarsity Press, 1983.

Gerstner, John H. *The Theology of the Major Sects.* Grand Rapids: Baker, 1960.

Geisler, Norman L., and Ron Rhodes. *When Cultists Ask: A Popular Handbook on Cultic Misrepresentations.* Grand Rapids: Baker, 1997.

Gomes, Alan W. *Unmasking the Cults.* Grand Rapids: Zondervan, 1995.

_____. *Truth and Error: Comparative Charts of Cults and Christianity.* Grand Rapids: Zondervan, 1998.

Hoekema, Anthony A. *The Four Major Cults.* Grand Rapids: Eerdmans, 1963.

House, H. Wayne. *Charts of Cults, Sects and Religious Movements.* Grand Rapids: Zondervan, 1997.

Larson, Bob. *Larson's New Book of Cults.* Wheaton, Ill.: Tyndale, 1989.

Lewis, Gordon R. *Confronting the Cults.* Philadelphia: P&R, 1966.

McDowell, Josh, and Don Stewart. *The Deceivers.* San Bernardino, Calif.: Here's Life, 1992.

Martin, Walter R. *The Kingdom of the Cults.* Rev. 1997 ed. Minneapolis: Bethany, 1997. This edition contains a full-text CD-ROM.

_____. *Martin Speaks Out on the Cults.* Ventura, Calif.: Regal, 1983. (Former title: *Rise of the Cults.*)

Mather, George A., and Larry A. Nichols. *Dictionary of Cults, Sects, Religions and the Occult.* Grand Rapids: Zondervan, 1993.

Melton, J. Gordon. *The Encyclopedia of American Religions.* 5th ed. Detroit: Gale Research, 1996.

Sire, James W. *Scripture Twisting: Twenty Ways the Cults Misread the Bible.* Downers Grove, Ill.: InterVarsity Press, 1980.

Tucker, Bruce. *Twisting the Truth.* Minneapolis: Bethany, 1987.

Tucker, Ruth A. *Another Gospel: Alternative Religions and the New Age Movement.* Grand Rapids: Zondervan, 1989.

2 | JEHOVAH'S WITNESSES

The world was shocked to learn that on November 8, 1978, more than nine hundred people had perished in Jonestown, Guyana, in a mass suicide (some people would say murder) carried out by the leader of the People's Temple, Jim Jones. Almost one-third of those who died of a cyanide-laced punch, or were shot, were children. This was the final act after forty-two rehearsals.[1] Nearly fifteen years later, on April 19, 1993, the world was again shocked as the news media reported that a fifty-one-day standoff in Waco, Texas, had ended with the burning of the Branch Davidian compound. Those who died in the conflagration numbered eighty-six. "What happened behind the walls, gunfire and flames of Waco on Monday may never be clear, but it was reported that [Branch Davidian leader David] Koresh tightly controlled his flock—and two dozen children died."[2]

Three years after the Guyana tragedy, an article in *Christianity Today* quoted former Jehovah's Witness insider Bill Cetnar as calling the Witnesses the "number one killer cult" because of its prohibition of blood transfusions. Cetnar "says it has been responsible for more premature deaths than the horror of Jonestown."[3] The article continues:

> Accepting the American Red Cross statistic that about 100 persons in every 1,000 need transfusions to survive at one time or another, Cetnar believes thousands of JWs have refused transfusions and entered early graves. "That's bigger than Jim Jones."[4]

Capitalizing on the Branch Davidian disaster, ex-Witness David A. Reed wrote an article entitled "More Dead Than Waco." He declared:

> Jehovah's Witnesses have been dying one at a time: refusing vaccinations between 1931 and 1952, refusing organ transplants between 1967 and 1980, and refusing blood transfusions and certain blood fractions since the mid-1940's.
>
> No one seems to have kept statistics on the number of JW deaths. And, because they have happened just one at a time, they haven't captured world headlines. But with the steady accumulation of a man dying here, a child there, a woman in another place, an infant somewhere else—for nearly 50 years—the JW death toll keeps adding up. How many, altogether, have followed the Watchtower to their deaths?[5]

Just as the followers of Jim Jones and David Koresh believed that their leaders spoke for God, Jehovah's Witnesses believe that the ban on blood is Jehovah's law and that they should die, if necessary, rather than receive a transfusion. Can this be true? One newspaper reported this:

> "If a doctor says you cannot survive without blood, then we would rather die than take a blood transfusion."
>
> So said William L. Barry, a Jehovah's Witness official, in defending the religious group's stand against the ingestion of blood. Witnesses believe blood transfusions are a form of feeding on blood—intravenous feeding—and that the Bible forbids it.
>
> Barry spoke on "Jehovah's Witnesses and the Question of Blood" to 20,000 followers.[6]

As Reed and others have pointed out, "Adding to the JW tragedy is the fact that the Watchtower Society has changed its mind on medical matters [vaccinations and organ transplants] and can be expected to change its mind again."[7] In the meantime, "perhaps the most frightening aspect of the JW tragedy is that the general public is unaware of its scope," and the Witnesses continue to recruit about 300,000 converts a year.[8]

This is only one of a number of teachings that should warn the reader that Witness beliefs not only may be unbiblical but also can endanger, or even cost, one's physical life.

In 1957 Marcus Bach identified the Jehovah's Witnesses, with about 600,000 "publishers," as "the fastest-growing religious movement in the world."[9] While growth has not always been as significant as Bach's statement would suggest, the Witnesses have made impressive gains, reaching a peak of more than 6 million active members in 235 lands in the 2000 service year.[10] That the outreach and influence of this organization greatly exceed its membership becomes evident from the circulation figures of the magazines and books published by the Watchtower Bible and Tract Society of Brooklyn, New York.

The work of the Witnesses among nominal Christians, new converts, and on the mission field has caused a great deal of confusion and heartache. This is because this cult denies most of the major doctrines of evangelical Christianity.

This brief survey presents a few highlights of the Witnesses' history, doctrines, false prophecies, publications, and outreach program. The study concludes with some suggestions on dealing with the adherents of this cult and their doctrinal views, with appropriate Scriptures. An annotated bibliography lists materials for further study. The organizations listed at the end of the chapter are sources for books, tracts, videos, and tapes.

History

The history of the Witnesses may be conveniently divided into four periods, coinciding with the four presidents who have led the movement. The fifth president was named in December 1993.

Charles Taze Russell (1879–1916). Russell founded *Zion's Watch Tower*—now *The Watchtower*—in 1879 and Zion's Watch Tower Tract Society in 1884 (later renamed). In addition to his speaking and editorial work, Russell penned six volumes entitled *Studies in the Scriptures* (originally *Millennial Dawn*), which appeared between 1886 and 1904. By the time of his death in 1916, the legal and doctrinal foundation of the Society had been established.

"Judge" Joseph F. Rutherford (1917–1942). The second president—under whose leadership the name "Jehovah's Witnesses" was taken in 1931—was a prolific writer. In addition to his speaking and editorial work and the publication of dozens of booklets, Rutherford wrote an average of one new book each year. A number of doctrinal and scriptural reinterpretations marked his administration. Rutherford became the "new oracle of God's message for this age," and Russell's writings and interpretations were often neglected or rejected for not being abreast of progressive light. By 1938 the independent congregations of Russell's day were brought under "theocratic" control—subservient to the Society's headquarters in Brooklyn.

Nathan H. Knorr (1942–1977). Following Rutherford's death in 1942, Knorr officially took over the leadership of the Witnesses, a movement then numbering slightly more than 115,000 people. As a result of Knorr's organizational ability, great growth took place in the areas of membership, outreach, buildings, and publications.

Frederick W. Franz (1977–1992). Franz began his residence at Watchtower headquarters in 1920. "Although he was not immediately chosen as one of the society's officers, his close friendship with Knorr and his role as the primary source of Watch Tower doctrine gave him immense, if indirect authority."[11] Franz was not an administrator but a "writer and researcher. . . . One could say that Franz was the molder and shaper of Watchtower theology for more than 70 years," says ex-JW Paul Blizard. Blizard also believes that Franz was a ghostwriter for many of Rutherford's books.[12] How important was Franz to the Jehovah's Witnesses? Blizard answers, "It is likely that aside from founder Charles Taze Russell, no person influenced Watchtower beliefs more than Franz."[13] It is well known that Franz was the principal "translator" of the Witnesses' *New World Translation*. Franz became president of the Watchtower Society in 1977, having previously been the vice president. He was ninety-nine years old when he died.[14]

Seventy-two-year-old Milton G. Henschel, formerly vice president, was named as the new president when Franz died. On October 7, 2000, it was announced that the Society's corporate structure had been reorganized. President Milton Henschel and other Governing Body members who were serving as officers and directors voluntarily removed themselves from these positions in all the corporate bodies.[15]

DOCTRINES

Jehovah's Witnesses deny many important doctrines of biblical Christianity. First, they deny the Trinity, accepting only "Jehovah" as God. They reject the deity of Christ, taking instead the Arian view that he was created by God. The Holy Spirit, they say, has no personhood, being only "God's active force."

Jehovah's Witnesses also deny that man has an immortal soul. It should be noted that the Scriptures apply the term *immortality* to man's future body. Christians use the term in reference to man's soul or spirit as it continues to exist after death. Since people do not have immortal souls, according to Watchtower doctrine, the lost will not suffer eternal punishment. Rather, they will be annihilated.

The Witnesses deny the biblical view of the atonement. They regard Christ's death only as that of a perfect man, exactly equal to Adam. They also deny his bodily resurrection, teaching that he arose as a spirit creature who materialized a body on various occasions in order to be seen by his disciples. Similarly, they deny the bodily, visible return of Christ, teaching that he "returned" invisibly in 1914 and that there was an invisible "rapture" in 1918.

Jehovah's Witnesses are works-oriented. They deny that salvation is by faith alone and insist that salvation is impossible outside of their organization. The born-again experience, they claim, is only for 144,000 of the Witnesses, including believers since the time of Christ.

Among their other characteristic doctrines is the idea that the Bible cannot be understood today without the guidance of the Society. They teach that if a Witness receives a blood transfusion willingly, it will result in his eternal death. Witnesses refuse to serve in the military and to salute the flag—to salute the flag would be an act of idolatry. Holidays and celebrations, such as Christmas, Easter, and birthdays, are rejected as pagan in origin. In their view, the present gathering of Jews in Palestine is not a fulfillment of prophecy. Israel has been set aside, and God's promises are being realized in "spiritual Israel," the Jehovah's Witnesses.

PUBLICATIONS

The printed page has been one of the most effective tools of the Witnesses. Their two semimonthly magazines, *The Watchtower* and *Awake!* had publication figures in January 2001 of 23 million and almost 20.7 million per issue, respectively. *The Watchtower* is the theological publication of the Society. Also, the publication of one or more books each year, with first editions of between one and five million copies, has a real impact.

The *New World Translation of the Holy Scriptures* was completed in 1960 and has been revised several times. Anthony Hoekema, in agreement with many others, says that it "is by no means an objective rendering of the sacred text into modern English, but is *a biased translation in which many of the peculiar teachings of the Watchtower Society are smuggled into the text of the Bible itself.*"[16]

The Witnesses have also published two Greek interlinear New

Testament texts. The older work is *The Emphatic Diaglott*, translated by Benjamin Wilson, a Christadelphian. *The Kingdom Interlinear Translation of the Greek Scriptures*, published in 1969 and revised in 1985, combines the Greek text edited by Westcott and Hort with the Society's translation and an improved text of the *New World Translation*. Both works clearly reveal a doctrinal bias. Two topically arranged handbooks (with verses frequently quoted out of context) should be mentioned: *"Make Sure of All Things; Hold Fast to What Is Fine"* (1965) and *Reasoning from the Scriptures* (1985). A Bible dictionary, *Aid to Bible Understanding*, which reflects the Witnesses' understanding on many of the topics explained, was completed in 1971. This was replaced in 1988 by the two-volume *Insight on the Scriptures*. In 1973 the *Comprehensive Concordance of the New World Translation* was published. A Jehovah's Witness can now "study" the Bible and never leave Watchtower Society publications.

PROPHETIC SPECULATION (FAILURE)

Claiming divine insight,[17] the publications distributed by the Jehovah's Witnesses and their predecessors, the Bible Students, have promoted a message of urgency—Armageddon is near—for more than one hundred years. In reality, they have succeeded in creating an illusion of urgency. Many have joined the Witnesses as a result of the Armageddon message. Many have also left the Witnesses because Armageddon has failed to come. It would take a book-length treatment to adequately show the extent of the erroneous speculations that have characterized the movement.[18]

The Witnesses are not reluctant to expose the failures of others. The March 22, 1993, issue of *Awake!* contains three articles under the title "The World's End—How Near?" The story of the boy who cried "Wolf! Wolf!" is told and an application is made: "So it has become with those who proclaim the end of the world. Down through the centuries since Jesus' day, so many unfulfilled predictions have been made that many no longer take them seriously." A footnote attempts to explain away the erroneous predictions made in Watchtower publications (without any specifics). The reader is told that "Jehovah's Witnesses, in their eagerness for Christ's second coming, have suggested dates that turned out to be incorrect"—but they are not false prophets.[19] To call their predictions "suggested dates," however, is to gloss over the true nature of their speculations.

Do the following quotations from Watchtower pronouncements or publications—taken from hundreds that could be cited and given with the year in which each statement was made—sound like mere suggestions?

1877: "THE END OF THIS WORLD . . . is nearer than most men suppose." (Barbour and Russell, *Three Worlds*, 17).

1886: "The Marshalling of the hosts for the battle of the great day of God Almighty, is in progress while the skirmishing is commencing" (*Watch Tower Reprints*, 17).

1889: "The 'battle of the great day of God Almighty' . . . which will end in A.D. 1914 . . . is already commenced" (Russell, *The Time Is at Hand*, 101).

1894: "But bear in mind that the end of 1914 is not the date for the *beginning*, but for the end of the time of trouble" (*Watch Tower Reprints*, 1677).

1904: "The stress of the great time of trouble will be on us soon, somewhere between 1910 and 1912—culminating . . . October 1914" (Russell, *The New Creation*, 579).

1915?: "The present great war in Europe is the beginning of the Armageddon of the Scriptures" (*Pastor Russell's Sermons*, 676).

1925: Predicted for 1925: "The old order of things, the old world, is ending." "We are standing at the very portals of that blessed time! [Golden Age of the Kingdom]. . . . Deliverance is at the door!" (Rutherford, *Millions Now Living Will Never Die*, 97, 105).

1926: "All the nations and kingdoms of earth are rapidly marching to the great battle of God Almighty" (*Watch Tower*, July 15, 1926, 216).

1931: "His day of vengeance is here, and Armageddon is at hand and certain to fall upon Christendom, and that within an early date" (Rutherford, *Vindication I*, 147).

1935: "Armageddon is about to begin" (Rutherford, *Universal War Near*, 48).

1939: "The time for the battle of the great day of God Almighty is very near." "The disaster of Armageddon is just ahead" (Rutherford, *Salvation*, 310, 361).

1943: "The final end of all things of this world is at hand, and the post-war arrangement will not save them" (*Watchtower*, May 1, 1943, 139).

1955: "The war of Armageddon is nearing its breaking out point" (*You May Survive Armageddon into God's New World*, 331).

1962: "Armageddon, the battle of the great day of God Almighty, is at the door. . . . This worldly generation, therefore, has not much longer to live" (*Watchtower*, July 1, 1962, 389).

1969: "All the evidence in fulfillment of Bible prophecy indicates that this corrupt system is due to end in a few years." (*Awake!* May 22, 1969, 15).

1971: "Shortly, within our twentieth century, the 'battle in the day of Jehovah' will begin against . . . Christendom" ("*The Nations Shall Know That I Am Jehovah*," 216).

1974: "Reports are heard of brothers selling their homes and property and planning to finish out the rest of their days in this old system in pioneer service. Certainly this is a fine way to spend the short time remaining before the wicked world's end" (*Kingdom Ministry*, May 1974, 3).

1984: "Some of that 'generation' [of 1914] could survive until the end of the century. But there are many indications that 'the end' is much closer than that!" (*Watchtower*, March 1, 1984, 18–19).

2000: "Yes, we stand at the very threshold of the fulfillment of Jehovah's decree against Satan and his entire wicked system." "Jehovah's rocking of the nations at Armageddon is just ahead" (*Watchtower*, January 15, 2000, 7, 19).

On February 10, 1975, Franz, then Watchtower vice president, spoke to twenty thousand Witnesses in the Los Angeles Sports Arena. In his talk, "Time in Which We Are Now Interested," he stated that six thousand years of human history would definitely end on September 5, 1975. Said Franz, "We do not necessarily have to insist or even expect that everything is going to be through and over with by September 5 of this year." How much time would be left if all was not realized in 1975? Was there time to realize

> human aspirations, getting married and raising a family—kids; or going to college for a few years and learning engineering and finding a fine job as an engineer . . . or some other prominent, fine paying job[?] No! The time does not allow for that, dear friends. . . . Evidently there is not much time left."[20]

It has now been twenty-six years, and Franz's "evidently there is not much time left" has joined all the other false predictions of an organization of false prophets. Can the Watchtower Society escape the conclusions of its own statements and Deuteronomy 18:20–22?

Program

All movements have a program of some kind to bring in the converts. William Schnell, the author of *Thirty Years a Watch Tower Slave*, explained the Witnesses' "seven-step program" in the mid-1950s. The program remains basically the same: (1) Get literature into the hands of people through house-to-house or other outreach. (2) Follow up with a return visit or visits to determine and encourage interest. (3) Try to arrange a "Bible study" (a study using a recent Watchtower book). (4) Get the person showing interest to come to the congregational "Bible study." (5) Bring those showing interest to the "Watchtower study." (6) Encourage attendance at the "Theocratic Ministry School" and "Service meeting" (where Witnesses are trained in their public speaking and outreach program). (7) Dedicate the person's life to Jehovah in baptism.

Being born again is not part of this conversion process. That experience is only for the 144,000, according to the Society.

Dealing with the Witnesses

The individual Witness is trained in a particular doctrinal system. He is committed to the Society without reservation as "God's channel." He has been brainwashed, a fact to which many former Witnesses have attested. He normally denies having been born again and cannot give a testimony of an accomplished personal salvation.

In dealing with such a Witness, it does not help to argue or get sidetracked. Focus on the primary doctrines: the person and work of Christ are vital. Give your personal testimony of salvation. Don't talk with the Witness without your Bible. Pray that he will be saved.

Christians must be prayerful, persistent, and patient in dealing with Jehovah's Witnesses. One may never see the results of one's witnessing to them. But, as ex-Witnesses Leonard Chretien and Marjorie Chretien tell us:

Christians have an opportunity to reach out in love to Jehovah's Witnesses. True, it is necessary to be prepared, so as not to become entangled in their web. But when a Witness knocks on our door, we can plant a seed of doubt or perhaps water what someone else has planted. Thousands of Witnesses have left the Watch Tower and become Christians in the truest sense. We can find them in various churches and fellowships throughout the world.[21]

In recent years, many Jehovah's Witnesses have left the movement. Some have come to Christ through reading and studying the Bible, but most have heard the gospel and accepted Christ as the result of the testimonies and ministry of concerned Christians.

SELECT REFERENCES

- **The Trinity:** Matt. 3:16–17; 28:19; John 14:26; 15:26; 1 Cor. 12:3–6; 2 Cor. 13:14; Eph. 2:18; 3:1–5, 14–17; 4:4–6; 5:18–20; 1 Peter 1:2; Jude 20–21.
- **The deity of Christ:** Isa. 9:6 (cf. Isa. 10:21); John 1:1, 23 (cf. Isa. 40:3); John 8:58; 12:37–41 (cf. Isa. 6:1–10); Heb. 1:1–12 (cf. Ps. 102:25–27); Rev. 22:13.
- **The personhood of the Holy Spirit:** Matt. 28:19; John 14:26; 16:13; Acts 10:19–20; Rom. 8:26–27; 1 Cor. 12:11.
- **The bodily resurrection of Christ:** Ps. 16:9–10 (cf. Acts 2:25–31); Mark 16:6; Luke 24:3–8 (cf. John 2:19–22); Luke 24:36–43; Rom. 8:11; 1 Cor. 15:1–15.
- **Salvation by faith:** Rom. 4:5; 5:8–11; Eph. 2:8–10; 2 Tim. 1:9; Titus 3:4–8; 1 John 5:11–13.
- **Born again:** John 3:3, 5, 7; 1 John 5:1–5. (See Luke 13:28–29 and Matt. 8:11. Old Testament saints will be found in the "kingdom of God" or "kingdom of heaven.")

- **The soul (spirit):** Acts 2:27; 1 Thess. 5:23; Heb. 12:23; Rev. 6:9–11; 20:4.
- **Eternal punishment:** Matt. 25:46; 2 Peter 2:17; Jude 13; Rev. 19:20 with 20:10. The Greek word *basanizo*, "to torment" (Rev. 20:10), in every place where it appears in the New Testament, speaks of pain and conscious suffering (cf. Mark 5:7; Luke 8:28; 2 Peter 2:8; Rev. 9:5; 12:2).
- **The visible return of Christ:** Zech. 12:10; Matt. 23:39; 24:30; Acts 1:11; 1 Thess. 4:16–17; Rev. 1:7.
- **The message of the early church:** Acts 2:22–40; 3:13–26; 4:2, 10–12, 33; 5:30–32, 42; 8:4–6, 35; 9:20; 10:39–43; 11:20, 26; 13:28–41; 16:30–32; 17:2–4, 18, 31; 18:5; 19:13; 20:21; 24:24; 26:22–23.

SELECT BIBLIOGRAPHY

Barnes, Peter. *Out of Darkness into Light.* San Diego: Equippers, Inc., 1992. Barnes was a JW for thirty years and served as a circuit overseer. He presents his testimony of deliverance from the JWs and gives insights into their thinking, methods, and practices and how to answer and evangelize them.

Bergman, Jerry. *Jehovah's Witnesses and the Problem of Mental Illness.* Clayton, Calif.: Witness Inc., 1992.

_____. *Blood Transfusions: A History and Evaluation of the Religious, Biblical, and Medical Objections.* Clayton, Calif.: Witness Inc., 1994.

Bowman, Robert M., Jr. *Jehovah's Witnesses, Jesus Christ, and the Gospel of John.* Grand Rapids: Baker, 1989. Bowman focuses on the JW mistranslations of John 1:1 and 8:58, with an appendix on 20:28.

_____. *Understanding Jehovah's Witnesses: Why They Read the Bible the Way They Do.* Grand Rapids: Baker, 1991. Bowman explains that the purpose of "this book is to offer a hermeneutical analysis of the Jehovah's Witnesses' interpretation of the Bible" (12).

_____. *Why You Should Believe in the Trinity: An Answer to Jehovah's Witnesses.* Grand Rapids: Baker, 1989. An answer to the Witnesses' booklet *Should You Believe in the Trinity?* published in 1989.

Chretien, Leonard, and Marjorie Chretien. *Witnesses of Jehovah.* Eugene, Ore.: Harvest House, 1988. The Chretiens were Jehovah's Witnesses for twenty-two years. They explain that the book "was written to expose the Watch Tower as a false religion, and not as a persecution or vendetta" (7). A videocassette with the same title is available from Good News Defenders, P.O. Box 8007, La Jolla, CA 92038.

Countess, Robert H. *The Jehovah's Witnesses' New Testament.* 2d ed. Phillipsburg, N.J.: P&R, 1987. In his conclusion he writes, "In the opinion of this investigator the *New World Translation of the Christian Greek Scriptures* must be viewed as a radically biased piece of work. At some points it is actually dishonest. At others it is neither modern nor scholarly" (93).

Finnerty, Robert U. *Jehovah's Witnesses on Trial: The Testimony of the Early Church Fathers.* Phillipsburg, N.J.: P&R, 1993. Finnerty demonstrates by specific examples how the Witnesses have misrepresented the Fathers in their publications.

Franz, Raymond. *Crisis of Conscience.* Atlanta: Commentary, 1983. Franz was a third-generation Jehovah's Witness who lived for sixty years among them, the last nine as a member of the Governing Body. "Those years led to the crisis of conscience which is the theme of this book" (book jacket). The 1992 edition has an index.

_____. *In Search of Christian Freedom.* Atlanta: Commentary, 1991. At the end of this 732-page sequel to *Crisis of Conscience,* Franz repudiates orthodox Christianity.

Gruss, Edmond C. *Jehovah's Witnesses—Their Monuments to False Prophecy.* Clayton, Calif.: Witness Inc., 1997. An in-depth examination of three JW monuments: The Great Pyramid of Egypt, once viewed as "the Bible in Stone," and "Beth-Sarim" and "Beth-Shan," two homes built to house Abraham, Isaac, Jacob, David and other "ancient worthies" predicted to return in the 1930s and early 1940s.

_____. *We Left Jehovah's Witnesses—A Non-Prophet Organization.* Nutley, N.J.: P&R, 1974. The book features the personal testimonies of six couples who left the Jehovah's Witnesses.

_____. *Jehovah's Witnesses: Their Claims, Doctrinal Changes and Prophetic Speculation.* Fairfax, Va.: Xulon Press, 2001.

Harris, Doug, and Bill Browning. Rev. ed. *Awake! to the Watch Tower.* Morden Surrey, UK: Reachout Trust, 1993. "The overall aim of this book is to encourage you to be able to reachout and share with the next Jehovah's Witness that calls at your door" (9).

Hoekema, Anthony A. *Jehovah's Witnesses.* Grand Rapids: Eerdmans, 1963. This book is an updated portion of material appearing in *The Four Major Cults* (Grand Rapids: Eerdmans, 1963). It is a scholarly presentation of the Witnesses' theology and a refutation of their denials of the deity of Christ and eternal punishment.

Jonsson, Carl Olof. *The Gentile Times Reconsidered.* 3d ed. Atlanta: Commentary, 1998. An in-depth examination and refutation of the Witnesses' crucial "Gentile times" 1914 chronology.

Lundquist, Lynn. *The Tetragrammaton and the Christian Greek Scriptures.* 2d ed. Portland, Ore.: Word Resources, Inc, 1998. Lundquist concludes that there is no evidence "that the Tetragammaton was ever used by the original Greek Scripture writers" (151).

Magnani, Duane, with Arthur Barret. *The Watchtower Files.* Minneapolis: Bethany, 1985. This book contains documentation from more than 150 Watchtower publications.

Martin, Walter R. *Jehovah of the Watchtower.* Minneapolis: Bethany, 1982. This is a republication of Martin's classic study on the Jehovah's Witnesses. Martin presents the history and doctrines of the Witnesses and a biblical response to their teachings.

Penton, M. James. *Apocalypse Delayed: The Story of Jehovah's Witnesses.* Toronto: University of Toronto, 1985. Penton, a professor of history and religion at Lethbridge University in Canada, is a fourth-generation ex-Witness. Updated in a 2d edition (1997).

Quick, Kevin R. *Pilgrimage Through the Watchtower*. Grand Rapids: Baker, 1989. Quick presents his search for truth and how he found the answer in Jesus Christ.

Reed, David A. *Behind the Watchtower Curtain: The Secret Society of Jehovah's Witnesses*. Southbridge, Mass.: Crowne, 1989. This book was "written to answer claims made by the Watchtower Organization, expose the false teaching, cultic practices, and to lay bare the secrets of the Watchtower Organization" (back cover).

_____. *How to Rescue Your Loved One from the Watchtower*. Grand Rapids: Baker, 1989.

_____. *Jehovah's Witnesses Answered Verse by Verse*. Grand Rapids: Baker, 1986. Reed examines the favorite texts used by Witnesses in support of their doctrines, as well as many they ignore. A chapter on sharing the gospel with the JWs and Reed's testimony conclude the book.

_____, ed. *Index of Watchtower Errors*. Compiled by Steve Huntoon and John Cornell. Grand Rapids: Baker, 1990. The teachings of Watchtower leadership from 1879 to 1989 are arranged chronologically and topically.

Rhodes, Ron. *Reasoning from the Scriptures with the Jehovah's Witnesses*. Eugene, Ore.: Harvest House, 1993. Rhodes provides well-organized answers to the doctrinal errors taught by the Jehovah's Witnesses and leading questions to challenge their confidence in the Watchtower Society.

Rogerson, Alan. *Millions Now Living Will Never Die*. London: Constable, 1969. This book contains a good treatment of the history of the movement.

Schnell, William J. *Thirty Years a Watch Tower Slave*. Grand Rapids: Baker, 1956. Schnell relates his experiences and reveals the inner workings of the Society during those years.

Watters, Randall. *Refuting Jehovah's Witnesses*. Rev. ed. Manhattan Beach, Calif.: Free Minds, 1992. Watters's book covers such subjects as the Trinity, the soul, the resurrection, the cross, holidays, war, blood, hell, and salvation. Written after many contacts with Witnesses, this book is an excellent resource.

ORGANIZATIONS

Some organizations with ministries to Jehovah's Witnesses and materials for Christian training and outreach.

Free Minds Inc.
P.O. Box 3818
Manhattan Beach, CA 90266
Phone 310-545-7831 Fax 310-545-0068
Website www.freeminds.org

This site includes more than one hundred Watchtower-related websites, plus a number of foreign language sites and others for related information.

Witness Inc.
P.O. Box 597
Clayton, CA 94517
Phone 925-672-5979 Fax 925-672-8230
Website www.witnessinc.com

3 | THE LATTER-DAY SAINTS (MORMONS)

On April 6, 1830, Joseph Smith Jr. (1805–1844) founded the Church of Christ (the original name) with six charter members at Fayette, New York. By 2000 its membership had climbed to 11 million. This growth has been explained by some observers as the result of three main factors: missionaries, money, and magnificence. One does not have to look far to find each of these factors illustrated in the Church of Jesus Christ of Latter-day Saints. For example, in 2000 there were 60,000 missionaries serving the LDS church. Another important factor is the media. The Mormon leadership has found that advertising and television and radio productions have resulted in many converts.[1] The November 13, 2000 *U.S. News and World Report* identified the LDS Church as "one of the world's richest and fastest growing religious movements."

This chapter will examine a number of important questions. How has the Mormon leadership historically viewed non-Mormon churches? Has this appraisal changed? Was there a universal apostasy, as Mormons claim? How might Mormonism be characterized as a theological system? What are the Mormons' sources of doctrinal authority? What do Mormons believe? How do the meanings of the terms employed by Mormons compare with the Bible and evangelical understanding? What Bible references may be used to refute key Mormon doctrines? How might the evangelical believer effectively share the gospel with Mormons? The chapter concludes with an appendix of witnessing references from the *Book of Mormon,* a select bibliography, and a list of ministries that provide materials for study and for outreach.

THE EXPOSURE OF RELIGIOUS ERROR

Those who view and expose the Mormon church as a false religion are frequently criticized by Mormons and sometimes even by evangelical Christians. In reply to such criticism, it should be pointed out that the initial attack on one's religion was launched not by orthodox Christians but rather by the founder of Mormonism, Joseph Smith. *Joseph Smith's Testimony,* written in 1838 and currently published and distributed by the LDS church, relates the following:

> My object in going to inquire of the Lord was to know which of all the sects was right, that I might know which to join. . . .
> I was answered that I must join none of them, for they were all wrong and the Personage who addressed me said that all their creeds were an abomination in His sight; that those professors were all corrupt; that "they draw near to me with their lips, but their hearts are far from me; they teach for doctrines the commandments of men, having a form of godliness, but they deny the power thereof."
> He again forbad me to join any of them.[2]

The Mormons view their church as the restored church of Jesus Christ and all other professing Christian groups as apostate. This is illustrated by *A Uniform System for Teaching Investigators,* a booklet once used by Mormon missionaries in their proselytizing work. In it the potential convert is led to say concerning other churches and his own: "They are false. . . . *There was a complete apostasy and my church is false.*"[3] Similarly, Apostle Bruce McConkie characterizes non-Mormon Christianity and churches as "perverted Christianity," "so-called Christianity," "apostate Christendom," and "false latter-day churches."[4] Orson Pratt, selected in 1835 as one of the original Twelve Apostles, claimed that the Roman Catholic Church was founded by "the Devil," that it was the "whore of Babylon," that the Protestant denominations were "her harlot daughters," and that "neither Catholics nor Protestants are members of the true Church."[5] It is hypocritical for Mormons to criticize non-Mormons for doing what the Mormons have been doing all along.

But in recent years a new Mormon strategy has emerged. Ex-Mormon James R. Spencer and others with ministries to Mormons have identified a new public relations effort by the Mormon church in which it

> seeks to minimize the doctrinal differences between Mormons and other Christians. It is attempting to be recognized as a legitimate expression of Christianity. Local Mormon leaders request to be included in city-wide Christian gatherings . . . , and they want to sit on local ministerial boards. Frequently Latter-day Saints plead with Christian neighbors to accept them as brothers.[6]

At the same time, fundamental Mormon doctrines have not changed. Spencer states: "That is evident in the message Mormon missionaries teach privately in Christian homes. In that setting they continue to declare themselves to be representatives of the One True Church."[7] He believes that "the reason for the new strategy is that the Mormon Church wants to be perceived in a positive light so that it can continue to penetrate the Christian community with its radical gospel message."[8]

Robert M. Bowman Jr., of Watchman Fellowship, says that Mormons "have sought to soften this claim [that their religion is the *only* one that is Christian] and are now denying that Mormonism has the harsh view of orthodox Christianity for which it is reputed."[9] This is done by adopting "strained interpretations of some of their leaders' statements."[10] For example, they take Smith's testimony ("I was answered that I must join none of them, for they were all wrong") and apply it only to the churches and ministers in the Palmyra area, not to all Christian churches.[11] But if this interpretation is correct, why was a restoration needed? And what about the many other harsh statements from Mormon sources that disagree with such an interpretation?

Bowman cites an extended passage from McConkie, in which he quotes from Smith's testimony and 1 Nephi 14:9–10, which are given the traditional interpretation. McConkie concludes, "'Thus we come back to Alma's teaching that unless men are in the sheepfold of Christ, their shepherd is the devil and they will be rewarded by him whom they list [i.e., choose] to obey (Alma 5:41).' "[12] McConkie's book, which was published in 1985, supports the traditional Mormon position "that all other churches are of the devil."[13]

Since the beginning of this movement, and today, the issue is clear: either orthodox Christianity or Mormonism is false. There can be no compromise on this matter.

Was There a Universal Apostasy?

This is a crucial question, for without a universal apostasy of the primitive church, the Mormon claim to be the restored church falls. The teaching that there was such an apostasy is presented in many LDS publications. But this claim is unscriptural and unhistorical. Mormons often misuse the sources they cite in support of their views.

Apostle James E. Talmage states the Mormon position and its significance in these words:

The significance and importance of the great apostasy, as a condition precedent to the re-establishment of the Church in modern times, is obvious. *If the alleged apostasy of the primitive Church was not a reality, The Church of Jesus Christ of*

Latter-day Saints is not the divine institution its name pro-claims.[14]

Mormons find important confirmation for the claimed universal apostasy in Smith's account of his First Vision, which he said took place in the spring of 1820. He reported that in answer to his prayer asking which of the churches he should join, he was told that "he must join none of them, for they were all wrong."[15] The significance of Smith's experience is explained in the introduction to *History of the Church:* "This is a tremendous arraignment of all Christendom. It charges a condition of universal apostasy from God. . . . *Nothing less than a complete apostasy from the Christian religion would warrant the establishment of the Church of Jesus Christ of Latter-Day Saints.*"[16]

In the LDS brochure *The Falling Away and the Restoration of the Gospel of Jesus Christ Foretold,* quotations are taken from the New Testament (Paul and Peter), Martin Luther, John Wesley, Roger Williams, and Thomas Jefferson to support the Mormon claim of to-tal apostasy and a restoration.[17]

The Mormon arguments for the alleged universal apostasy and restoration may be summarized: (1) The Bible predicts such an apos-tasy and restoration. (2) Various observers (primarily churchmen) agree that such an apostasy took place. (3) Joseph Smith's First Vision in 1820 is the ultimate confirmation. These three arguments will now be examined.

The Bible predicts a universal apostasy. The Bible does predict an apostasy (a "falling away"), and biblical writers even warn that it had already begun during the first century (2 Thess. 2:3; 1 Tim. 4:1–3; 2 Tim. 3:1–5; 4:3–4; 1 John 2:18–19; 4:3). Mormon writers cite a number of Bible references in an attempt to prove their position,[18] but an examination of them reveals that not one of them speaks of the apostasy as being total, and some of them do not even apply to the church or the church age.

Mormon Heber C. Snell, identified as a former LDS Institute director, questioned the legitimacy of the Mormon use of some of these texts:

> Numerous texts of the Bible (e.g. Is. 24:5; Amos 8:11, 12; 2 Tim. 4:3, 4; 2 Pet. 2:1–12) [all cited by Talmage] are said by Mormon writers to point toward the complete apostasy of the ancient Christian Church. Thorough study of such texts, taking into account their history, will usually show that they are descriptive of conditions in the writer's own time or of events which, in his view, will shortly occur. It would be difficult indeed to prove that the Bible writers had their eyes fixed on specific events to take place centuries after their own day. If space permitted, many examples of questionable interpretations of biblical texts could be cited from Mormon writings. . . .
>
> The Bible, in my view, has been too much used by Church theologians as a repository of proof texts, with little or no regard for the historical background or context for the sections cited.[19]

The claim of a universal apostasy finds no support from Scripture.

Observers agree that a universal apostasy took place. Space does not permit a full examination of the Mormon misuse of quotations from Martin Luther, John Wesley, Roger Williams, and Thomas Jefferson, which I have discussed elsewhere.[20] But I can state that the Mormon brochure handles sources in an unscholarly or dishonest manner. It shows an ignorance of the beliefs of the men cited, which are incompatible with the Mormons' position.

In support of their views, Mormons cite Paul in 2 Thessalonians 2:2–3 and Peter in Acts 3:20–22.[21] The passage in 2 Thessalonians does teach that the second coming of Christ would be preceded by an apostasy. But it does not teach that genuine Christians would fall away or that apostasy would be universal. That notion is contradicted by such passages as Matthew 24:10–13; John 6:37–40; 10:28; Romans 5:6–10; 8:38–39; 1 Timothy 4:1; 2 Timothy 4:18.

The "restoration of all things" mentioned in Acts 3:20–21 is interpreted by the Mormons to mean that after the universal apostasy, the gospel would be restored by divine agency through Joseph Smith. But to interpret this passage in such a way is to lift it from its context. The "restoration" spoken of in verse 21 is said to be that "which God has spoken by the mouth of all His holy prophets since the world began." Hans-George Link explains:

> This sentence accords with the eschatological hope of OT prophecy and Judaism. . . . The *apokatastasis panton* does not mean the conversion of mankind, but the restoration of all things and circumstances which the OT prophets proclaimed, i.e. the universal renewal of the earth.[22]

This restoration would see the fulfillment of Isaiah's prophecy of "new heavens and a new earth" (Isa. 65:17; see also Isa. 66:22; 2 Peter 3:13; Rev. 21:1) with the second coming of Christ and the messianic age.

Joseph Smith's First Vision confirms it. The importance of the First Vision to the Mormon church is summarized by Wesley P. Walters: "Mormon leaders have repeatedly asserted that the foundation of their church rests on the truthfulness of Joseph Smith Jr.'s First Vision story. If that story is false, they have declared, the whole of Mormonism is a fraud."[23]

Realizing the importance of this event to Mormon claims, in the mid-1960s Walters began a historical investigation of the Palmyra Revival. His findings were published in the fall of 1967 and reprinted as the booklet *New Light on Mormon Origins*.[24] His study was then expanded and published in the spring 1969 issue of *Dialogue: A Journal of Mormon Thought*, along with a rebuttal by Mormon scholar Richard L. Bushman and a reply by Walters.[25] At the same time, Milton V. Backman Jr. argued in *BYU Studies* that the 1820 revival and the First Vision were authentic, and in 1971 his book *Joseph Smith's First Vision* was published.[26]

In 1980 Walters published "Joseph Smith's First Vision Story Revisited." In this article, Walters surveyed the three Mormon responses to his original study: (1) to ignore the evidence and assert that there was a revival, (2) to attempt to verify a revival in 1820, and (3) to claim that Smith's account is too ambiguous to ascertain what he meant. After an examination of each of these approaches, Walters concluded, "In our judgment none of these have shaken the evidence that proves Joseph's story a fabrication."[27] Walters's judgment is warranted. He did his homework. His research is solid.

In summary, there was no 1820 revival, no First Vision, no confirmation of a universal apostasy, and therefore no basis for a restoration and the Mormon church.

MORMONISM AS A SYSTEM

The Lutheran theologian F. E. Mayer declares: "As a religious system Mormonism is a mixture of theosophy, spiritism, and elements of paganism, under a thin veneer of Christian terminology. As a philosophy it is slightly materialistic and approaches Islam."[28] According to Mayer, Mormon theology teaches at its heart

> that man, an eternally preexistent soul, is placed upon earth in order to gain "the remission of his sins" through obedience to the laws and regulations laid down by the priesthood and ultimately that he reaches perfection by a continual advance and eternal progress. In the interest of this central doctrine the Mormons have developed their theology and worship.[29]

These statements indicate that many non-Christian sources and teachings are embodied in the Mormon system.

THE SOURCES OF MORMON DOCTRINE

Mormonism finds doctrinal authority in five sources: the four "Standard Works" (the Bible, the *Book of Mormon, Doctrine and Covenants,* and *The Pearl of Great Price*) and revelations delivered by church leaders.

1. The King James Version of the Bible is accepted as "the word of God as far as it is translated correctly" (Articles of Faith, art. 8). Joseph Smith began a revision of the King James Version in 1831 and evidently completed that work in 1833. This revision has been published by the Reorganized Church of Jesus Christ of Latter Day Saints and is designated the "Inspired Version." (This group followed Joseph Smith III as the legitimate successor to his father rather than Brigham Young and eventually established their headquarters in Independence, Missouri.)

2. It is claimed that the *Book of Mormon* presents God's dealings with the Western continent, just as the Bible presents God's dealings with the Eastern continent. According to a statement printed on the front cover, it is "Another Testament of Jesus Christ."

3. *Doctrine and Covenants* is important as a source of some of the distinctive doctrines of Mormonism, such as celestial marriage and baptism for the dead. A number of the early revelations that were published in 1833 were changed when they were republished in *Doctrine and Covenants* in 1835.[30]

4. *The Pearl of Great Price* is a compilation of several writings: the *Book of Moses,* the *Book of Abraham,* a portion of Smith's translation of the Bible (Matt. 24), a portion of *Joseph Smith's Testimony,* and the *Articles of Faith.*

5. Further revelations through the leadership of the Mormon church are the fifth source of authoritative doctrine. Brigham Young University professor C. C. Riddle, citing a church authority, writes: "He said that the most important scriptures that the Church has today are the words of [then] President McKay. And they are scripture."[31]

Mormon writers make it clear that the Bible is subordinated to the distinctively Mormon authorities. William E. Berrett writes: "Whenever any discrepancies were found between the Book of Mormon text and the Bible account, Joseph Smith followed the Book of Mormon and thereby set an example to the Church."[32] Joseph Fielding Smith states: "Guided by the *Book of Mormon, Doctrine and Covenants*, and the Spirit of the Lord, it is not difficult for one to discern the errors in the *Bible*."[33]

MORMON DOCTRINE

Mormon doctrine is quite complex, but the following summary should suffice.

God. The Trinity is rejected, and the three persons of the Godhead are viewed as separate and distinct. God the Father has a physical body, and the Holy Spirit is a personage of Spirit. Joseph Smith stated: "God himself was once as we are now, and is an exalted man, and sits enthroned in yonder heavens! . . . He was once a man like us."[34] There is a plurality of gods.

Man. Before men inhabit the earth, they exist as spirits. Man was "created" in the physical image of God. The Garden of Eden was located in Independence, Missouri. The fall accomplished good. Original sin is rejected.

Christ. The difference between other men and Christ is one of degree—not of kind. The scriptural teaching on the virgin birth is rejected. Brigham Young stated that "Jesus Christ was not begotten by the Holy Ghost."[35] Christ's birth was the result of a physical union between God the Father and Mary. Leading LDS authorities have taught that Jesus was a polygamist.[36] Christ's death guarantees that all will be resurrected. Individual salvation is gained by the person in the degree to which he believes and obeys the Mormon gospel. The doctrine of blood atonement teaches that "there are some serious sins for which the cleansing blood of Christ does not operate, and the law of God is that men must have their own blood shed to atone for their sins."[37]

Church and ordinances. God's church entered into apostasy and remained in that state until 1830. The true church was reestablished with the restoration of the Aaronic and Melchizedekian priesthoods (conferred upon Joseph Smith and Oliver Cowdery). Baptism is absolutely necessary for salvation. Baptism for the dead is performed (based upon 1 Cor. 15:29). The Lord's Supper is administered weekly, and water is used.

Eschatology. Before Christ returns to rule over Zion and Jerusalem, there are three "gatherings": (1) the Ephraimites (Mormons) to Zion (i.e., Independence, Missouri), (2) the Jews to Palestine, and (3) the Lost Ten Tribes to Zion. There is a one-stage advent, with a resurrection at the beginning of the millennium—the First Resurrection. Those raised are the believing dead and those who never heard the gospel. The wicked are burned up and suffer punishment in preparation for the postmillennial period. Satan is bound, and there is peace on the earth. The wicked are raised after the millennium (one thousand years). Satan has his last fling, and some follow him in defeat. The saved spend eternity in the Celestial, the Terrestrial, or the Telestial Kingdom. There is opportunity for advancement within each.

A helpful survey of Mormon theology is A *Study of the Articles of Faith*, by James E. Talmage, who was one of the Twelve Apostles of the church. The *Articles of Faith* set forth the basic doctrines of the LDS as written by Joseph Smith in thirteen articles. They are included in *The Pearl of Great Price*. The non-Mormon scholar Anthony A. Hoekema has an excellent survey of Mormon doctrine in *Mormonism.*

A REFUTATION OF MORMON DOCTRINE

The gist of some major Mormon doctrines or denials is given below, and appropriate Bible and other references in refutation are cited. (See additional references in the next section, "The Semantic Problem.")

- **Plurality of gods:** Isa. 43:10–11; 44:6, 8; James 2:19. (See also the *Book of Mormon*, Alma 11:27–29, and the appendix at the end of this chapter.)
- **God is an exalted man:** Num. 23:19; Mal. 3:6; John 4:24 (cf. Luke 24:39); Rom. 1:22–23; 1 Tim. 1:17.
- **Preexistence of man:** Genesis 2:7 indicates that man experienced his creation on earth. Christ was preexistent, but there is no mention of man's preexistence—John 3:31; 8:23.
- **The fall was "a blessing in disguise":**[38] Rom. 5:12–21; 8:19–22.
- **Rejection of original sin:** Ps. 51:5; Rom. 5:12–21; Eph. 2:1–3.
- **Rejection of the virgin birth:** Matt. 1:18–20; Luke 1:26–35.
- **Rejection of salvation by grace through faith alone:** John 6:28–29; Rom. 3:21–30; 5:1; Gal. 2:16, 21; Eph. 2:8–10; Phil. 3:9; Titus 3:5–7.
- **Some sins are beyond the blood of Christ (blood atonement):** 1 John 1:7–9.
- **The church went into apostasy and required restoration:** The Bible denies that the apostasy was universal, requiring a restoration: Matt. 16:18; 1 Tim. 4:1, "*some* will depart from the faith" (not "all").
- **The Aaronic and Melchizedekian priesthoods were restored:** Heb. 7:12, 24; 1 Peter 2:9; Rev. 1:5–6. Every believer

becomes a priest through redemption. Christ alone is our great High Priest (Heb. 9:24–26). The word *unchangeable* in Hebrews 7:24 means not transferred to another. It is the peculiar possession of Jesus Christ: "His priesthood is untransferable" (Goodspeed), "permanent" (NIV).[39]

- **Joseph Smith was a prophet of God:** See *The Testing of Joseph Smith Jr.—Was He a Prophet?* by James D. Bales. Gordon R. Lewis states, "Fifty-eight prophecies of Joseph Smith examined in detail by G. T. Harrison failed to come to pass."[40] Smith failed the test of Deuteronomy 18:20–22.
- **The restored gospel is Mormonism:** Paul warns of "a different gospel" (Gal. 1:8–9). A true restoration must agree with that which it restores. This is not true of Mormonism.

THE SEMANTIC PROBLEM

One of the difficulties a Christian experiences in sharing his faith with a Mormon is the semantic problem—the redefinition of terms. Former Mormon Marvin Cowan explains: "When Mormons and Bible believing Christians try to communicate, there is usually a problem because the LDS use Biblical terms which are defined by sources other than the Bible."[41] What are these terminological differences? The following list of terms, with their contrasting LDS and biblical meanings (adapted from one prepared by Sandra Tanner of Utah Lighthouse Ministry),[42] will help in "scaling the language barrier."[43]

TERMINOLOGY DIFFERENCES

Preexistence

LDS: Everyone preexisted—we all exist eternally.

Bible: Only Christ preexisted—not man (John 8:58; Col. 1:17). We didn't have a spiritual existence prior to earth (1 Cor. 15:46).

Fall

LDS: The fall brought mortality and physical death—not fallen nature. Adam was given two conflicting commandments and was supposed to fall.

Bible: God tempts no one (James 1:13–14). Man is basically sinful (Rom. 8:5–8; 1 Cor. 2:14).

Sin

LDS: Sin involves specific acts—not man's basic nature.

Bible: We are in spiritual rebellion until conversion (Eph. 2:3; Rom. 5:6). We do not just commit sins—we are sinful (Matt. 1:21).

Repentance

LDS: We need only to repent of individual acts—not sinful nature.

Bible: We must repent of basic rebellion (Jer. 17:9; Luke 5:32).

Atonement—Salvation by grace

LDS: Christ's death brought release from the grave and universal resurrection. Salvation by grace is universal resurrection. Beyond this man must earn his place in heaven.

Bible: Salvation is not universal but based on the belief of each individual (Rom. 1:16; Heb. 9:28; Eph. 2:8–9).

Redeemed

LDS: People are redeemed from mortal death only—not sinful rebellion or spiritual death.

Bible: Christ redeems from more than mortal death. He redeems us from spiritual death (Rom. 6:23; Eph. 2:1).

Gospel

LDS: The gospel consists of the Mormon church system and doctrines.

Bible: The gospel is the message of Christ's death and resurrection as atonement for our sins (1 Cor. 15:1–4; Gal. 1:8).

Born again

LDS: New birth is by baptism into the LDS church.

Bible: We are spiritually dead until our spiritual rebirth (1 Peter 1:23; 2 Cor. 5:17).

True church

LDS: Only the Mormon church is true. The true church was taken from earth until Joseph Smith restored it.

Bible: As born-again Christians we are part of God's true church (1 Cor. 12:12–14; Matt. 18:19–20; Matt. 16:18).

Authority—Priesthood

LDS: Only LDS have authority to baptize, ordain, etc. Mormons have a two-part system of priesthood—Melchizedek and Aaronic.

Bible: Christ brought an end to the Aaronic priesthood and is the only High Priest after the manner of Melchizedek (Heb. 5:9; 2 Tim. 2:2).

Baptism

LDS: Baptism must be performed by the LDS priesthood.

Bible: Emphasis is on the believer—not priestly authority (Mark 16:15–16).

Sons of God

LDS: We are all literal spirit children of God.

Bible: We become children of God at conversion (John 1:12).

Eternal life

LDS: Eternal life consists of exaltation in the Celestial Kingdom. There will be childbearing in heaven. One must have a temple marriage.

Bible: Eternal life is not limited to certain ones in heaven. There is no mention of parenthood or temple marriage. Eternal life is given to all Christians (1 John 5:12–13).

Immortality

LDS: A universal gift, immortality is the ability to live forever but is not the same thing as eternal life.

Bible: There is no distinction between immortality and eternal life (2 Tim. 1:10).

Heaven

LDS: Heaven is divided into three kingdoms—Celestial, Terrestrial, and Telestial. There is a place for almost everyone (misuse of 1 Cor. 15:40–41).

Bible: There are only two conditions—everlasting punishment or life eternal (Matt. 25:31–46).

Kingdom of God

LDS: The kingdom of God is the Celestial Kingdom—only those in the Celestial Kingdom are in God's presence. Those in the Terrestrial or Telestial Kingdoms are not in the presence of the Father.

Bible: All of the redeemed will be in God's presence (Rev. 21:1–3). All believers are part of God's kingdom (Matt. 13:41–43).

Hell

LDS: Hell as an institution is eternal—inmates come and go as in jail. They do not spend eternity there but stay until they have paid their debts to God.

Bible: There is no mention of people getting out of hell (Rev. 21:8; Matt. 13:24–43, 47–50; Luke 16:26).

Godhead

LDS: God the Father is a resurrected man with a physical body. Christ is a separate resurrected man with a physical body. The Holy Ghost is a separate man with a spiritual body. They are three totally separate gods.

Bible: God is not a man (Num. 23:19). There is only one God (Isa. 43:10–11; 44:6; 45:21–22). The Father is a spirit and invisible (John 4:24; 1 Tim. 1:17).

Holy Ghost

LDS: The Holy Ghost is a separate God from the Father and the Son and is different from the Holy Spirit. The Holy Ghost is a person—the Holy Spirit is an influence from the Father and not personal.

Bible: The same Greek word is used for Holy Ghost and Holy Spirit (1 Cor. 3:16 and 6:19).

Virgin birth

LDS: God, as a resurrected, physical man, is the literal Father of Jesus in the same manner in which men are conceived on earth. Matthew 1:18 is in error.

Bible: Mary was "with child of the Holy Spirit" (Matt. 1:18).

WITNESSING TO MORMONS

Sandra Tanner, from her experience and as a former Mormon, gives the following suggestions for witnessing more effectively to Mormons.[44]

1. You are already witnessing to your LDS friends—one way or another.
2. Start with a positive witness for Christ.
3. If they say they believe like you, ask them to define their terms. Also ask for references from the Bible.
4. Be aware of LDS teaching and pet arguments so you won't get caught off guard. (Not to argue but to better understand and be prepared.)
5. Make a list of Scriptures that refute their claims (even memorize them) and keep it in your Bible.
6. Stress Christ and the need of committing one's life to Him. The gospel is the good news of Christ's atoning work, not a church system.

7. Don't get sidetracked defending your denomination—their first need is Christ.

8. If they say the Bible has been changed to the point it no longer is reliable for doctrine, kindly ask them for documentation. Such claims should be challenged. (A good book on this is *The New Testament Documents: Are They Reliable?* by F. F. Bruce, InterVarsity Press.)

9. Challenge them to study the Bible. If Mormonism is a "restoration" of Christ's church, it will agree with the Bible (Acts 17:11–12).

10. Pray for God's love and patience. You are to plant and water, but God gives the increase (1 Cor. 3:6). Winning a Mormon takes TIME.

11. Challenge them to think for themselves—truth can stand up to examination (2 Tim. 2:15).

12. Sharing is not arguing! Don't raise your voice or argue (2 Tim. 2:23–26; Titus 3:2–9). Is your love showing?

13. Share with them how you saw yourself as a sinner, separated from God and your repentance and turning to Christ for salvation.

14. Keep grace and works in proper order. Explain how works are a result of grace, not a way to earn it (Gal. 5:22–23; Eph. 2).

15. Mormons limit the result of the Fall (LDS say it brought mortality but not a sinful nature, as man is supposed to be a god in embryo)—thus they limit the need of atonement (they say Christ brought resurrection to all, but our place in heaven is based on our good works). A Mormon doesn't usually understand he is a lost sinner in need of salvation. Salvation means something to you only when you are lost (Luke 7:36–47). They believe they commit sin but don't understand man's basic sin-nature.

16. A Mormon quickly senses if you are talking from genuine concern and conviction or if you are just out to put down Mormons. Check your attitude. You hinder the work of God if your motive is less than to share Christ's love.

"Always be full of joy in the Lord; I say it again, rejoice! Let everyone see that you are unselfish and considerate in all you do" (Phil. 4:4–5—LB).

APPENDIX: WITNESSING REFERENCES FROM THE BOOK OF MORMON (1981 ED.)[45]

There is only one God—
- Alma 11:26–29 (pages 235–36): Amulek: No more than one God.
- 2 Nephi 31:21 (114–15): Father/Son/Holy Ghost "is one God without end."
- Mosiah 13:34 (174): God will take the form of man.
- Mosiah 15:1–4 (175–76): Christ is Father and Son, one God.
- Alma 11:44 (236–37): Father/Son/Holy Spirit "is one Eternal God."
- 3 Nephi 11:27 (429): Father/Son/Holy Ghost "are one."
- 3 Nephi 11:36 (430): "The Father, and I, and the Holy Ghost are one."
- Testimony of Three Witnesses: Father/Son/Holy Ghost "is one God."

God is unchangeable, and eternal progression is impossible—
- Mosiah 3:5 (151–52): God is "from all eternity to all eternity."
- 3 Nephi 24:6 (455): "I am the Lord, I change not."
- Mormon 9:9–10 (485): God does not vary or change.
- Mormon 9:19 (486): God is an "unchangeable Being." He "changeth not."
- Moroni 7:22 (522): God is "from everlasting to everlasting."
- Moroni 8:18 (526): God is not "a changeable being; but he is unchangeable from all eternity to all eternity."

God is a Spirit and could not be a glorified man—
- Alma 18:2–5 (253–54): God as "Great Spirit."
- Alma 18:24–28 (255): "this Great Spirit, who is God."
- Alma 22:9–11 (264): God "is that Great Spirit."

Salvation is by grace, through faith—

- 2 Nephi 10:24 (80): It is "only in and through the grace of God that ye are saved."
- Mosiah 3:17–18 (153): Salvation is only through the blood.
- Mosiah 5:7 (158): One is "spiritually begotten . . . through faith."
- Alma 22:14 (264): The works of man merit nothing.
- Ether 3:14 (493): They who believe shall become "my sons and daughters."
- Moroni 7:26 (523): "by faith, they become the sons of God."

You must be born again—

- Alma 5:14 (218): "Have ye spiritually been born of God? . . . experienced this mighty change in your hearts?"
- Alma 22:15–16 (264): To have "eternal life" and be "born of God," thou must "repent of all thy sins . . . [and] call on his name in faith."

Baptism for the dead will not help them—

- Alma 34:32–35 (295): There is no repentance after death [strong].
- 2 Nephi 9:38 (76): All "who die in sins . . . remain in sins."
- Mosiah 3:25 (154): The wicked are sent to "endless torment, from whence they can no more return."
- Mosiah 16:5 (178): The devil has "all power" over the unsaved.
- Mosiah 16:11 (179): The evil go to "endless damnation."
- Mosiah 26:25–27 (198): The unsaved go "into everlasting fire."

Hell is eternal—

- Jacob 3:11 (123): Hell is a "lake of fire and brimstone."
- Jacob 6:10 (133): Hell is "forever and ever."
- 2 Nephi 9:16 (74): The "lake of fire and brimstone . . . [remains] forever." [The word is not in the original MS of the 1830 *Book of Mormon*.]
- 2 Nephi 28:21–23 (108): The devil says, "There is no hell."

Polygamy is an abomination—

- Jacob 2:24, 28 (121)—compare to *Doctrine and Covenants* 132:1.
- Mosiah 11:2 (167): Polygamy is a sin and abominable.
- Ether 10:5 (505): Polygamy is not right "in the sight of the Lord."

Errors in the *Book of Mormon*—

- Saved by grace after all you can do? (2 Nep. 25:23 [99–100]).
- How could Moroni "read" Hebrews 13:8 and James 1:17 (Mormon 9:9 [485]) when the New Testament never reached America?
- Helaman 12:25–26 (397), ostensibly written in 7 B.C., says "we read," quoting 2 Thessalonians 1:9 and John 5:29, decades before they were written.
- Jesus, "a Son of God"? (Alma 36:17 [299]).
- Mosiah 21:28 (188) says King Mosiah had a gift from God, but the original manuscript of the *Book of Mormon* refers to "King Benjamin."
- In the former edition of the *Book of Mormon*, Jacob 7:27 (135) has the French word *adieu* used by people speaking "Reformed Egyptian" around 500 B.C. But the French language did not exist until about A.D. 700. This passage has been changed to "I bid farewell" in the 1981 edition.
- 2 Nephi 3:11–16 (60–61) predicts the coming of Joseph Smith from the loins of Joseph, son of Lehi. Yet Lehi's descendants were wiped out (Morm. 6:11 [479]; 8:2–3 [481]), while Joseph Smith's ancestors came from England.

SELECT BIBLIOGRAPHY

Bannister, S. I. *For Any Latter-day Saint: One Investigator's Unanswered Questions.* Fort Worth: Bible Publications, Inc., 1988.

Beckwith, Francis J., Norman Geisler, Ron Rhodes, Phil Roberts, Jerald Tanner, and Sandra Tanner. *The Counterfeit Gospel of Mormonism.* Eugene, Ore.: Harvest House, 1998.

Blomberg, Craig, and Stephen E. Robinson. *How Wide the Divide? A Mormon and Evangelical Conversation.* Downers Grove, Ill.: InterVarsity Press, 1997. Some reviewers' comments: "A landmark in Evangelical LDS dialogue blurs the essential differences between Christianity and Mormonism" (Timothy Oliver, "Disguising the Divide," *Watchman Expositor* 15, 4, 1998, 22). ". . . One of the most ill-conceived and dangerous books ever written" (Jay Crosby, "How Wide the Divide?" *The Evangel*, September/October; November/December 1997, 3). "And if a Christian layperson comes across this book, and this book only, would they not be badly misled concerning the real issues and the full teaching of the LDS Church?" (James White, *Is the Mormon My Brother?* [Minneapolis: Bethany, 1997], 183). See also chapter 11, "How Wide the Divide?"

Bowman, Robert M., Jr. "How Mormons Are Defending Their Faith." *Christian Research Journal* (fall 1988), 22–24.

Brodie, Fawn M. *No Man Knows My History.* 2d ed. New York: Knopf, 1971. The best biography of Joseph Smith, written by the niece of a former president of the LDS church, David O. McKay.

Cares, Mark J. *Speaking the Truth in Love to Mormons.* Milwaukee: WELS Outreach Resources, 1998.

Cowan, Marvin W. *Mormon Claims Answered.* Rev. ed. Salt Lake City: Marvin W. Cowan, 1989.

Farkas, John R., and David A. Reed. *Mormonism: Changes, Contradictions, and Errors.* Grand Rapids: Baker, 1995.

_____. *Mormons: How to Witness to Them.* Grand Rapids: Baker, 1997.

Hoekema, Anthony A. *Mormonism.* Grand Rapids: Eerdmans, 1963. Presents a concise treatment of Mormon history, sources of authority, doctrines, and the genuineness of the *Book of Mormon.*

Larson, Charles M. *By His Own Hand Upon Papyrus.* Grand Rapids:

Institute for Religious Research, 1992.

Larson, Stan. *Quest for the Golden Plates: Thomas Ferguson's Archeological Search for The Book of Mormon*. Salt Lake City: Freethinker Press, 1996.

McKeever, Bill. *Answering Mormons' Questions*. Minneapolis: Bethany, 1991.

McKeever, Bill, and Eric Johnson. *Questions to Ask Your Mormon Friend*. Minneapolis: Bethany, 1994.

_____. *Mormonism 101*. Grand Rapids: Baker, 2000.

Marquardt, Michael H., and Wesley P. Walters. *Inventing Mormonism: Tradition and the Historical Record*. Salt Lake City: Smith Research Associates, 1994.

Persuitte, David. *Joseph Smith and the Origins of the Book of Mormon*. Jefferson, N.C.: McFarland, 1985.

Petersen, LaMar. *The Creation of the Book of Mormon: A Historical Inquiry*. Salt Lake City: Freethinker Press, 1998.

Reed, David A., and John R. Farkas. *Mormons Answered Verse by Verse*. Grand Rapids: Baker, 1992.

Reynolds, Leslie. *Mormons in Transition*. 2d ed. Grand Rapids: Baker, 1998.

Rhodes, Ron, and Marian Bodine. *Reasoning from the Scriptures with the Mormons*. Eugene, Ore.: Harvest House, 1995.

Roberts, R. Philip, with Tal Davis and Sandra Tanner. *Mormonism Unmasked: Confronting the Contradictions Between Mormon Beliefs and True Christianity*. Nashville: Broadman & Holman, 1998.

Scott, Latayne. *Ex-Mormons: Why We Left*. Grand Rapids: Baker, 1990. The experiences of eight ex-Mormons who became Christians.

_____. "Mormonism and the Question of Truth." *Christian Research Journal* (summer 1992): 24–29.

Tanner, Jerald, and Sandra Tanner. *Mormonism—Shadow or Reality?* 5th ed. Salt Lake City: Utah Lighthouse Ministry, 1987. The Tanners have written numerous books; this is their best. In 1980

Moody Press released a condensed and updated version of an earlier edition of this book as *The Changing World of Mormonism*. A further condensing of the material at a reasonable cost is found in *Major Problems of Mormonism*, published by the Tanners in 1989. It is recommended that the reader obtain their book list at the Utah Lighthouse Ministry address below.

Van Gorden, Kurt. *Mormonism.* Grand Rapids: Zondervan, 1995.

White, James R. *Is the Mormon My Brother? Discerning the Differences Between Mormonism and Christianity.* Minneapolis: Bethany, 1997. White's book presents a response to *How Wide the Divide?*

Walters, Wesley P. "Mormonism." In *Evangelizing the Cults*, edited by Ronald Enroth. Ann Arbor, Mich.: Servant, 1990.

_____. *New Light on Mormon Origins From the Palmyra NY Revival.* El Cajon, Calif.: Mormon Research Ministry, 1997 (first printed in 1967).

MATERIALS

Tracts, pamphlets, cassettes, and books for study and distribution may be obtained from the following sources.

Utah Lighthouse Ministry
P.O. Box 1884
Salt Lake City, Utah 84110
Phone 801-485-0312
Website www.utlm.org
Salt Lake City Messenger

Mormonism Research Ministry
P.O. Box 20705
El Cajon, CA 92021-0955
Phone/Fax 619-447-3873

Website www.mrm.org
Quarterly *Mormonism Researched*

UMI Ministries
P.O. Box 348
Marlow OK 73055
Phone 800-654-3992
Website www.umi.org
The Evangel

Concerned Christians
P.O. Box 18
Mesa, AZ 85211
Phone 480-833-2LDS
Website www.ConcernedChristians.org
Newsletter *The Cross*

Berean Christian Ministries
P.O. Box 1091
Webster, NY 14580-7791
Phone 716-872-4033
Website www.frontiernet.net/~bcmmin
Quarterly *Newsletter*

Concerned Christians and Former Mormons
P. O. Box 3554
Mission Viejo, CA 92691
Phone 800-215-5018

4 CHRISTIAN SCIENCE

The Church of Christ, Scientist, founded by Mary Baker Eddy in the last quarter of the nineteenth century, has presented a challenge to orthodox Christianity in its theology and stress on healing. Many people have left denominational churches to become Christian Scientists because of a healing experience. The membership of this movement is not available because its *Church Manual* instructs, "Christian Scientists shall not report for publication the number of the members of The Mother Church, nor that of the branch churches."[1]

After decades of decline, the worldwide membership has been estimated at between 75,000 and 100,000, and some scholars have observed that there might be more Christian Scientists outside the church than there are in it.[2] At one time it was also estimated that approximately 80 percent of Christian Scientists were in the United States and that 75 percent were women.

In the following survey of Christian Science, attention is given to its founder, developments since her death, the group's use of censorship, the question whether Christian Science is Christian, and its doctrine. A select bibliography concludes the chapter.

THE FOUNDER OF CHRISTIAN SCIENCE

Apart from Mary Baker Eddy, Christian Science would not exist. Mary Baker was born in Bow, New Hampshire, in 1821. Her family

was devoutly religious, and she grew up in an orthodox Congregational church. In *Retrospection and Introspection*, Mrs. Eddy explains
how she reacted against the Reformed faith—in particular, the doctrine of predestination.[3] According to Walter Martin and Norman
Klann, her childhood was

> marked continually by a strange illness which seemed to grow
> in severity with Mary's increasing years. Young Mary, history
> tells us, was quieted during these fits by rocking in a specially
> built cradle made of an old sofa where she remained until she
> fell asleep. As a small child she had often been subject to fre-
> quent fits evidenced by a peculiar physical lethargy erupting
> into violent spasms of pronounced hysteria and ending even-
> tually in unconsciousness. Mary Baker was also plagued with
> a neurotic temper which exhibited itself whenever her wishes
> were denied and her anger aroused.[4]

Her personal problems, emotional and physical, continued beyond her youth and help to explain the emphasis of her religion on
the healing of mind and body.

Mary Baker was married three times. Her first husband, George
Glover, died shortly before the birth of their only child. Her second
marriage was to Daniel Patterson, a dentist; this ended in a divorce,
she being the innocent party. Her third husband, Asa Eddy, died of a
chronic heart condition, but Mrs. Eddy claimed that he had been
killed by "mesmeric poison."[5]

The turning point in Mrs. Eddy's life began in 1862, when she became a patient and student of P. P. Quimby of Portland, Maine, who
was the founder of mental healing in America. Raymond J. Cunningham continues:

> Then, in the ten years following that healer's death (1866),
> she compounded his system of mental therapeutics with an
> idealistic metaphysics and a pantheistic theology to create a

distinctive creed, summarized in a brief doctrinal formula known as the "Scientific statement of being."

"There is no life, truth, intelligence, or substance in matter. All is infinite Mind and its infinite manifestation, for God is All in all, Spirit is immortal Truth; matter is mortal error. Spirit is the real and eternal; matter is the unreal and temporal. Spirit is God, and man is His image and likeness; hence, man is spiritual and not material."

Consequently, "the only reality of sin, sickness, or death is the awful fact that unrealities seem real to human, erring belief."[6]

Other key dates in the life of Mrs. Eddy and the development of Christian Science include

1866: She claimed that as a result of a serious fall on a slippery walk (Feb. 1), she discovered the principles of Christian Science.[7] Her account of the severity of the accident was contradicted by the attending physician, Alvin Cushing, in an affidavit of more than one thousand words.[8]

1875: The first edition of *Science and Health* was published. In 1883 *with Key to the Scriptures* was added to the title. This book has been revised, rewritten, and polished grammatically and structurally—despite Mrs. Eddy's claim to divine inspiration:

> I should blush to write of *Science and Health with Key to the Scriptures* as I have, were it of human origin and I apart from God its author, but as I was only a scribe echoing the harmonies of heaven in divine metaphysics, I cannot be supermodest of the Christian Science textbook.[9]

1879: The Church of Christ, Scientist, was organized in Charlestown, Massachusetts. In 1892 this became the First Church of Christ, Scientist, in Boston—The Mother Church.

1895: The *Church Manual* was published. It established the permanent procedures for the government of the church. Christian Science is a highly authoritarian organization because of this publication, for it states: "This Manual shall not be revised without the written consent of its author."[10]

1910: Mrs. Eddy "passed on" on December 3, 1910. Since her death, the leadership of the movement has been in the hands of a "self-perpetuating board of directors whose members choose their own successors—a structure that today leaves church critics with no direct power to change the church."[11]

DEVELOPMENTS SINCE 1910

Reporter Bob Baker says that Christian Science became "the fastest-growing American denomination."[12] Religious census reports for 1906, 1926, and 1936 indicate that the church in the U.S. experienced rapid growth, especially for the two decades after 1906 (1906—85,717; 1926—202,098; 1936—268,915).[13] (Census figures would not represent the total membership.) Baker continues: "By the 1960s, however, membership in the church was plummeting, the number of full-time practitioners was decreasing (there are only 3,000 today [1992], compared to 11,000 in 1950) and the Monitor was losing millions of dollars each year."[14]

Until 1961 the respected *Christian Science Monitor* "even turned a profit. Then, as national advertising drifted to television, the Monitor's losses built up, totaling $166 million between 1970 and 1987, according to confidential church documents provided to The Times."[15] Despite efforts to rejuvenate the paper by hiring a new manager and a new editor in the early 1980s, "by 1985, the Monitor was still losing $16 million a year, its circulation mired near 150,000, down from a high of 170,000 in the 1950s, and [manager] Hoagland decided that the paper could not be made profitable."[16] What could be done to change the situation? Hoagland convinced church leaders that a profit could be realized and a wider audience could be reached through a venture into radio and television and the addition of a new publication. An ambitious program was initiated to expand into each of these areas. "He began to pour tens of millions of dollars into *World Monitor* magazine, a nightly cable-TV news program, a Boston UHF station and, especially, a 24-hour cable service, Monitor Channel, founded in May [1991]."[17] The Monitor Channel shut down on June 28, 1992.[18] "The church said it rejected four proposals for purchase of the Monitor Channel . . . that has cost the church about $250 million."[19] Church members were also told that $325 million had been spent on television between 1984 and 1992 and that $900 million had been spent on the *Christian Science Monitor* and the periodicals *Christian Science Journal, Sentinel,* and *Herald.*[20]

"To some distinguished Christian Scientists," wrote *New York Times* reporter Peter Steinfels, "the church's new media empire was the religious equivalent of junk bonds." They objected because it "was financially imprudent" and, more important, "a distraction from spiritual renewal."[21]

A second major issue that brought strong criticism and division from within the church was the church's publication in 1991 of *Destiny of the Mother Church,* by church member Bliss Knapp—apparently to obtain a large sum of money. The church had rejected his book for publication in 1948 (after it was published privately in 1947) because it came close to deifying Mrs. Eddy.[22] The title and question in a *Time* article summarized the matter: "Tumult in the Reading Rooms: Christian Science reverses its stand on an 'unsound' book. Was it to fulfill the terms of a $90 million will?"[23] This question was answered in the affirmative by disillusioned Christian Scientists, who accused "church leaders of compromising doctrinal principles for dollars."[24]

The wills of Knapp, his wife, and his sister-in-law required that the church "publish the book as 'authorized' Christian Science literature and display it prominently in 'substantially all' Christian Science reading rooms" within twenty years (by May 1993) to receive the money held in trust.[25] "A Los Angeles Superior Court granted the request by two rival beneficiaries—Stanford University and the Los Angeles County Museum of Art—to delay payment of the $98 million." A settlement was approved on December 15, 1993, in which the church would receive 53 percent of the trust and the remainder would be divided between the university and the art museum.[26]

Christian Science has also made the news in recent years when children with treatable illnesses died. Instead of consulting doctors, parents resorted to prayer and Christian Science practitioners.[27]

CHRISTIAN SCIENCE CENSORSHIP

The authors of *The Christian Science Myth* considered the subject of censorship to be so significant that they devoted a chapter to it (chap. 7). They described it as "one of the most distinguishing characteristics of the Christian Science religion."[28] The appearance of a chapter from this book in the January 1955 *Eternity* magazine and the subsequent publication of the entire exposé brought Christian Science opposition.[29]

The most well-known attempt at censorship concerned the publication of *Mrs. Eddy: The Biography of a Virginal Mind*, by Edwin F. Dakin, in 1929.[30]

Other writers have also recognized the power of the Christian Science Committee on Publication. Lutheran author George Wittmer writes, "The powerful forces of Christian Science censorship have been marshaled again and again to suppress writings that were unfavorable to the cause of this sect."[31] Catholic journalist William J. Whalen observes: "In recent years the Committee's methods of boycott and intimidation have managed to stifle nearly all published criticism of the cult."[32]

Carolyn Poole, formerly a third-generation Christian Scientist, observes on the basis of her experience that Christian Science "practices censorship, in effect, by discouraging members from reading any unauthorized literature, which means any religious material that is not sold in the reading rooms or printed by the Christian Science publishing house."[33] This is true today.

IS CHRISTIAN SCIENCE CHRISTIAN?

Why do evangelical Christians state that Christian Science is not Christian and therefore that its followers are not Christians? A simple answer is provided by some former Christian Scientists: "Because Christian Science rejects every single basic Christian doctrine, it is viewed by the entire Christian community as a non-Christian cult."[34]

In his theological analysis of Christian Science, P. G. Chappell agrees and offers some additional insights to explain the problem:

> Theologically, the Church of Christ, Scientist, does not concur with the basic tenets of historic orthodox Christianity. Although it uses the theological vocabulary of traditional Christianity, *it assigns metaphysical meanings to terms.* The sources of authority for the church are the Bible and Eddy's writings. *Members accept Eddy's writings as divine revelation and interpret the Bible allegorically through her works.* The most significant authority for the church is Science and Health. . . . Eddy referred to this volume as containing the perfect word of God, and thus was divine and infallible teaching.[35]

Anthony Hoekema's study of Christian Science publications also confirms its theology as non-Christian.

CHRISTIAN SCIENCE DOCTRINE

The following quotations are taken from the conclusions reached by Hoekema in *The Four Major Cults.* His study is based on primary sources, and the interested reader should check this source for the reasons behind the conclusions.

The Bible:

Science and Health declares the Bible to be "our sufficient guide to eternal life,"[36] but, as Hoekema comments, "In actual practice, however, Christian Scientists accept the Bible only as interpreted by Mrs. Eddy, whose book *Science and Health* . . . is really their ultimate source of authority, and is thus placed above the Bible."[37]

God:

"God, to the Christian Scientist, is divine Mind, and Mind is all that truly exists. . . . Christian Science repudiates the orthodox Trinity."[38]

Man:

"Christian Science, in its anthropology, denies the reality of the body, of sin and the fall, and repudiates man's temporality and finiteness."[39]

Jesus Christ:

In summary, Christian Science denies the unity of the person of Jesus Christ, Jesus' present existence, the absolute necessity for Jesus' earthly mission, the incarnation of Christ, the Virgin birth of Jesus, the sinlessness of Jesus, the full deity of Jesus, and Jesus' genuine humanity. In addition, Christian Scientists reject Jesus' suffering, death, physical resurrection, and ascension into heaven.[40]

It is clear that Christian Scientists repudiate the teaching which is the heart of the gospel: that Jesus Christ suffered and died on the cross in order to bear the burden of God's wrath against sin, so that we might be saved through his blood. We are left with a Jesus who was merely an example.[41]

Salvation:

For Christian Science salvation from sin is accomplished when one ceases to sin, or when one stops believing that there is such a thing as sin. In either event, the death of Christ has nothing to do with salvation; if Christ had never existed, it would have made no real difference.[42]

Eschatology:

Christian Science "repudiates every major tenet of Christian eschatology."[43]

Having concluded that Christian Scientists reject every major doctrine of historic Christianity, Hoekema then states:

> Christian Scientists, therefore, have no more right to apply to themselves the title *Christian* than have Buddhists or Hindus—with whose teachings, indeed, Christian Science has greater affinity than with those of Christianity. We conclude that, strictly speaking, Christian Science is neither Christian nor science.[44]

CONCLUSION

A refutation of Christian Science doctrine has not been included in this study because the natural, normal interpretation of the Bible, as well as common sense, provides a complete exposé.[45] The approach to Scripture followed by Mrs. Eddy ignores or "violates all recognized canons of biblical interpretation."[46] It must be admitted that Mrs. Eddy did have some unusual talents and that she built what was one of the most powerful churches in America. But, as the Bible and a study of her theology clearly show, she was not a trustworthy channel of divine revelation.

SELECT BIBLIOGRAPHY

Bates, Ernest S., and John V. Dittemore. *Mary Baker Eddy, the Truth and the Tradition*. New York: Knopf, 1932. "Devastating in its documentary evidence" (*The Christian Science Myth*, 35).

Dakin, Edwin F. *Mrs. Eddy: The Biography of a Virginal Mind*. New York: Scribner's, 1929.

Fraser, Caroline. "Suffering Children and the Christian Science Church." *The Atlantic Monthly*, April 1995, 105–20.

Gottschalk, Stephen. *The Emergence of Christian Science in American Religious Life*. Berkeley: University of California Press, 1973. Gottschalk, a Christian Scientist, has written a comprehensive and scholarly interpretation of the development of Christian Science.

Hartsook, Andrew W. *Christian Science after 1910*. Santa Clarita, Calif.: The Bookmark, 1993. Written by a Christian Scientist, it documents the basic reasons for the decline of the church.

Hoekema, Anthony A. *The Four Major Cults*. Grand Rapids: Eerdmans, 1963. The section on Christian Science (171–221) is also published as a booklet.

Kramer, Linda S. *The Religion That Kills: Christian Science: Abuse, Neglect, and Mind Control*. Lafayette, La.: Huntington House, 2000.

Martin, Walter R., and Norman H. Klann. *The Christian Science Myth*. Rev. ed. Grand Rapids: Zondervan, 1955. An able treatment of Christian Science history, doctrines, censorship, and cures, including a refutation of their theology.

Milmine, Georgine. *The Life of Mary Baker G. Eddy and the History of Christian Science*. 2d ed. Grand Rapids: Baker, 1971. This book was reprinted by the University of Nebraska Press in 1993. As originally published, it had only Milmine as the author. "It was later realized that Willa Cather probably wrote the biography using Milmine's research" (Kramer, *The Religion That Kills*, 107).

Scott, Latayne C. *Why We Left a Cult.* Grand Rapids: Baker, 1993.
Two of the six accounts were written by former Christian Scientists.
Swan, Rita. "Children, Medicine, Religion, and the Law." *Advances in Pediatrics* 44 (1997): 491–543.

FURTHER INFORMATION

The official Christian Science website is www.tfccs.org. An independent CS publications and information website is www.christian-science.org.

Christian Way
P.O. Box 39607
Phoenix, AZ 85069
An evangelical ministry of former Christian Scientists
Phone 602-973-4768 Fax 602-789-7165
Website www.christianway.org

5 | UNITY SCHOOL OF CHRISTIANITY

The Unity School of Christianity, begun by Myrtle Fillmore and Charles Fillmore in the late 1880s, has become one of the best-known healing cults of American origin. Unity claims a following of millions, and it has been characterized as "the largest mail order religious concern in the world."[1] The impressive headquarters of this movement are located in Unity Village, on about sixteen hundred acres near Lee's Summit, Missouri. In the brief treatment that follows, Unity's history, outreach, and doctrines are surveyed. The cult is then viewed and evaluated in the light of the Bible and orthodox Christian scholarship. A select bibliography concludes the chapter.

HISTORY

The Unity story began in Kansas City, Missouri, when in 1886 (possibly 1885) Myrtle and Charles Fillmore attended a lecture given by Eugene B. Weeks. He represented the Illinois Metaphysical College, founded by Emma Curtis Hopkins, a former associate of Mary Baker Eddy and an editor of the *Christian Science Journal*.[2] Myrtle had suffered for years with tuberculosis and malaria, and "from her earliest childhood, she had been taught to think of herself as an invalid."[3] Of the ideas presented by Weeks, one stood out in Myrtle Fillmore's mind: *"I am a child of God and therefore I do not inherit sickness."*[4] According to her testimony, her entire life changed with the acceptance of this statement, and in two years she was "no longer an invalid."[5] The story of her healing was set forth in *How I Found Health*.

Charles Fillmore, who had been a cripple from youth as a result of a skating accident,[6] also applied the healing principles discovered by his wife. He saw results and wrote: "My chronic pains ceased. My hip healed and grew stronger, and my leg lengthened until in a few years I dispensed with the steel extension that I had worn since I was a child."[7]

The Fillmores wanted to share their newfound faith with others, and in 1889 the first issue of *Modern Thought* was published. At this time they were affiliated with Christian Science and were spreading Mrs. Eddy's philosophy through their publication. They were also ordained in that church. But a short time later they ended their formal ties with Christian Science because "it seemed to them that Mrs. Eddy and some of her followers were exhibiting feelings of exclusivity in the revelations from God."[8]

The Fillmores' religious philosophy was clearly stated: "We see the good in all religions and we want everyone to feel free to find the Truth for himself wherever he may be led to find it."[9] In developing their religious system, the Fillmores were extremely eclectic, a fact that will be developed later. In the spring of 1891, the term "Unity" was taken as the name of the organization. This name was aptly chosen, for it embodied the central principle of the group: "Unity of the soul with God, unity of all life, unity of all religions, unity of the spirit, soul and body; unity of all men in the heart of the truth!"[10]

Because of his dislike for dogma, it was thirty years before Charles Fillmore was induced to write a statement of faith. And even then he cautioned:

> We . . . are hereby giving warning that we shall not be bound by this tentative statement of what Unity believes. We may change our mind tomorrow on some of the points, and if we do, we shall feel free to make a new statement of faith in harmony with the new viewpoint.[11]

Myrtle Fillmore died in 1931. Charles Fillmore then married Cora G. Dedrick, who had served as private secretary to him and his wife. He died in 1948. The great growth of Unity was largely due to the Fillmores' two sons, Lowell and Rickert, who became president and secretary, respectively. Rickert died in 1965 and Lowell in 1975. The leadership of Unity is still in the Fillmore family. Grandson Charles R. Fillmore, who served as president (1972–1987), is presently chairman of the board, and great-granddaughter Constance Fillmore is currently president.[12]

The growth of the movement may be attributed to its emphasis on love, healing, and prosperity, Unity's ability to spread its message through the printed page, and Silent Unity. Silent Unity is a twenty-four-hour, 365-days-a-year prayer ministry that people can contact for prayer.[13] It received two million requests in 1997.

OUTREACH

The Unity outreach program is worldwide. In 1988 Unity was actively involved with 4 million people in 160 countries. Silent Unity handled 650,000 phone calls and 2.7 million letters. *Daily Word* went out to almost 3 million homes, and *Unity* magazine had more than 400,000 subscribers. Unity published hundreds of thousands of pamphlets, and more than a hundred Unity-published books were in print. The mail operation averaged "more than 300,000 pieces of mail each working day." "The Unity Printing Department is one of the largest and best equipped in the Midwest."[14] In addition, Unity has a continuing education program, with resident and extension programs.

For twenty-three years, Unity produced "The Word," a one-minute inspirational message, which was aired over hundreds of radio stations and a number of television stations. In May 1992 it was decided to stop producing the series.[15] Unity's worldwide outreach cannot be ignored.

DOCTRINES

That the Fillmores were eclectic in formulating Unity's doctrinal system has already been mentioned. Charles Ferguson was right when he stated that Unity "was undoubtedly joined by an umbilical cord to the New Thought, and sired by Christian Science."[16] All three stress healing, but there are also a number of differences. While recognizing these, J. K. Van Baalen states, "We maintain, however, that they are as much alike as triplets."[17]

Reflecting on its eclectic nature, F. E. Mayer comments that "Unity has elements of Quakerism (Inner Light), of Christian Science (healing), of Theosophy (reincarnation), of Rosicrucianism (cosmic unity), of Spiritism (the astral or physical self), of Hinduism (idealism)."[18]

Gordon Lewis has carefully examined Unity's doctrinal position, and he concludes that this cult differs from orthodox Christianity in at least seven essential respects:

(1) *The Bible is not divine revelation* but merely fallible human witness to revelation. It may be reinterpreted at will in accord with Fillmore's flashes of insight.
(2) *Man's primary problem is not sin* before a holy God but mistakes in thinking. So man's primary need is not for the gospel of redemption but examples of denials and affirmations.
(3) *Jesus is not God* incarnate but a man who effectively demonstrated the Christ ideal.
(4) *Jesus made no real atonement* [at Calvary] for man's sin but exemplified the power of mind over matter.
(5) *Christ's resurrection was no miracle* but another demonstration of thought control.
(6) *Faith is a magic wand* which uses divine principle to satisfy personal desires.
(7) *In place of divine grace* through faith alone Unity stresses human striving to overcome the lower by the higher self.[19]

In addition, the doctrine of reincarnation should also be mentioned:

> We believe that the dissolution of spirit, soul, and body, caused by death, is annulled by rebirth of the same spirit and soul in another body here on earth. We believe the repeated incarnations of man to be a merciful provision of our loving Father to the end that all may have opportunity to attain immortality through regeneration, as did Jesus. "This corruptible must put on incorruption."[20]

Scripture's answer is clear:

> It is appointed for men to die once, but after this the judgment. (Heb. 9:27)

> Therefore, just as through one man sin entered the world, and death through sin, and thus death spread to all men, because all sinned. (Rom. 5:12)

> We are confident, yes, well pleased rather to be absent from the body and to be present with the Lord. (2 Cor. 5:8)

> For to me, to live is Christ, and to die is gain. But if I live on in the flesh, this will mean fruit from my labor; yet what I shall choose I cannot tell. For I am hard pressed between the two, having a desire to depart and be with Christ, which is far better. (Phil. 1:21–23)

> For we know Him who said, "Vengeance is Mine; I will repay, says the Lord." And again, "The Lord will judge His people." It is a fearful thing to fall into the hands of the living God. (Heb. 10:30–31)

EVALUATION

A number of evangelical writers and theologians have written on the Unity School of Christianity and what it would mean to accept this cult's teachings. Some of these conclusions are cited.

J. Oswald Sanders writes:

> We would say that the greatest danger in this movement lies in the many beautiful and true sentiments contained in its literature which would appeal to the uninstructed leading them to believe that they are imbibing true Scripture teaching. Satan does his most dangerous work when he is masquerading as an angel of light.
>
> With an impersonal God, a Christ degraded to the level of man, and man elevated to deity, with a denial of sin and consequent emasculation of the atonement, with self regeneration and the Hindu doctrine of reincarnation, we are amazed at the temerity of its promoters in designating it a school of "Christianity."[21]

Walter R. Martin concludes:

> In order to join the Unity School of Christianity (the Unity cult), it must be understood that one would have to renounce every basic doctrine of the Christian faith, deny the deity, physical resurrection and personal second coming of our Lord, and believe in the reincarnation of the soul as over against the doctrine of the physical resurrection of the body.[22]

Russ Wise explains:

> Since Unity does not recognize the work of Christ on the cross (the Atonement), but rather accepts evolution as a positive ingredient in man's spirituality, it is only logical that they

embrace reincarnation as a valid system for spiritual enlightenment. As you can see then, Unity is not based on biblical
teaching. To the contrary, it is heavily influenced by Eastern
thought and belief. Unity is a classic New Age cult and is not
Christian in any aspect of its doctrine or teaching.[23]

Ruth A. Tucker notes Unity's nonorthodox theology and a significant influence of its philosophy:

> Unity's acceptance of non-Christian tenets such as reincarna-
> tion and its rejection of various biblical tenets have placed the
> movement outside traditional Christian orthodoxy, but there
> have been other movements and individuals regarded by
> some to be within the framework of orthodoxy that have been
> deeply influenced by the same philosophy of positive think-
> ing. The Modern Faith movement that focuses on health and
> wealth—as proclaimed by such preachers as Charles Capps,
> Kenneth Hagin, and Kenneth Copeland—is an example of
> this, as is the theme of positive thinking which is preached by
> such mainline celebrity preachers as Norman Vincent Peale
> and Robert Schuller.[24]

That Unity's doctrines are nonbiblical and thus non-Christian has
been stated by every evangelical scholar who has written on the subject. And, as Tucker reminds the reader: "More than any other established alternative religion, Unity has embraced the New Age
Movement. The religious philosophy of Unity is entirely compatible
with New Age concepts."[25]

CONCLUSION

With Unity, as with Christian Science, the refutation of the system is provided by a natural, normal interpretation of the Bible. In

dealing with adherents of the Unity School of Christianity, it is necessary to define terms that are employed. It is also important to stress

- that God is a person, not a principle,[26]
- that man is a lost, depraved, and helpless sinner in need of God's grace for salvation,
- that redemption as set forth in the Bible is vastly different from that propagated by Unity.

Pertinent are these words from the pen of the apostle John: "Beloved, do not believe every spirit, but test the spirits, whether they are of God; because many false prophets have gone out into the world" (1 John 4:1).

Select Bibliography

There are no books and only a few booklets (many out of print) that have been written by evangelical scholars exclusively on the Unity School of Christianity. Most treatments are included in books that deal with a number of cults. The Unity School of Christianity materials are voluminous and easy to obtain from Unity or from public libraries.

Examination and Refutation of Unity

Ankerberg, John, and John Weldon. *Encyclopedia of Cults and New Religions.* Eugene, Ore.: Harvest House, 1999. Unity is treated on 540–76.

Duncan, Homer. "An Evaluation of the Unity School of Christianity." Lubbock, Tex.: Missionary Crusader, n.d. This sixteen-page study shows that Unity teachings contradict the Bible.

Juedes, John P. "Mail Order Christianity: Is a Word from Unity a Word from God?" *Personal Freedom Outreach Newsletter,* January–March 1987, 4–6.

Lewis, Gordon R. *Confronting the Cults.* Philadelphia: P&R, 1966. Unity is treated on 131–61.

McClain, Elissa L. "Should the Church Apologize to Unity?" *Christian Research Journal* (winter/spring 1987), 31. She sees "mind-science" thinking infiltrating the evangelical church.

McDowell, Josh, and Don Stewart, *Handbook of Today's Religions.* Nashville: Thomas Nelson, 1983. Unity is treated on 131–35.

Martin, Walter R. *The Kingdom of the Cults.* Rev. ed. Minneapolis: Bethany, 1985. Unity is treated on 275–94.

———. *Unity.* Grand Rapids: Zondervan, 1957. This thirty-two-page booklet deals with history, doctrine, and refutation.

Talbot, Louis T. *What's Wrong with Unity School of Christianity?* Findlay, Ohio: Dunham, 1956. This sixty-four-page booklet deals with history, doctrines, and refutation. It is compiled from a four-part series that appeared in *The King's Business* (October 1955 to January 1956).

Tucker, Ruth A. *Another Gospel: Alternative Religions and the New Age Movement.* Grand Rapids: Zondervan, 1989. Unity is treated on 177–90.

Van Baalen, J. K. *The Chaos of Cults.* 4th rev. ed. Grand Rapids: Eerdmans, 1962. Unity is treated on 128–45.

Van Gorden, Kurt. "The Unity School of Christianity." In *Evangelizing the Cults*, edited by Ron Enroth, 139–53. Ann Arbor, Mich.: Servant, 1990.

Whalen, William J. *The Unity School of Christianity.* Chicago: Claretian, 1966. This is a booklet by a Catholic journalist.

Wise, Russ. "Unity School of Christianity." Richardson, Tex.: Probe Ministries, www.prob.org/docs/unity (1995).

UNITY MATERIALS

When the writer visited Unity Village during the summer of 1971, the following Unity books were recommended as basic for an introduction to Unity: *Lessons in Truth* (Cady), *Christian Healing and Dynamics for Living* (C. Fillmore), *What Are You?* (Shanklin). *The Metaphysical Bible Dictionary* (C. Fillmore) explains Unity's metaphysical language.

The book *The Household of Faith (The Story of Unity)*, by James D. Freeman and the booklets *The Adventure Called Unity* and *Unity's Statement of Faith* are also helpful. The video cassette *On Wings of Truth: The Unity Way to Health, Prosperity and Love* (1988) "incorporates Unity philosophy, history and practical self-development instructions."

The official Unity website is www.unityworldhq.org.

6

WORLDWIDE
CHURCH OF GOD:
FROM ARMSTRONGISM
TO THE N.A.E.

I first became aware of Herbert W. Armstrong and the Radio Church
of God (the Worldwide Church of God since 1968) shortly after
World War II through listening to "The World Tomorrow" broadcast.
It has been estimated that this radio program (when Armstrong's son,
Garner Ted, was the speaker) had the potential to be heard by 95 percent of the population of America and Canada. In addition, it
reached all the continents of the world.[1]

From listening to the program, I first concluded that Armstrong belonged in the doctrinal camp of the Jehovah's Witnesses—the cult in which
I was reared. Later I learned that his theological system was far more complex. In "Herbert Armstrong: Mr. Confusion," Roger Campbell expresses
the typical experience and conclusion of other writers on the subject:

> After being asked about Herbert Armstrong, I set out to iden-
> tify him. I soon discovered, however, that pigeonholing this
> fellow's teaching was no simple task. Just when I thought I
> had him labeled with one of the well-known cults, another of
> his teachings would come to my attention that would divorce
> him from that group. Here was sort of an hybrid-heretic who

seemingly had jumped the fences of three or four mistaken groups to take along some peculiar and unscriptural doctrine of theirs to make it his own.[2]

While the discerning Christian would soon realize that much of Armstrong's message was less than orthodox, many who were contacted by his ministry did not have this discernment, and confusion resulted.

What is the history of the Worldwide Church of God (WCG) and its founder? What are the major doctrines known as Armstrongism? What place did prophetic speculation have in the WCG? What happened after Armstrong's death in 1986? What churches were formed by WCG splinter groups? For further study, a select bibliography, which includes WCG recommendations, is presented.

HISTORY

Herbert W. Armstrong was born in Des Moines, Iowa, in 1892. Although he "was brought up in a respectable Protestant church of traditional Christianity,"[3] his early years were characterized by a disinterest in religion. At the age of eighteen, after graduation from high school, he began a career in public relations and advertising. He married Loma Dillon in 1917. The Armstrongs moved to the Pacific Northwest, and in 1926 Herbert was motivated to study the Bible through the influence of his wife, who began observing the seventh-day Sabbath. She had been brought to this position by Mrs. Ora Runcorn, a family friend, who was a member of the Church of God (Stanberry, Missouri), "an early offshoot of the Seventh-day Adventist Church."[4] After investigation, Mr. Armstrong also was converted and began keeping the Sabbath. He later identified himself with the Church of God and was ordained in 1931.

When doctrinal disputes rent the Church of God, a sizable portion of the membership withdrew and set up a new headquarters in

Salem, West Virginia, in 1933. Armstrong joined this faction but afterward broke from it and established the Radio Church of God.

A radio ministry began in January 1934, over the one-hundred-watt station KORE in Eugene, Oregon. The first issues of *The Plain Truth* were also run the same year on a borrowed mimeograph. These events were later seen as having great prophetic import: "What was actually happening, back in 1934, was precisely this: Jesus Christ (Rev. 3:8) was opening the gigantic mass-media DOOR of radio and the printing press for the proclaiming of His same original GOSPEL to all the world!"[5]

In *A True History of the True Church*, Herman L. Hoeh explains the importance of Herbert W. Armstrong to God's program:

> Jesus chose Paul, who was highly educated, for spreading the gospel to the Gentiles. He later raised up Peter Waldo, a successful businessman, to keep His truth alive during the Middle Ages. In these last days WHEN THE GOSPEL MUST GO AROUND THE WORLD, Jesus chose a man amply trained in the advertising and business fields to shoulder the mission—HERBERT W. ARMSTRONG.[6]

How did the Worldwide Church of God under Armstrong's leadership view all other churches? "There is ONLY ONE WORK that is preaching the true gospel. . . . THIS IS THAT WORK. Every other work rejects the message of Jesus Christ—rejects His RULE through His LAWS. There is no exception!"[7]

In 1947 Armstrong moved his ministry to Pasadena, California, where he expanded his radio outreach. He also established Ambassador College, to train church leaders to organize his followers into small congregations. The work grew in the 1950s and 1960s with the purchase of more radio time on stations in the United States and Canada, and then in other countries, where church offices were opened.[8]

The 1970s brought a number of problems to the Armstrong empire. "Confidence in the Armstrong cause was eroding quite rapidly

by the beginning of 1970 as a credibility gap continued to widen regarding his 1972 prophecies."[9] (He had predicted that in 1972 "the
Great Tribulation would begin and that the WCG would be miracu-
lously transported to Petra, Jordan, where the church would be physically protected." The "booklet *1975 in Prophecy* predicted the return
of Christ in that year").[10] The years 1972 through 1974 were also critical, with dozens of ministers and thousands of members leaving or
being disfellowshiped.[11] The *Los Angeles Times* published a number
of articles dealing with the difficulties the church was experiencing,
with such headlines as: "Founder of Church Fights Defections,"
"Garner Ted Show to End," "Father Banishes Garner Ted Armstrong," "State Files Suit against Armstrong's Empire," and "Receiver
Takes Over Armstrong Empire."

While other splits from the Worldwide Church of God had oc-
curred during the decade, the most significant one was brought about
by the June 1978 excommunication of Garner Ted Armstrong, heir
apparent to the Armstrong empire. The following month, he announced that he had formed his own church, the Church of God, International, in Tyler, Texas, and that he would resume his religious
broadcasting.[12]

From small beginnings in 1934, the WCG emerged as a potent
religious force. When Herbert W. Armstrong died in 1986, 120,000
people attended services each week, annual income was about $200
million, *The Plain Truth* circulation was more than 8 million (and
claimed more than 20 million readers), and *The World Tomorrow* television program was "one of the most watched religious programs in
America."[13] Joseph Tkach Sr., who had served as director of church
administration, had been named by Armstrong as his successor.

ARMSTRONGISM

Joseph Tkach Jr., present WCG Pastor General, articulates what
many other researchers have also determined: "Mr. Armstrong was

nothing in his theological approach if not eclectic. He borrowed and adapted most of his 'unique' teachings from others."[14] He concludes: "Contrary to what we formerly believed, none of our distinctive doctrines was specially revealed to Mr. Armstrong—at least not in the way the term 'specially revealed' is commonly understood."[15]

A number of writers on the WCG refer to the doctrines advanced by Armstrong as "Armstrongian theology" or "Armstrongism."[16] What are some of these doctrines once held by the WCG but no longer taught?

The doctrine of the Trinity was condemned as a pagan doctrine. God the Father had a human form and "all the bodily parts we have." While Christ was deity and coeternal with God, he was a *separate God from the Father.*" Christ became the Son of God only when he was born of the Virgin Mary.[17] "Herbert W. Armstrong's position was really polytheistic: he taught that there were two separate God-beings in the God-family and that our ultimate destiny was to be God as God is God in that family."[18] Jesus inherited the sinful nature of Adam and could have sinned.[19] At his resurrection "God the Father did not cause Jesus Christ to get back into the body which had died."[20] The Holy Spirit is not a member of the Godhead, and his personhood is denied. He is an "it," a manifestation of God's power.[21]

No one was saved at the present time, because no one can be born again until the resurrection. "Until then, a believer was only conceived, not born."[22]

> We also claimed that while Christ died for the sins of the world, believing in Christ was insufficient to gain salvation; the believer must also obey Christ. That obedience . . . included adherence to the Saturday Sabbath, to dietary laws (as in Leviticus 11), and observance of religious festivals, new moons, and holy days. We taught that only those who obeyed all the commandments . . . could achieve salvation. . . . While salvation was a gift, one had to qualify to receive this free gift.[23]

There was only one true church, the WCG. "All others were false and apostate. We labeled Roman Catholicism 'the Great Whore of Babylon' (from Revelation 17) and called Protestants her harlot daughters." The true church was destroyed, and the gospel was no longer preached beginning in about A.D. 53.

> The truth reappeared nineteen centuries later under the leadership of Mr. Armstrong. He was Christ's apostle in the last days who would restore lost truth to the church in order to prepare for Christ's imminent Second Coming. . . .
>
> The WCG interpreted the Bible to discourage members from voting, to prohibit righteous people from serving in the military, marrying after being divorced, relying on doctors (for anything other than accidents, "repair surgery" or childcare), using cosmetics, or observing Christmas, Easter and birthdays. No other church followed all these strict practices, therefore, they were apostate and we were righteous.
>
> Because this was true, we distanced ourselves from every other "Christian falsely so-called" and all other denominations. We became isolated and set apart.[24]

As to whether the church was under the Old or the New Covenant, Armstrong concluded that "we were 'between' the two covenants. Such a pronouncement gave Mr. Armstrong a platform from which to pick and choose which items from the Old Covenant and which items from the New Covenant would apply to us."[25]

Armstrong's version of British Israelism was one of his cardinal teachings. A chapter of Tkach's *Transformed by Truth* ("The Central Plank Cracks") is devoted to the subject. He explains its significance:

> We believed that we were the true Israel. We observed the Sabbath and the feasts for a very good reason. We were biological descendants of Abraham. We were not Gentiles. This

doctrine formed the basis for how we lived each day and for our view of the world and its future in prophecy.[26]

Sabbath keeping was viewed as

> the *sign* that the United States was one of the ten lost tribes of Israel. . . .
> If Americans lost the Sabbath, they wouldn't know who they were; they would lose the knowledge that they were really Israel. . . . Our whole commission was to tell people to start keeping the Sabbath; then they would recover their identity and then they would be ready for the Lord's imminent Second Coming. . . . He claimed British-Israelism held the key to unlocking biblical prophecy. . . .[27]

What about these doctrines of Armstrongism and the WCG today? Tkach responds: "Today we reject what is well known as 'Armstrongism,' that is, adherence to the teachings of Herbert W. Armstrong in lieu of biblical evidence to the contrary. We have accepted the primacy of the Bible and of the gospel."[28]

PROPHETIC SPECULATION

One additional subject characterized Armstrong's teaching. In the past, one of the most prominent features of Armstrongism was the attention given to prophecy. Tkach explains: "One of the more peculiar dynamics of WCG history is that our flagship publication, *The Plain Truth* magazine, formerly contained vast amounts of prophetic speculation."[29] After reviewing a number of examples from the late 1970s and early 1980s, he admits: "While we did manage a few correct calls, we also made more than *one hundred* prophetic predictions that failed. . . . For fifty years we predicted the end of the world would come in just four to seven short years."[30]

Twenty years before Tkach's admission, former WCG staff member Marion McNair devoted two chapters of *Armstrongism: Religion or Ripoff?* to documenting the false predictions of Herbert W. Armstrong and his associates. He lists twenty-one major failed prophecies made between 1938 and mid-1945 and forty for the years 1947 to 1972.[31] In spite of this disastrous record, Garner Ted Armstrong claimed that "major events now taking place in the world were being predicted 35 years ago in *The Plain Truth.*"[32] However, a review of some of the predictions made in 1940 and 1941 reveals prophetic failure, not success. It was predicted that Armageddon was only three to four years away, Britain would be invaded and conquered, the U.S. and Britain would "annihilate the Turks from off the earth," America would be conquered and its people transplanted to other lands, the Italians would capture Egypt and Palestine, and Hitler would be the victor in the invasion of Russia.[33] The events of history have demonstrated that Herbert W. Armstrong and his associates failed the prophetic test recorded in Deuteronomy 18:20–22.

From Armstrongism to the N.A.E

Space does not permit a detailed account, but shortly after Herbert W. Armstrong's death, reports of changes in WCG doctrines began to appear. Beginning in 1987, under the leadership of Joseph Tkach Sr., major doctrinal changes were announced, and Armstrong's books and booklets were either revised or not reprinted.[34] These developments were noted by a number of scholars, cult watchers, former and present members, and the secular press. As might be expected, these changes produced an exodus of members and pastors from the church, and new churches, loyal to Armstrong's teachings, were formed. Two years after his death, church membership peaked at 126,800 members, with 150,000 in attendance.[35] The current WCG website records that there are only about 30,000 members in the U.S. and 50,000 members worldwide.[36]

In his article on the WCG written in 1995, outside observer Phillip Arnn writes: "In the last nine years, Tkach has overturned every major unbiblical doctrine held by that organization."[37] And Ruth Tucker adds: "The 'changes'—as they are referred to by insiders—are truly historic. Never before in the history of Christianity has there been such a complete move to orthodox Christianity by an unorthodox fringe church."[38]

On May 7, 1997, under the leadership of Joseph Tkach Jr., who succeeded his father in 1995, the Worldwide Church of God became a member of the National Association of Evangelicals (N.A.E.).[39]

In his article in the winter 1996 *Christian Research Journal*, Joseph Tkach Jr. looks back over the momentous changes of doctrine in the WCG during the previous ten years:

> Gone are our obsession with a legalistic interpretation of the Old Testament, our belief in British Israelism, and our insistence on our fellowship's exclusive relationship with God. Gone are our condemnations of medical science, the use of cosmetics, and traditional Christian celebrations such as Easter and Christmas. Gone is our long-held view of God as a "family" of multiple "spirit beings" into which humans may be born, replaced by a biblically accurate view of one God who exists eternally in three Persons, the Father, the Son, and the Holy Spirit.
>
> We have embraced and now champion the New Testament's central theme: the life, death, and resurrection of Jesus Christ. . . . We proclaim the sufficiency of our Lord's substitutionary sacrifice to save us from the death penalty of sin. We teach salvation by grace, based on faith alone, without resort to works of any kind. We understand that our Christian works constitute our inspired, grateful response to God's work on our behalf . . . and by these works we do not "qualify" ourselves for anything.
>
> . . . Christians are under the New Covenant, not the Old. This teaching resulted in our abandoning past requirements

that Christians observe the seventh-day Sabbath as "holy time," that Christians are obligated to observe the annual festivals commanded to Israel in Leviticus and Deuteronomy, that Christians are required to triple tithe, and that Christians must not eat foods that were "unclean" under the Old Covenant [one is reminded of Galatians 4:31–5:1].[40]

WORLDWIDE CHURCH OF GOD SPLINTER GROUPS

It is difficult to keep up with the many divisions in the movement established by Herbert W. Armstrong in 1934. In *Transformed by Truth*, Tkach lists more than one hundred Worldwide Church of God splinter groups that left the movement between 1970 and 1996. Only three of these are identified by Tkach as having a membership of more than three thousand: Philadelphia Church of God (1989), Global Church of God (1992), and United Church of God (1995).[41] This last church was much larger: "In early 1995, hundreds of ministers and 12,000 members left to form the United Church of God."[42]

How do these new churches view Armstrong's teachings? Tkach quotes from the writings of each of them as they *affirm* the "18 Truths Restored by Herbert W. Armstrong" or the WCG system of doctrine in place when Armstrong died.[43] Gerald Flurry, who founded the Philadelphia Church of God, claims that his church "is the only one that is remaining faithful to the truth found in Armstrong's teaching."[44]

Each of these churches has also experienced divisions, with new organizations being formed. It is also of interest that the men who led in the organization of the Global Church of God (Roderick Meredith) and United Church of God (David Hulme) were fired from leadership positions in their churches in 1998. They went on to start yet other ministries: Living Church of God (Meredith) in San Diego, California, and Church of God, an International Community (Hulme) in Pasadena, California.[45]

In 1998 the board of Garner Ted Armstrong's Church of God, International, which he founded in Tyler, Texas in 1978, revoked his ministerial credentials because of a "sexual harassment suit by a Tyler masseuse and the discovery that Armstrong had a five-year extramarital affair." Armstrong then founded the Intercontinental Church of God and the Garner Ted Evangelistic Association, also in Tyler, Texas.[46]

Herbert W. Armstrong is dead, the WCG has renounced his teachings, but Armstrongism lives on in many WCG splinter organizations.

Select Bibliography

Developments and Theology under Herbert W. Armstrong

Anderson, Stanley E. *Armstrong's 300 Errors Exposed by 1300 Bible Verses.* Nashville: Church Growth, 1973.

Benware, Paul N. *Ambassadors of Armstrongism: An Analysis of the History and Teachings of the Worldwide Church of God.* Nutley, N.J.: P&R, 1975. This book was republished in 1984 by Christian Literature Crusade and included a revised appendix, which updated developments through 1982.

Campbell, Roger F. *Herbert W. Armstrong and His Worldwide Church of God: A Critical Examination.* Fort Washington, Pa.: Christian Literature Crusade, 1974.

DeLoach, Charles F. *The Armstrong Error.* Plainfield, N.J.: Logos, 1971. Written by a former member.

Hinson, William B. *The Broadway to Armageddon.* Nashville: Religion in the News, 1977. Written by a former WCG minister.

Hopkins, Joseph M. *The Armstrong Empire: A Look at the Worldwide Church of God.* Grand Rapids: Eerdmans, 1974. The best treatment of the subject for the period covered.

Lowe, Harry W. *Radio Church of God: How Its Teachings Differ from Those of Seventh-day Adventists*. Mountain View, Calif.: Pacific Press, 1970. Lowe is an Adventist.

McNair, Marion. *Armstrongism: Religion or Rip-Off? An Exposé of the Armstrong Modus Operandi*. Orlando: Pacific Charters, 1977. The most revealing of the books by former members.

Marson, Richard A. *The Marson Report Concerning Herbert W. Armstrong*. Seattle: Ashley-Calvin Press, 1970. Written by a former member.

Martin, Walter R. Herbert W. *Armstrong and the Radio Church of God in the Light of the Bible*. Rev. ed. Minneapolis: Bethany, 1968.

Robinson, David. *Herbert Armstrong's Tangled Web: An Insider's View of the Worldwide Church of God*. Tulsa: John Hadden, 1980. Written by a former WCG minister who served in varying capacities in the church and came to know many of its leaders.

Sumner, Robert L. *Armstrongism: The "Worldwide Church of God" Examined in the Searching Light of Scripture*. Brownsburg, Ind.: Biblical Evangelism Press, 1974.

DEVELOPMENTS SINCE HERBERT W. ARMSTRONG'S DEATH

Alnor, William A. "Unprecedented Changes Affect Worldwide Church of God." *Christian Research Journal* (spring 1991), 5–6.

Arnn, Phillip. "The Worldwide Church of God." *Watchman Fellowship Profile*, 1995.

Adams, John S. "The Plain Truth about the Worldwide Church of God." *The Baptist Bulletin*, July 1998, 23–26.

Davies, Eryl. "The Worldwide Church of God," (in 3 parts) *Evangelical Times* (August 1998), 20; (September 1998), 25–26; (October 1998), 11.

Ditzel, Peter. "From the Plain Truth to the Real Truth: A Former Worldwide Church of God Writer Tells Why He Left." *The Quar-*

terly Journal (October-December 1995), 4, 11–14. A revealing
and insightful testimony.

―――――. "Transforming the Truth: The Worldwide Church of God
Continues to 'Make' History," *The Quarterly Journal* (July-
September 1998), 5–12. A former WCG worker expresses some
reservations about the church.

Frame, Randy. "Worldwide Church of God Edges Toward Orthodoxy." *Christianity Today*, November 9, 1992, 57–58.

Gomes, Alan W. "The Worldwide Church of God: Acknowledging
the 'Plain Truth' about the Trinity?" *Christian Research Journal*
(spring/summer, 1994), 29–31, 39–40.

LeBlanc, Doug. "The Worldwide Church of God: Resurrected into
Orthodoxy." *Christian Research Journal* (winter 1996), 6–7,
44–45.

Martin, Tim. "The Philadelphia Church of God." *Watchman Fellowship Profile*, 2000.

Neff, David. "The Road to Orthodoxy." *Christianity Today*, October
2, 1995, 15.

Stammer, Larry B. "Denomination Riven by Dramatic Changes in
Doctrine," *Los Angeles Times*, September 26, 1995, A-3, A-37.

Tkach, Joseph W., Jr. "A Church Reborn." *Christian Research Journal*
(winter 1996), 53.

Trott, Jon. "The Saga of a 'Cult' Gone Good." *Cornerstone* 26, 111
(1997), 41–44.

WORLDWIDE CHURCH OF GOD

Statement of Beliefs of the Worldwide Church of God (1995). Presents
a brief summary of the new doctrinal position of the WCG to this
point. In the introduction it is explained: "The Spirit of God leads
the Church into all truth (John 16:13). Accordingly, this Statement of Beliefs does not constitute a closed creed. The Church
constantly renews its commitment to truth and deeper under-

standing and responds to God's guidance in its beliefs and practices."

"A Brief List of Doctrines of the Worldwide Church of God" is also found on the WCG official website. The following publications are recommended "for further information on the history of the church" in "Transformed by Christ: A Brief History of the Worldwide Church of God" www.wcg.org/lit/AboutUs/history (1998).

Tkach, Joseph, Jr. *Transformed by Truth*. Sisters, Ore.: Multnomah, 1997.

Nichols, Larry, and George Mather. *Discovering the Plain Truth: How the Worldwide Church of God Encountered the Gospel of Grace*. Downers Grove, Ill.: InterVarsity Press, 1998.

Martin, Walter. *Kingdom of the Cults*. 1997 rev. ed. Minneapolis: Bethany, 1997. Appendix A.

Tucker, Ruth. "From the Fringe to the Fold: How the Worldwide Church of God Discovered the Plain Truth of the Gospel." *Christianity Today*, July 15, 1996, 26–32.

SPIRITUALISM (SPIRITISM)

The notoriety over Bishop James Pike's bestseller, *The Other Side* (1968), and his televised séance with Arthur Ford on September 3, 1967, did much to bring Spiritualism back into prominence for the first time in about fifty years. Currently another revival of Spiritualism is taking place in America and other places in the world, such as Europe and South America. This time it is called channeling—explained as voluntary spirit possession.[1] And, according to a *USA Today*-CNN-Gallup poll (1994), almost seventy million Americans believed that communication with the dead is possible.

Some Christians call this phenomenon Spiritualism, while others prefer the term *Spiritism*. "Spiritualism" is the title commonly used by its adherents, and " 'Spiritism' is a kind of nickname given to the Spiritualist Movement by its opponents."[2]

In the following survey, several important matters are investigated. What is Spiritualism's modern history? What is its appeal? What manifestations are attributed to it? How might these be explained? What do Spiritualists teach? What do Christians who were formerly mediums say about Spiritualism? What does the Bible say about it? The concluding select bibliography lists materials for further study.

HISTORY

The beginnings of the movement are lost in antiquity, but modern Spiritualism dates from March 31, 1848, in the psychic experiences of Margaret Fox and Kate Fox in Hydesville, New York.[3] Some Spiritualists say the modern movement began three years earlier with the spirit-controlled writings of Andrew Jackson Davis. The movement reached its zenith in the United States during the 1850s, when it was estimated that there were 1.5 to 2 million Spiritualists.

The first National Convention of Spiritualists met in Chicago in 1864. At the second National Convention in Philadelphia the next year, after some debate and opposition, the American Association of Spiritualists was established. But its continued existence would be short-lived. Because of opposition to organization, dwindling attendance at subsequent conventions, and ideological differences, "in 1875, no one thought of keeping the association alive. State and local organizations persisted. . . . Spiritualism reverted back to the loose networks more consistent with its religious beliefs."[4] At the same time, Spiritualist camp meetings were thriving, with up to 12,000 in attendance.[5]

In 1893 the first Delegate Convention of Spiritualists of the United States assembled in Chicago and organized what is today known as the National Spiritualist Association of Churches (N.S.A.C.), and Spiritualism as an organized religion began.[6] Because it is the oldest American Spiritualist organization, "most of the other Spiritualist associations derive from it." Groups have separated from the N.S.A.C. over such issues as the authority of the Bible (Progressive Spiritualist Church), the belief in reincarnation (National Spiritual Alliance; General Assembly of Spiritualists), and racial segregation (National Colored Spiritualist Association).[7] Many Spiritualists in America belong to other organizations or are not affiliated with any group.

The National Spiritualist Association of Churches has influence beyond its membership through its distribution of Spiritualist literature, its Morris Pratt Institute (in Wauwatosa, Wisconsin), and the publication of *The National Spiritualist Summit,* a monthly magazine.[8]

The Declaration of Principles of the N.S.A.C. appears on the back cover of the current issues of *The National Spiritualist Summit.* As J. Gordon Melton says, "Most Spiritualists would also agree with the basic statements concerning God, ethics, and the afterlife included" in this declaration.[9]

THE APPEAL OF SPIRITUALISM

It is a mistake to view Spiritualism primarily as a psychic phenomenon. It is that, but it is also a religion. "Spiritualism is the science that investigates, analyzes and classifies, all things dealing with Spirit in its various manifestations. It constitutes a true religion when one lives in accordance with its teachings."[10]

The reasons for Spiritualism's appeal are not difficult to ascertain. The question of what lies beyond death draws many people. The desire to keep in touch with the departed attracts others. Still other people are lured by curiosity. Spiritualism claims to give concrete proof of life after death and enlightenment. This is illustrated in an excerpt from *The National Spiritualist:*

> All religious groups are largely theoretical, with respect to theology and practice with the exception of Spiritualism which does not theorize, but which has a direct contact with the teachers and loved ones in the greater life. Spiritualism does not promise a sometime uncertain future in another life after death, it teaches and gives the student experience of spiritual life here and now. Such direct contact and full realization is bliss beyond compare. There are no ceremonies in the Spiritualist church which are not understood by all who participate, no mysteries of theology, all that is required is that the

Spiritualist shall be earnest in his desire for more light and more understanding of the beauty of contact with universal truth.

. . . Therefore since life is a school, why waste time any longer in a theatrical kindergarten? Graduate to the understanding of Spiritualism which is the science, philosophy and religion of enlightenment.[11]

THE MANIFESTATIONS AND INTERPRETATIONS OF SPIRITUALISM

Traditional Spiritualism, with its inevitable séances, claims a number of manifestations that are usually classified as either physical or mental. Some examples of the physical phenomena are table tipping, slate writing, rappings, materialization, levitation, and Ouija board operation. Examples of mental phenomena include automatic writing, clairvoyance, and speaking in a trance. Many additional examples of each category could be listed.

How are the phenomena to be explained? Spiritualists argue that the genuine manifestations (not frauds or merely psychic force) are proof of contact with departed spirits.

Christians see the phenomena as explainable in three possible ways: trickery, psychic force, and demonic activity. Which of the three explanations applies in an individual case is not always easy to determine. It is proved that some Spiritualists have employed trickery. That psychic force[12] can be operative has also been demonstrated, and Spiritualists admit that sometimes the messages received reflect the mind of the sitter.[13] They even admit that the "spirit world contains evil spirits" and "untruthful and deceiving spirits" and that advice received has at times led to tragic results.[14] Christianity teaches that the spirits contacted are not those of the dead but rather fallen angels (demons) who impersonate the dead to deceive and to possess those who call upon them.[15] This is why the Bible strongly condemns spiritism.

THE TEACHINGS OF SPIRITUALISM

F. E. Mayer accurately states that "as a religious system spiritualism must be characterized as a complete denial of every Christian truth."[16] The questions and answers below are all taken from *The A.B.C. of Spiritualism,* a booklet currently published and distributed by the National Spiritualist Association of Churches.

11. *Is not Spiritualism based upon the Bible?*
    No. The Bible so far as it is inspired and true is based upon Mediumship and therefore, both Christianity . . . and Spiritualism rest on the same basis.

    Spiritualism does not depend for its credentials and proof upon any former revelation.

16. *Do Spiritualists believe in the divinity of Jesus?*
    Most assuredly. They believe in the divinity of all men. Every man is divine in that he is a child of God, and inherits a spiritual (divine) nature. . . .

17. *Does Spiritualism recognize Jesus as one person of the Trinity, co-equal with the Father, and divine in a sense which divinity is unattainable by other men?*
    No. Spiritualism accepts him as one of many Savior Christs, who at different times have come into the world to lighten its darkness and show by precept and example the way of life to men. It recognizes him as a world Savior but not as "the only name" given under heaven by which men can be saved.

19. *Does not Spiritualism recognize special value and efficacy in the death of Jesus in saving men?*
    No. Spiritualism sees in the death of Jesus an illustration of the martyr spirit, of that unselfish and heroic devotion to hu-

manity which ever characterized the life of Jesus, but no special atoning value in his sufferings and death.

21. *From the standpoint of Spiritualism how is the character and work of Jesus to be interpreted?*

   Jesus was a great Mediator, or Medium, who recognized all the fundamental principles of Spiritualism and practiced them. . . .

86. *Does Spiritualism recognize rewards and punishments in the life after death?*

   No man escapes punishment, no man misses due reward. The idea of an atoning sacrifice for sins which will remove their natural consequences (pardon) is simply ludicrous to the inhabitants of the spirit spheres.

88. *Do the departed, according to Spiritualism, find heaven and hell as depicted by Church teaching?*

   Not at all. . . . They deny any vision of a great white throne, any manifestations of a personal God, any appearance of Jesus, or any lake of fire and torment for lost souls. . . .

Additional denials of biblical doctrine could be quoted, but it is obvious that Spiritualism represents a system that rejects orthodox Christianity.[17]

Two Former Spiritualists

Raphael Gasson and Victor Ernest were mediums before they became Christians. Both have written books relating their experiences.

In *The Challenging Counterfeit,* Gasson writes:

The journey, for me, from Satan to Christ, was a long and weary one, taking dangerous pathways, bringing many bitter experiences and battles against principalities and powers, almost costing my life, before I reached that place called Calvary—where the Lord Jesus Christ met my need as a sinner as I surrendered my life to Him.[18]

We find that Spiritualism is one of the most fiendish of Satan's methods of instilling lying deceptions into the minds of people. Having tested the spirits and the claims they make through their mediums, we most certainly find them contrary to the Word of God.[19]

In *I Talked with Spirits*, Ernest explains how demon interference continued years after his conversion:

Sometimes my memory would go blank; other times my throat would constrict and I couldn't speak. As soon as I prayed for help through the power of Jesus' blood, the attack ceased and I continued. These assaults continued sporadically for thirteen years. . . .[20]

Ernest gives the following account of a question-and-answer séance that took place shortly before his conversion:

When the trumpet returned for my third and last question, I reviewed what the spirit had said. "O spirit, you believe that Jesus is the Son of God, that he is the Savior of the world—do you believe that Jesus died on the cross and shed his blood for the remission of sin?"
The medium, deep in a trance, was catapulted off his chair. He fell in the middle of the living room floor and lay groaning as if in deep pain. The turbulent sounds suggested spirits in a carnival of confusion.[21]

These quotations reveal the source and dangers of Spiritualism and the deliverance to be found in Christ.

THE BIBLE ON SPIRITUALISM

Spiritualists often argue as though Spiritualism were the true successor of Christianity as set forth in the New Testament. For example:

> How—it may be asked—could Christianity be opposed to Spiritualism when the Christian Religion was really born in a Séance? The real beginning of Christianity, its motive power, its great impetus, came—not from the birth or death of Jesus—but from Pentecost, the greatest Séance in history.[22]

Spiritualists do admit that there are "a few isolated passages" in the Old Testament that forbid "the practice of communicating with spirits."[23] This statement fails to recognize that in Israel necromancy (consulting the dead) was "viewed as flagrant apostasy from Jehovah and as a crime punishable by the severest penalties."[24] The Bible declares:

> Give no regard to mediums and familiar spirits; do not seek after them, to be defiled by them: I am the Lord your God. (Lev. 19:31)

> And the person who turns after mediums and familiar spirits, to prostitute himself with them, I will set My face against that person and cut him off from his people. (Lev. 20:6)

> A man or a woman who is a medium, or who has familiar spirits, shall surely be put to death; they shall stone them with stones. Their blood shall be upon them. (Lev. 20:27)

> There shall not be found among you anyone . . . who practices witchcraft, or a soothsayer, or one who interprets omens, or a sorcerer, or one who conjures spells, or a medium, or a spiritist, or one who calls up the dead. (Deut. 18:10–11)

[Manasseh] consulted spiritists and mediums. He did much evil in the sight of the Lord, to provoke Him to anger. (2 Kings 21:6)

Moreover Josiah put away those who consulted mediums and spiritists . . . that he might perform the words of the law which were written in the book that Hilkiah the priest found in the house of the Lord. (2 Kings 23:24)

So Saul died for his unfaithfulness which he had committed against the Lord, because he did not keep the word of the Lord, and also because he consulted a medium for guidance. But he did not inquire of the Lord; therefore He killed him, and turned the kingdom over to David the son of Jesse. (1 Chron. 10:13–14)

And when they say to you, "Seek those who are mediums and wizards, who whisper and mutter," should not a people seek their God? . . . To the law and to the testimony! If they do not speak according to this word, it is because there is no light in them. (Isa. 8:19–20)

After examining these and other passages, J. Stafford Wright concludes:

Whatever may be the precise rendering of any single passage, it is beyond doubt that the Old Testament bans any attempt to contact the departed. This is true of the law, the historical books, and the prophets. Is there the slightest sign that the New Testament lifts the ban?[25]

CONCLUSION

Spiritualism must be rejected not only because what it teaches is unbiblical but also because of the harm it can bring to those who devote themselves to it. As Gasson has warned, *"The way into Spiritualism is extraordinarily easy, the way out is extremely dangerous."*[26]

SELECT BIBLIOGRAPHY

Ankerberg, John, and John Weldon. *The Facts on Spirit Guides.* Eugene, Ore.: Harvest House, 1988.

Ernest, Victor H. *I Talked with Spirits.* Wheaton, Ill.: Tyndale, 1970.

Gasson, Raphael. *The Challenging Counterfeit.* Plainfield, N.J.: Logos, 1966.

Martin, Walter R. *The Kingdom of the Cults.* Rev. ed. Minneapolis: Bethany, 1985. Spiritism is treated on 227–45.

Mayer, F. E. *The Religious Bodies of America.* 4th ed. St. Louis, Mo.: Concordia, 1961. Spiritualism is treated on 563–67.

Melton, J. Gordon. *Encyclopedic Handbook of Cults in America.* New York: Garland, 1986. Spiritualism is treated on 81–86.

Miller, Elliot. *A Crash Course on the New Age Movement.* Grand Rapids: Baker, 1989. Chapters 8 and 9 are entitled "Channeling: Spiritistic Revelation for the New Age."

Parker, Russ. *Battling the Occult.* Downers Grove, Ill.: InterVarsity Press, 1990.

Pember, G. H. *Earth's Earliest Ages.* Old Tappan, N.J.: Revell, n.d. Spiritualism is treated on 243–391.

Unger, Merrill F. *Biblical Demonology.* 9th ed. Wheaton, Ill.: Scripture Press, 1971.

_____. *Demons in the World Today.* Wheaton, Ill.: Tyndale, 1971.

_____. *The Haunting of Bishop Pike: A Christian View of the Other Side.* Wheaton, Ill.: Tyndale, 1971.

Van Baalen, J. K. *The Chaos of the Cults.* 4th rev. ed. Grand Rapids: Eerdmans, 1962. Spiritualism is treated on 31–61. The case of the witch (medium) of Endor is discussed on 51–54.

Wright, J. Stafford. *Christianity and the Occult.* Chicago: Moody, 1971.

SPIRITUALIST MATERIALS

The A.B.C. of Spiritualism, The "Why's" of Spiritualism, History of the National Spiritualist Association of Churches, and many other materials are published and distributed by the National Spiritualist Association of Churches. The Morris Pratt Institute Association, the Educational Bureau of the N.S.A.C. (11811 Watertown Plank Rd., Wauwatosa, WI 53226), provides a book list of several hundred books and tapes that the institute sells. Its website is morrispratt.org. The official monthly magazine of the N.S.A.C. is *The National Spiritualist Summit,* which has been published since 1919.

8 | SEVENTH-DAY ADVENTISM

In *Another Gospel: Alternative Religions and the New Age Movement*, Ruth A. Tucker writes:

> It could easily be argued that a survey of Seventh-day Adventism does not belong in a book of this nature. Indeed, the controversy has raged for decades as to whether this religious group is a "cult" or an evangelical Protestant denomination.[1]

She later adds:

> No reputable scholar would claim that the Seventh-day Adventists are "cultic" to the same degree as the Mormons, for example. Yet, the history, and even present-day doctrine, of this group could be said to have cultic characteristics.[2]

What these cultic characteristics are will be discussed later in the chapter.

Of the many groups that have been identified as cults, the Seventh-day Adventist Church is one of the most puzzling for the researcher. Evaluations of this group range from strong opposition to approval with reservations. Some of the strongest voices against the recognition of Adventism as an evangelical body have been former adherents (D. M. Canright, E. B. Jones, R. A. Greive, G. Hunt, W. Slattery, and

S. Cleveland).[3] In 1963 Calvin Theological Seminary professor Anthony A. Hoekema included the Seventh-day Adventists in *The Four Major Cults*. In addition to the chapter on Seventh-day Adventism, Hoekema devoted a separate section to the question "Is Seventh-day Adventism a Cult?" At the end of the survey, after acknowledging "certain soundly Scriptural emphases in the teaching of Seventh-day Adventism," he writes:

> It is, however, my conviction that the Adventists have added to these Scriptural doctrines certain unscriptural teachings which are inconsistent with the former and undermine their full effectiveness. It is also my conviction that, because of the Adventists' acceptance of these additional teachings, Seventh-day Adventism must be classified, not as an evangelical church, but as a cult.[4]

In 1956 the Adventists were accepted as evangelical (while recognizing some doctrinal errors) by Walter R. Martin, E. Schuyler English (*Our Hope*, November 1956), and Donald Grey Barnhouse (*Eternity*, September 1956). Martin presented a full account of his findings and conclusions in *The Truth About Seventh-day Adventism*, published in 1960. In the foreword, Barnhouse explains:

> As a result of our studies of Seventh-day Adventism, Walter Martin and I reached the conclusion that Seventh-day Adventists are a truly Christian group, rather than an antichristian cult. . . .
>
> Let it be understood that we made only one claim; i.e., that those Seventh-day Adventists who follow the Lord in the same way as their leaders have interpreted for us the doctrinal position of their church, are to be considered true members of the body of Christ. We did not, and do not, accept some of their theological positions which we consider to be extravagant, or others which we consider to be non-biblical.[5]

In an article in *Christianity Today*, Martin concluded that while the Adventist church "is essentially a Christian denomination, . . . in the overall perspective, its theology must be viewed as more hetero-dox than orthodox, and that its practices in not a few instances might be termed divisive."[6]

While not an answer to Martin's book, Norman F. Douty's *Another Look at Seventh-day Adventism* (1962) should be read if one wants the other side of the issue. Douty concluded that as

> long as Adventism denies, explicitly or implicitly, doctrines which the church of Christ as a whole has always declared; and declares, explicitly or implicitly, doctrines which the church of Christ as a whole has always denied, it cannot be es-teemed a Scriptural church.[7]

It is clear that the Adventist leaders who met with Martin and other evangelicals wished recognition as an evangelical body, but the distinctive doctrines of this group have perpetuated its isolation from many evangelicals. In 1957 the Review and Herald Publishing Association published *Seventh-day Adventists Answer Questions on Doctrine*, which, as the title page states, was written by "a Representative Group of Seventh-day Adventist leaders, Bible Teachers and Editors." The writers of this book explain that their aim "was to set forth our basic beliefs in terminology currently used in theological circles. This was not to be a new statement of faith, but rather an answer to specific questions concerning our faith."[8] This volume was the first comprehensive statement of the Seventh-day Adventist "denomination in the area of church doctrine and prophetic interpretation."[9] The book was obviously an effort to give the Adventist answer to the question whether it should be viewed as a sect or as an evangelical body. Many reviewers of this book concluded with John H. Gerstner that they were "still unconvinced of Seventh-day Adventism's adequate creedal orthodoxy."[10]

There is much within the Seventh-day Adventist Church that is praiseworthy: its emphasis on public health and medical missions, its recognition of the sanctity of the home and marriage, its separation from worldliness, its educational and publishing programs, and its adherence to many orthodox doctrines. Undoubtedly many Adventists are truly regenerate people.

Adventist growth and outreach was substantial during the 1970s, and the church's membership was 3.2 million in 1979 (566,000 in North America). Work was being done in a hundred languages in 192 countries. Statistics on Adventist medical, welfare, radio ("Voice of Prophecy"), educational, and publishing activities are equally impressive. As one of the fastest growing churches in the world, at the end of 2000 it was reported that SDA membership had reached 11.3 million in 206 countries.[11]

In the survey that follows, there is a brief discussion of the origin of Seventh-day Adventism. The experience of R. A. Greive, an SDA pastor who was excommunicated, is presented, and it illustrates why many people find it difficult to recognize the SDA Church as an evangelical body. A brief survey of developments since 1956 will help to place this church in clearer perspective and will explain why there are conflicting evaluations of it. A select bibliography with annotations will help the reader to go beyond this introduction.

HISTORY

The Seventh-day Adventist Church arose out of the expectation of Christ's imminent advent that swept through America and many parts of South America, Africa, and Asia in the early decades of the nineteenth century. In America, William Miller (1782–1849) led the movement. After his conversion, he joined the Baptist church in 1816 and later became a licensed minister. Miller took an interest in prophetic themes, and after two years of diligent study he concluded that Christ would return in 1843. He lectured widely, and "Adventist congregations were raised up in more than a thousand places, numbering some fifty thousand believers."[12]

The Lord did not return on the date set—March 21, 1843—but, after recalculation, the date was pushed back by a year. When Christ again did not appear on the appointed day, another way of reckoning time was adopted, and October 22, 1844, was then set. But when this day passed without Christ's return, the majority of Miller's followers left the movement. Miller admitted his mistake and did not accept any of the new theories proposed after "the Great Disappointment." He never became a Seventh-day Adventist.[13]

Seventh-day Adventism began with the conclusion of Hiram Edson (received in a vision) that October 22, 1844, was the correct date but that they had been wrong about what would take place on that day. This reinterpretation produced the Adventists' doctrines of the heavenly sanctuary and the investigative judgment.[14]

Of the Millerites who did not drop out of the movement, three groups emerged with distinctive doctrines:

> the group headed by Hiram Edson in western New York State, which emphasized the doctrine of the heavenly sanctuary; the group in Washington, New Hampshire, which along with Joseph Bates, advocated the observance of the seventh day; and the group around Portland, Maine, which held that Ellen G. White was a true prophetess, whose visions and words were to be followed by Adventists.[15]

By 1855 the three groups merged and headquarters were established at Battle Creek, Michigan. Ellen G. White (1827–1915) played the leading role in the history and doctrinal formation of the movement. "Almost every aspect of the belief and activity of the Seventh-day Adventists was encouraged or inspired by a vision or word from Mrs. White."[16] In 1860 the name "Seventh-day Adventist" was officially adopted, and in 1863 the General Conference (the ruling body of the church) was organized. The headquarters were moved to Takoma Park, Maryland, in 1903.

How Should the SDA Church Be Viewed?

Lengthy articles and books have been written discussing whether or not the Seventh-day Adventist Church should be considered evangelical. The testimony of R. A. Greive, "Why I Was Excommunicated from the SDA Church," published in 1958, helps one to understand why many find it difficult to accept the Adventists as evangelical. Greive did not write as an uninformed outsider or as a novice. In his article, he states that he "was a Seventh-day Adventist pastor for 30 years and the former president of the North New Zealand Conference of the Seventh-day Adventist Church." The account is also valuable because it was written after the SDA Church was declared to be an evangelical Protestant denomination by Martin, Barnhouse, and others, who were assured that *Seventh-day Adventists Answer Questions on Doctrine* accurately presented SDA beliefs.[17] Grieve wrote:

> [About two] years ago certain American editors reported that the Seventh-day Adventist church had reworked its theology to the point that the SDA movement should now be considered evangelical.
>
> At the very moment these Christian editors in America were extending the right hand of fellowship to the leaders of Adventism, I and three other SDA ministers were being tried for heresy in Australia. What I saw at that trial convinced me how hopelessly mistaken were these American editors.
>
> It all began when we four ministers came with hungry, seeking hearts to the New Testament revelation of the Gospel. We made the great discovery of the doctrine of justification and found its dynamics too much to contain in earthen vessels. We literally spilled over with the good news. Many in our congregations came to believe in Biblical justification and many of us hailed it as the dawn of a new day for Adventism. But its triumph was short-lived.

We ministers were placed on trial and when we failed to recant were summarily dismissed from the SDA ministry. But we did not go alone. Spiritually-enlightened members numbering more than 100 resigned from their SDA churches seeking to find fellowship and happiness within various branches of God's earthly church. This was not a mass movement from one Adventist church but an intelligent separation on the part of schoolteachers, businessmen and other thinking people from many places in Australia and New Zealand.

They moved out because they were convinced that the basic doctrines and prophetical interpretations of their church were at variance with the revelation of Scripture.

Our crime consisted in sharing the good news that God in Christ had completely forgiven us our sins, so blotting out the record of wrong doing that the judgment and condemnation resulting therefrom was entirely lifted and the believer restored to sonship and heirship with Christ. These New Testament concepts conflicted with the published statements of Ellen G. White who had declared, "It is impossible that the sins of men should be blotted out until after the judgment (commencing in 1844) at which their cases are to be investigated" (*Great Controversy*, p. 485). Hence we were indicted for believing that the Bible alone was the sole source of faith and doctrine and was its own interpreter as against the overriding authority of the writings of Ellen G. White.

The point of issue was whether a Seventh-day Adventist minister could lay aside the authority of Mrs. White's writings in favor of the Bible and still be a minister of the SDA church. The answer at our trial was an unequivocal *no*.

These heresy trials were to us ordeals by fire. There was all the evidence of carefully-planned psychological warfare. There was also the make-believe of prayer and investigation of the themes of salvation as presented. But back and behind everything was the resolve on the part of the 13 men on the committee to force a surrender to the E. G. White interpretations, no matter what evidence there was to the contrary.

When the committee failed to break down a defendant a private session with the chairman and his secretary was held. At this private session all subtleties were cast aside. And when we failed to recant we were excommunicated and ruined over night.

We who were once the ardent supporters of the SDA church now see that it is not in the Protestant succession. We also know that SDA special doctrines—Sabbath, sanctuary, investigative judgment, remnant church—are unalterable, unchangeable beliefs. To change any one of these doctrines is to compromise the prophetic standing of Mrs. White and that the SDA leaders will never do because it is their firm belief that Mrs. White's prophetic gift is the outstanding mark of their remnant church.

In theory Adventists exalt the Bible above the writings of Mrs. White. In practice they do exactly the opposite. The psychological power and effects of *her* writings and interpretations so subtly enslave the minds of ministers and members alike that I doubt if ever they realize that it is her revelations they are believing and not those of the Bible. As an illustration of this subtle enslavement, more than 30 years ago as a young minister entering upon his life work, I read the Epistle to the Hebrews in the Greek text and was astonished and mystified that I could not fit my Adventist beliefs of the sanctuary into the teaching of this portion of Scripture. My faith in the writings of Mrs. White were such that unhesitatingly I laid the Bible teaching aside in favor of what my church taught.

During our trials F. G. Clifford, head of the SDA church here, put it on record as the denominational position that "the writings of Mrs. White are inspired by the same Spirit that inspired the Bible; therefore we must have the same faith in the writings of Mrs. White as we have in the Bible." Again, "This is our denominational position, that God forgives neither absolutely nor finally."

Consistent with the SDA demand for implicit faith in Mrs. White is a recent article appearing in the *Australasian Record* titled, "The Unchanging Unchangeable Truth." It was written by the head of the Australasian SDA church. Said this learned gentleman: "No fresh presentation, or clearer outline will ever change or diminish the force of the truth of the foundational doctrines which have made us a distinct people. Unfortunately some of our people have gained the impression that there is developing within the church some change in attitude toward the *Spirit of Prophecy* [writings of Mrs. White] and also toward the nature of the work of Christ in the cleansing of the sanctuary. It is even suggested by some that the General Conference [USA ruling body of SDAs] is considering the matter of presenting a changed viewpoint to our people on these subjects. *We desire to state unequivocally that such statements are not true; they do not bear a semblance of truth.*"

The writer of this article then quoted W. R. Beach, secretary of the General Conference, who had written to assure the Australasian division of SDAs that their fears of any impending changes in doctrine were altogether groundless. "We have made it clear here at the seminary and elsewhere," said Beach, "that there is no altering of our position, no new pronouncement. . . ."

The doctrinal and prophetical edifice of Adventism rests not on the Bible alone, but upon Mrs. White and the Bible. This duality of revelation under interpretation of the "secondary" revelation creates a freak religion that is in no way related to full-blooded Protestantism. When I was on trial the committee essayed to give me 16 quotations from extra-canonical sources to prove that a believer's sins are all upon the record until after the investigative judgment. But in their presentation there was not a single Bible text.

Adventism and justification cannot live together. At my trial the secretary reasoned thus: "If Brother Greive is right on justification and no record of a believer's sins remains upon the books, then verily there is no investigative judgment; and if there is no investigative judgment then no Adventist movement of 1844; and if no Adventist movement the whole prophetic interpretation of Daniel 8:13, 14 is gone."

But Seventh-day Adventism must not be dismissed as unworthy of notice. It has an attractive side and a driving force worthy of a better cause. Their members are selfless in their devotion and loyal to its creed and to its propagation. There is personal sacrifice in giving and service that is altogether astonishing. The expansion of their movement is phenomenal and their activities worldwide. Their members are honorable and lovable in the main. All this makes the task of their enlightenment one of the greatest facing Christendom today. And they are stuck in the mud of their pharisaic pride that "we are God's very own people. We have a prophetess that no other modern religion has. We keep the 10 commandments. We pay our tithes and offerings."

Indeed the task of winning them will be difficult. As an Adventist minister for 30 years, I know there will be no change from within. True, the cruder form of their doctrines is giving way to a more polished expression of the same. But the hard core of original Adventist doctrine persists. A few minor changes and modifications will never make Adventism a New Testament church in the Protestant succession. It will have to be rebuilt from the bottom up.[18]

How Should the SDA Church Be Viewed? Developments Since the 1950s

Why have evangelical scholars and others come to different conclusions concerning the Seventh-day Adventists?

Christian Research Institute writer Kenneth Samples answers that "a problem in past evangelical evaluations of Adventism has been the failure to recognize its theological diversity. Adventism is anything but monolithic. . . . While the 27 Fundamental Beliefs officially define" their "doctrine, there is much debate . . . concerning the meaning of such doctrines as atonement, sin, Christ's nature, authority, and, especially, the meaning of righteousness by faith."[19]

Ex-SDA Joan Craven provides further insight into why there are different perceptions of Adventism:

> Adventists themselves disagree as to whether they should be considered part of the evangelical movement. At one extreme are those who think it is impossible to maintain distinctive Adventists "truths" in an evangelical framework; many of these people are church administrators. At the other extreme are those who willingly scrap Adventist teachings if they appear to differ from evangelical doctrine; these people are largely pastors (or ex-pastors, if they have made their views known to administrators at the other extreme).
>
> Adventists who claim to be evangelical point to the church's official doctrinal positions as stated in the church manual. . . .
>
> By contrast, Adventists who do not wish to be identified with the evangelical movement point out that certain SDA teachings are held by few or no other Christian denominations. Fully half of the "Fundamental Beliefs" concern such teachings as the unchangeable seventh-day Sabbath, Christ's function in the heavenly sanctuary since 1844, and the prophetic ministry of Ellen G. White. . . . To join forces with evangelicals, these Adventists fear, would be to compromise distinctive SDA teachings and to risk diluting the message they believe God has given them.
>
> Evangelicals who look primarily at SDA statements about Scripture, the Trinity, and salvation tend to think of Adventists

as fellow evangelicals, while those who focus on peculiar doctrines may wonder if Adventists are even Christian.[20]

In the three decades since the late 1950s, there has been internal
debate over doctrinal positions that "has resulted in several distinct
factions and strong disagreements as to which doctrinal perspective
represents 'true Adventism.' Seventh-day Adventism is experiencing
an identity crisis."[21]

The 1960s and 1970s are characterized by Samples as a period "of
turmoil and doctrinal debate within" the movement, with "the central issue: Adventism's uniqueness. Would it continue in the direction
set in *QOD [Questions on Doctrine]*? Or would Adventism return to
more traditional understandings?"[22] The debate polarized two main
theological perspectives among North American Adventists, which
Samples calls "Evangelical Adventism" and "Traditional Adventism"
(or "Historic"). He traces the roots of evangelical Adventism to the
Adventists who dialogued with Martin and Barnhouse and to *Questions on Doctrine*. Traditional Adventism found fault with *Questions
on Doctrine*, with SDA theologian M. L. Andreasen "stating that it
had sold Adventism down the river," having "robbed Adventism of
some of its distinctiveness," and many "other prominent scholars believed that *QOD* had not reflected the beliefs and identity of Seventh-
day Adventism accurately enough."[23]

The five major doctrinal issues on which the evangelical Adventists differed from the traditional Adventists, according to Samples,
were righteousness by faith, the human nature of Christ, the events of
1844, assurance of salvation, and the authority of Ellen G. White.[24]

"The 1980s," writes Samples, "have been a time of real crisis
within Seventh-day Adventism as several representatives of Evangelical Adventism were fired or forced to resign because of their uncom-
promising views." In 1980 "Desmond Ford . . . challenged the biblical
validity of the sanctuary doctrine."[25] Ford, a popular and prominent
SDA theologian, "argued that that doctrine had no biblical warrant,
and was only accepted because of Ellen G. White."[26] Ford's "teach-

SEVENTH-DAY ADVENTISM

ing and ministerial credentials were removed," and as a result a number of Adventists in North America and Australia left the church.[27]

What was the outcome of the conflict between evangelical and traditional Adventism by the end of the decade? Samples concludes, "Denominational discipline in the 1980s against certain evangelical advocates gave a strong indication that there is a powerful traditionalist segment that desires to retain Adventism's 1844 'remnant identity.' "[28] In another article published in 1988, Samples says that traditional Adventism "appears to be moving further away from a number of positions taken in QOD."[29] It is disturbing that while Adventist leaders "have stated that the denomination stands by QOD, some of these same leaders have disfellowshiped scores of Adventists for affirming portions of QOD," and some "have referred to it as 'damnable heresy.' "[30]

What about evangelical Adventism? While having lost ground, "its supporters remain, though they are not nearly as prominent today."[31]

So, is traditional Adventism cultic? Samples draws this conclusion:

With respect to the charge that Traditional Adventism is a non-Christian cult, it must be emphasized that the structure of Adventism is largely orthodox (accepting the Trinity, Christ's deity, virgin birth, bodily resurrection, etc.). Presently, however, it would appear that Traditional Adventism is at least aberrant, confusing or compromising biblical truth (e.g., their view of justification, the nature of Christ, appealing to an unbiblical authority). It must also be stated that if the traditional camp continues in its departure from QOD, and in promoting Ellen White as the church's infallible interpreter, then they could one day be fully deserving of the title "cult," as some Adventists recognize. . . .

The crisis of the 1980s makes it plain that many in Adventist leadership are attentive to the vocal traditionalist segment, and, unfortunately, have headed Adventism in the wrong direction. If those in Adventist leadership who love the Reformation gospel (and there are still many) do not speak up and stand for their convictions, Adventism has little hope, because Traditional Adventism is theologically bankrupt. Its perverted gospel robs Adventist Christians of assurance and puts them on a treadmill of trying to measure up to God's holy law in order to be saved.[32]

And, in his *The Truth About Seventh-day Adventist "Truth"* (2000), Dale Ratzlaff concludes that some SDA teachings

militate against functional church unity. For all intents and purposes, Historic Adventists, who really believe the twenty-seven Fundamental Beliefs of the Seventh-day Adventist church, cannot work hand in hand with Evangelicals and see them as Christian brothers and sisters. Rather, the Adventist will always have a hidden, or not so hidden, agenda to convert the Evangelical to Adventist truth.[33]

SELECT BIBLIOGRAPHY

Barnett, Maurice. *Ellen G. White and Inspiration*. Louisville, Ky.: Gospel Anchor, 1983. The author asks, "Was she the 'spirit of prophecy' in the Seventh-day Adventist Church?" Barnett concludes that she was "a false prophetess" and a plagiarist.

Bird, Herbert S. "Adventists." In *The Encyclopedia of Christianity*, 79–93. Wilmington, Del.: National Foundation for Christian Education, 1964. Bird concludes: "If a reconciliation between S.D.A. and evangelical Protestantism is to be effected, it will require either that the former so revise its basic principles as practically to cease to be what it is, or that the latter deny the faith" (92).

_____. *Theology of Seventh-day Adventism*. Grand Rapids: Eerdmans, 1961. This is a good analysis of Seventh-day Adventism, but it is criticized by Martin. Chapter 8 deals with "Seventh-day Adventism and Evangelical Faith."

Canright, D. M. *Seventh-day Adventism Refuted.* Nashville: B. C. Goodpasture, 1962. "A reprint of a series of ten tracts copyrighted and published by D. M. Canright in 1889."

_____. *Seventh-day Adventism Renounced.* 14th ed., 1914. Reprint. Nashville: Gospel Advocate, 1961. This work was originally published in 1889. The author was an Adventist for twenty-eight years and a prominent SDA minister before he left. He presents reasons why he left the movement and refutes SDA doctrines. Norman F. Douty defends Canright against the Adventist attacks upon him in *The Case of D. M. Canright* (Grand Rapids: Baker, 1964).

Carson, D. A., ed. *From Sabbath to Lord's Day: A Biblical, Historical, and Theological Investigation.* Grand Rapids: Zondervan, 1982.

Cleveland, Sydney. *Whitewashed: Uncovering the Myths of Ellen G. White.* Glendale, Ariz.: Life Assurance Ministries, 2000. "During an extensive study of Ellen G. White's writings, [this former SDA pastor] discovered that she contradicted the Holy Bible, gave many false prophecies, and didn't even follow her own teachings" (back cover).

Craven, Joan. "The Wall of Adventism." *Christianity Today*, October 19, 1984, 20–25. Craven, a former Adventist, presents insights into Adventism.

Damsteegt, P. Gerard. *Foundations of the Seventh-day Adventist Message and Mission.* Grand Rapids: Eerdmans, 1977. This is a well-documented, comprehensive, and careful study. Damsteegt, an Adventist, traces the development of Adventist (Millerite) and SDA ideas and theology from the beginning of the nineteenth century to 1874.

Douty, Norman F. *Another Look at Seventh-day Adventism.* Grand Rapids: Baker, 1962. This is a careful study based upon *Questions on Doctrine* and other SDA sources. In his conclusion (182–89), Douty finds that Adventism is characterized by features that disqualify it as an evangelical body.

Gaustad, Edwin Scott, ed. *The Rise of Adventism.* New York: Harper, 1974. Gaustad has assembled a collection of lectures given by historians and has added an exhaustive bibliographic essay.

Gerstner, John H. *The Theology of the Major Sects.* Grand Rapids: Baker, 1960. Adventism is treated on 19–28. The portion on Adventism also appeared as a separate booklet: *The Teachings of Seventh-day Adventism.* Grand Rapids: Baker, 1978.

Gladson, Jerry. *A Theologian's Journey from Seventh-day Adventism to Mainstream Christianity.* Glendale, Ariz.: Life Assurance Ministries, 2000. Two appendices deal with the questions "What Do You Do with the Sabbath?" and "Is Seventh-day Adventism the True Church?"

Hoekema, Anthony A. *The Four Major Cults.* Grand Rapids: Eerdmans, 1963. Adventism is treated on 89–169. On 388–403 ("Is Seventh-day Adventism a Cult?") Hoekema argues that Adventism must be regarded as a cult because it manifests the traits distinctive of a cult.

Hunt, Gregory G. P. *Beware This Cult!* Belleville, Ontario: 1981. The subtitle explains the author's purpose: *An Insider Exposes Seventh Day Adventism and Their False Prophet Ellen G. White.*

Jewett, Paul K. *The Lord's Day: A Theological Guide to the Christian Day of Worship.* Grand Rapids: Eerdmans, 1971.

Lewis, Gordon R. *The Bible, the Christian, and Seventh-day Adventists.* Philadelphia: P&R, 1966. Lewis says on 28:

> If Adventism is not ardent evangelicalism or typical cultism then how shall it be classified? . . . Like Romanism Adventism has added to the Scripture a body of tradition it seems reluctant to break. Like Romanism Adventism depreciates the completeness of Christ's work of atonement, and like Romanism Adventism adds to grace the necessity of human works as a condition of salvation. . . .
>
> The error of Romanism and Adventism resembles that of the Galatians.

Martin, Walter R. *The Kingdom of the Cults.* Rev. 1997 ed. Minneapolis: Bethany, 1997. In Appendix C, he answers those who still find Adventism a cult and defends his position that they are not. See Martin's comments in note 17.

_____. *The Truth About Seventh-day Adventism*. Grand Rapids: Zondervan, 1960. Martin defends the SDA Church as evangelical, but he is also critical of a number of its distinctive doctrines. Ex-SDA Mary Lyons questions whether this book is "really 'The Truth' about the SDAs" in *The King's Business* (July 1960), 27–29.

Numbers, Roland L. *Prophetess of Health: A Study of Ellen G. White*. New York: Harper & Row, 1976. Exposes the myths and sources of Mrs. White's health care visions.

Paxton, Geoffrey J. *The Shaking of Adventism*. Grand Rapids: Baker, 1978. "A documented account of the crisis among Adventists over the doctrine of justification by faith" (front cover).

Ratzlaff, Dale. *Sabbath in Crisis*. Applegate, Calif.: Life Assurance Ministries, 1990. The author was a fourth-generation Adventist and pastor who resigned from the SDA ministry. "A biblical study of the Sabbath in the old and new covenants."

_____. *The Cultic Doctrine of Seventh-day Adventists*. Sedona, Ariz.: Life Assurance Ministries, 1996.

_____. *The Truth About Seventh-day Adventist "Truth": Questions to Ask Your Adventist Friends*. Glendale, Ariz.: Life Assurance Ministries, 2000.

Rea, Walter T. *The White Lie*. Turlock, Calif.: M. & R, 1982. Rea, a former SDA pastor, proves that Ellen G. White "was not original in her writings; her material was taken from other sources—on all subjects, in all areas, in all books" (199).

Samples, Kenneth R. "From Controversy to Crisis: An Updated Assessment of Seventh-day Adventism." *Christian Research Journal* (summer 1988), 9–14. See note 24.

_____. "The Recent Truth About Seventh-day Adventism." *Christianity Today*, February 5, 1990, 18–21. See note 19.

"Seventh-day Adventism: The Spirit Behind the Church" (video). Phoenix: Grace Upon Grace Productions, 1998.

Slattery, Wallace D. *Are Seventh-day Adventists False Prophets? A Former Insider Speaks Out*. Phillipsburg, N.J.: P&R, 1990. The author "explains why he and his wife left the SDA Church—and how they found new freedom in Christ" (cover).

ADVENTIST SOURCES

The official SDA website is www.adventist.org.

Seventh-day Adventists Answer Questions on Doctrine. Washington, D.C.: Review and Herald, 1957. This official statement of SDA doctrine answered questions submitted by Walter Martin. But it did not represent the views of more traditional SDAs (*Christianity Today* [December 19, 1960], 24); Geoffrey Paxton, *The Shaking of Adventism*, 153). "While Adventist officials have stated the denomination stands by QOD, some of these same leaders have disfellowshiped scores of Adventists for affirming portions of QOD" (Kenneth R. Samples, "From Controversy to Crisis," 14).

Seventh-day Adventists Believe . . . A Biblical Exposition of 27 Fundamental Doctrines. Hagerstown, Md.: Review and Herald, 1988. The most recent statement of SDA doctrine. ". . . Carefully researched, it represents an authentic exposition of Adventist beliefs" (viii).

NON-SDA ORGANIZATIONS

Life Assurance Ministries, Inc.
P.O. Box 11587
Glendale, AZ 85318
Phone 623-572-9549
Fax 623-572-3035
Websites www.LifeAssuranceMinistries.com www.ratzlaf.com
LAM writes, publishes, stocks, and sells books relevant to former SDAs, inquiring Adventists, Sabbatarians, and concerned evangelicals. It also provides links to other sites.

Seventh-Day Adventist Outreach
P.O. Box 39607
Phoenix, AZ 85069
Phone 602-973-4768

Fax 602-789-7165
Website www.SDAOutreach.org
Much helpful information, resources, and a bibliography of relevant materials are on this site. Some featured articles deal with the "Writings of Ellen G. White," "The Sabbath and Sunday," and "The State of the Dead."

The Ellen G. White Web Site
Website www.ellenwhite.org
This site provides a number of articles, online books, and other resources on Ellen G. White and her writings. Links to other websites are provided for further study.

Former Adventist Fellowship
Website www.FormerAdventist.com
Started by former SDAs; a number of ministries, meeting places, and testimonies of former Adventists are presented.

OCCULT OBSESSION
AND THE NEW CULTS

A strologers tell us that the Age of Aquarius is supposed to bring with it a new religious atmosphere. As John Godwin observed three decades ago, "It has become difficult to venture anywhere in contemporary America without being informed that the Age of Aquarius is upon us. There's no escaping the message."[1] (Many astrologers would say that the song from *Hair* announcing that "this is the dawning of the Age of Aquarius" is wrong. It "will not begin for about another 300 years.")[2] The designation "Age of Aquarius" has been replaced by the term "New Age."

Whatever one concludes concerning the Age of Aquarius, interest in religion, the occult, mysticism, and Eastern religions is high in America. Writing in 1978, John Weldon observed, "The last ten years have witnessed a virtual explosion of new religions."[3] Religion was one of the fastest growing fields of graduate study at secular universities. These facts are striking because during the 1960s some Protestant theologians were erroneously proclaiming the death of God and the imminent demise of religion. Vernon C. Grounds comments:

> In their learned opinion supernaturalism of any sort was no
> longer a believable option for intelligent people, just as fairy
> tales are incredible to a rational adult. In fact, those radicals
> prophesied that religion as a whole seemed slated to disap-

pear, a kind of cultural fog evaporating before the rising sun of scientific knowledge.

But to judge by the course of events in the early 1970s those radicals are going to be exposed as false prophets. Religion, whether traditional Christianity or the latest brand of spiritism, is not dying out by any means; instead, it is experiencing a tremendous upsurge.[4]

The significance of this upsurge was recognized and interpreted in a book put out by *U.S. News and World Report* in 1972, entitled *The Religious Reawakening in America*:

At a time when established religion has become an object of criticism, we have moved into what many consider to be one of the most religious periods in the history of the United States.

Young people particularly have sparked the revival of interest in spiritual values. Unfulfilled by the offering of the traditional church and the traditional temple, they have slipped into rebellion—not against God and religious values but against the "establishment" of Christian, Jewish, and other faiths. They are searching for new forms and ways of achieving spiritual satisfaction to offset the dulling and sterile effect of a highly materialistic and technological society.[5]

The revival of interest in religion and spiritual values led many to accept beliefs and practices that are antithetical to orthodox Christianity and Judaism. This is verified by Peter Rowley:

In 1970 about two and a half million people belonged to the new religions of America—Indian, Sino-Japanese, avant-garde Christian and others even more unusual. . . .

Reports indicate that growth in the latter part of 1970 may be as great as a million people seeking an answer to what seems to them a frightening world; young Americans and

some middle-aged and older ones all across the U.S. are join-
ing occult religions or following Eastern and Western gurus
and abandoning traditional Christianity and Judaism.[6]

A look at the contemporary scene would indicate that the trend of
the 1970s has continued to the present. As Christian sociologist
Ronald Enroth observes:

> Once upon a time it was possible to describe North American
> religious institutions in terms of that sacred canopy we often
> refer to as the Judeo-Christian tradition. . . .
>
> Today, all that has changed dramatically. In an increas-
> ingly pluralistic society, it is not unusual for individuals to af-
> filiate with sects and cults that have little directly to do with
> Protestantism, Catholicism, and Judaism. Along with
> churches and synagogues can be found mosques, temples,
> kingdom halls, meditation centers, and societies of all sorts.
> The diversity that constitutes the North American landscape
> in the 1990s . . . is more nontraditional and less familiar to
> even the religiously-oriented average citizen.[7]

What caused the renewed interest in the occult? What is responsible for the swing toward Eastern religion and mysticism? What are
some of the new religions (cults), and how do they differ from the established cults? These questions are reviewed in the material that follows. A select bibliography of materials for further study concludes
the chapter.

THE OCCULT OBSESSION

T. K. Wallace investigated what was behind the occult craze by
questioning people in bookstores that specialized in occult material.
What were these people seeking?

"I believe there's a master plan to the cosmos, and I want to learn it," said one person. "I need something like horoscopes or Tarot cards to make my decisions for me," said another. "My marriage is on the rocks. I need to find happiness somewhere," a third told me. Still another said, "My life is dull, and I must find something exciting."[8]

Russ Parker has worked with dozens of victims of the occult. From his experience he suggests several reasons why people get involved in the occult:

[1] **Fear of the Future** . . . Superstition and occult practices are attractive because they appear to meet a need for security regarding the future. [2] **The Desire for Power** . . . [3] **Fascination with the Supernatural:** Some people seem to be attracted by the unusual. . . . The various phenomena of occult meetings provide such people with a degree of meaning and fulfillment. . . . [4] **A Spiritually Impotent Church:** Many . . . have looked for a real spiritual experience within the church but have been disillusioned by its liberalism and unbelief. They begin to search elsewhere and are attracted to the occult with its demonstrations of spiritual power. . . . [5] **The Bankruptcy of Materialism** . . . For many . . . the pace of such [materialistic] living offers no fulfillment, and so they start to look for a spiritual center for their lives. This need for a spiritual center is clearly the force behind the rise in "new age" religions. . . . [6] **Occult Power and Deception:** Many people have found that, for them, the occult works. . . .

Whatever the reasons why people are attracted to the occult, many discover its power to be real. Because the occult works for them, we need to ask whether its power is from God or whether it is a deception.[9]

Many people have been influenced to study the occult by the many books on the subject, some of which have been bestsellers. It does not require a keen observer to discern the abundance of books on this topic in bookstores, on paperback racks in markets and drug stores, and in public libraries (I found several hundred books on astrology in the catalog of a local branch). The occult has been given much exposure in newspapers, magazines, comic books, movies, television, and contemporary music. Many public schools and colleges offer courses dealing with the occult, witchcraft, astrology, and like subjects. Many computer/video games involve the participant in occult themes.[10] The foregoing observations would not be complete without mentioning the best-selling Harry Potter children's books, authored by J. K. Rowling.[11] The occult is respectable today.

Dr. Stanley Krippner contends that the occult revival can be traced to the fact "that many people are having experiences that are not explained by tradition or by education." Occultism seems to promise an answer. Another authority says that many find the occult a place of "escape from the world's problems and from their own."[12] Additional suggestions might be given to explain the obsession with the occult; these could be found as one reads the ads in occult or New Age publications. Such words as *happiness, love, wealth, enlightenment, success,* and *healing* communicate the claimed advantages of occult involvement.[13]

An investigation of the popularity of the occult shows that interest in this subject and its influence in American life are far more widespread and serious than one would like to believe.

THE EASTERN INFLUENCE

What has caused the swing of many Americans, especially young people, to Eastern religion and mysticism? The answer is not simple, but some valuable suggestions have been given by Oswald Guinness. He sees three basic reasons:

1. Western science and philosophy became too mechanistic and rationalistic. They ended up with dry, arid linguistics and a cage-like universe. All this crippled human sensitivity, human imagination and sheer subjective experience. In reaction, many nineteenth-century western people were already turning toward the East. It gave them a basis for imagination and experience when the West was extremely dry and mechanistic.

2. . . . In the last 100 [now 130] years we've seen a resurgence of the whole Eastern culture. . . .

   The work of the various eastern apologists is most important of all. . . .

   They have traveled widely in the West and have tried to show that where western Christianity has failed and western, post-Christian philosophy has no answers, the East has provided the answers. They have a broad appeal on our campuses.

3. The third and most important factor behind the swing to the East is what Alan Watts calls parallelism. I call this dovetailing, the coinciding of post-Christian, western thinking and ancient eastern thinking. The primary cause of dovetailing has not been the direct intellectual influence of the East on the West. Rather, by playing with the options it has, the West has gotten to the place where its only choice is to adhere to what the East has always believed.[14]

Guinness makes another significant observation relative to Eastern religion and orthodox Christianity: "I'm appalled to see how many evangelical Christians accept eastern ideas uncritically without knowing where they came from. Many are completely naive."[15] Guinness concludes:

What can the Christian do in the light of this move toward the East? In a day when people are streaming out toward the East, the East is proving to be less than adequate at many points. We need to be among those who call our generation to be realistic, pointing out the errors in the direction they are going. We must show clearly that the East is no exit. And then we must demonstrate the alternative that Christianity offers.[16]

THE NEW RELIGIONS

As a teacher of a college course dealing with religions of America, it became obvious to me during the 1960s that the cult scene was changing and that a number of new religions (cults) were becoming important. (They were new to America, new as originating in America, or new as reflecting great growth in recent years. The term *cult* is being used in a broad sense.) The usual course at that time dealing with cults included such groups as the Jehovah's Witnesses, Mormons, Unity School of Christianity, Worldwide Church of God, and Christian Science. Among the new breed of cults confronting Christianity are Divine Light Mission, ECKANKAR, the Church of Scientology, Nichiren Shoshu (Soka Gakkai), the Church Universal and Triumphant (Summit Lighthouse), the Unification Church, Transcendental Meditation (TM), and the International Society for Krishna Consciousness (ISKCON—Hare Krishna).[17]

The older cults were perversions of biblical truth—heresy—holding doctrines that had been rejected by the church. The new cults are often closely related to Eastern religions and the occult rather than to Christianity, as the foregoing groups illustrate. But cults that deviate from mainstream evangelical Christianity are also well represented in such groups as The Family of Love (formerly the Children of God) and The Way International, Inc. (The Way).[18]

How many of these new religions are there? The numbers vary according to which source is consulted, and none can state accurately how many there are. But informed sources have estimated "anywhere from 2,500 to as high as 5,000."[19] In 1980 C.A.R.I.S. published

"America: A Mission Field," which listed about 1,300 cults, occult groups, and Eastern mystical groups, "which are only a *fraction* of what is in America today."[20] In the introduction to *Dictionary of Cults, Sects, Religions and the Occult* (1993), the authors state that "there are thousands of religious cults and sects in America today."[21]

CONCLUSION

What should the Christian's attitude and action be toward adherents of the new cults and the occult in this New Age of religious and occult confusion? The Christian must assert the claims of Christ: "I am the way, the truth, and the life. No one comes to the Father, except through Me" (John 14:6). The search in life for spiritual satisfaction, peace, happiness, fulfillment, excitement, help in decision making and in the problems of life can all be realized in a personal relationship with Jesus Christ. Many of the new cults speak of reincarnation. Christianity proclaims the resurrection of Jesus Christ from the dead (1 Cor. 15). The man "in Christ" has a satisfying present as well as a sure future (Phil. 4:19; Eph. 1:3–14). Guinness indicates that Eastern religion "is no exit," and the same may be said of the occult. Many religions, gurus, and saviors have come and gone, but "Jesus Christ is the same yesterday, today, and forever" (Heb. 13:8).

SELECT BIBLIOGRAPHY

Ankerberg, John, and John Weldon. *Encyclopedia of New Age Beliefs.* Eugene, Ore.: Harvest House, 1996.

_____. *Encyclopedia of Cults and New Religions.* Eugene, Ore.: Harvest House, 1999.

Bowman, Robert M., Jr. "What's New in the New Religions." *Moody Monthly* (November 1987), 69–74.

Enroth, Ronald. *The Lure of the Cults and New Religions.* Downers Grove, Ill.: InterVarsity Press, 1987.

_____. *Youth, Brainwashing and the Extremist Cults.* Grand Rapids: Zondervan, 1977.

Godwin, John. *Occult America.* Garden City, N.Y.: Doubleday, 1972.

Groothuis, Douglas R. *Unmasking the New Age Movement.* Downers Grove, Ill.: InterVarsity Press, 1986.

Hunt, Dave, and T. A. McMahon. *America The Sorcerer's New Apprentice: The Rise of New Age Shamanism.* Eugene, Ore.: Harvest House, 1988.

Kyle, Richard. *The Religious Fringe: A History of Alternative Religions in America.* Downers Grove, Ill.: InterVarsity Press, 1993.

Larson, Bob. *Larson's New Book of Cults.* Wheaton, Ill.: Tyndale, 1989.

McBeth, Leon. *Strange New Religions.* Rev. ed. Nashville: Broadman, 1977.

Mangalwadi, Vishal. *The World of Gurus: A Critical Look at the Philosophies of India's Influential Gurus and Mystics.* Rev. ed. Chicago: Cornerstone, 1992.

Martin, Walter R., ed. *The New Cults.* Santa Ana, Calif.: Vision House, 1980.

Mather, George A., and Larry A. Nichols. *Dictionary of Cults, Sects, Religions and the Occult.* Grand Rapids: Zondervan, 1993.

Melton, J. Gordon. *Encyclopedic Handbook of Cults in America.* Rev. ed. New York: Garland, 1992.

Muck, Terry. *Alien Gods on American Turf.* Wheaton, Ill.: Victor, 1990.

Needleman, Jacob. *The New Religions.* Garden City, N.Y.: Doubleday, 1970.

Neil, Stephen. *Christian Faith and Other Faiths.* Downers Grove, Ill.: InterVarsity Press, 1984.

Newman, Joseph, ed. *The Religious Reawakening in America.* Washington, D.C.: U.S. News, 1972.

Newport, John P. *Christ and the New Consciousness.* Nashville: Broadman, 1978.

Parker, Russ. *Battling the Occult*. Downers Grove, Ill.: InterVarsity Press, 1990.

Petersen, William J. *Those Curious New Cults in the 80s*. New Canaan, Conn.: Keats, 1982.

Rhodes, Ron. *The Culting of America*. Eugene, Ore.: Harvest House, 1994.

Rowley, Peter. *New Gods in America*. New York: McKay, 1971.

Sparks, Jack. *The Mind Benders: A Look at Current Cults*. Nashville: Thomas Nelson, 1977.

Watchman Fellowship. *Watchman Expositor 2000 Index of Cults and Religions*. Arlington, Tex.: Watchman Fellowship, 2000. "The 2000 edition contains over 1,200 entries—including cults, occult organizations, world religions, related terms, doctrines, and cross references."

Weldon, John. "A Sampling of the New Religions." *International Review of Mission* (October 1978), 407–26.

ASTROLOGY

The New Age movement, the Rosicrucians, and Edgar Cayce and the A.R.E., which are discussed later in this book, include astrology in their belief systems. The popularity of astrology is a major indication of the renewed interest in the occult. In the *New Age Almanac* we read:

> According to professional astrological societies, there are probably more than 10,000 professional astrologers in the United States, serving more than 20 million clients, in addition to those who read astrology magazines and the astrology column in the daily newspaper [about 80 percent have astrology columns].[1]

One cannot escape the fact that astrology is popular. It is related to such diverse subjects as health, physical fitness, diet, sex, birth control, marriage, dating, religion, politics, geography, psychology, meditation, earthquakes, the stock market, child rearing, pets, music, business, occupations, gambling, menus—and the list goes on.

Books on astrology have featured such titles as *Astrological Birth Control, Astrology and Horse Racing, Your Baby's First Horoscope, Your Dog's Astrological Horoscope, Cat Horoscope Book, Astrology for Teens, Earthquake Prediction, Financial Astrology, Astro Numerology, Astrology and Past Lives, Cooking with Astrology, Medical Astrology, Astrology for the New Age, Holistic Astrology, Reincarnation Through the Zodiac,* and *How to Find Your Mate Through Astrology.* Computers have been programmed to give personalized horoscopes, and on many "college campuses there are 24-hour-a-day computers that turn out horoscopes for the younger generation."[2] Four decades ago, Kurt Koch referred to astrology as "the most widely spread superstition of our time."[3] Statistics from other countries show Koch's statement to be true. Astrology's influence is not unique to America. In "Great Britain, more than two-thirds of the adult population read their horoscopes. In France 53 percent read their horoscopes daily; and in Germany the percentage who take astrology somewhat seriously is 63 percent."[4] Interest in, and the promotion of, astrology continued to be strong through the 1970s and 1980s up to the present.

Bernard Gittelson "calculated that the circulation of newspapers and magazines carrying astrological columns in the U.S., Europe, Japan, and South America totaled over 700 million or three-fourths of a billion."[5]

The basic belief of astrology is that the fixed stars, the sun, the moon, and the planets have a decisive influence on people and things. John Warwick Montgomery defines it as "the art of divining fate or the future from the juxtaposition of the sun, moon, and planets."[6] Astrology and Spiritualism vie for the distinction of being the most ancient.[7]

In the following treatment of astrology, several important questions are investigated. What has caused its resurgence and popularity? Does astrology work? What are its problems? What is the biblical perspective on astrology? A select bibliography of materials for further study concludes the survey.

ASTROLOGY'S RESURGENCE AND POPULARITY

An article printed in the *Los Angeles Times* in 1971 was captioned "Astrology Gaining New Acceptance in Europe—Pastime Once Left for Little Old Ladies Gets Most Serious Look in 300 Years." It went on to report that a Paris university professor, Michel Garquelin, traces the astrological revival to three major developments: the collapse of religious faith, a concurrent loss of confidence in pure reason as a guide to action and the spreading interest, particularly among the young, in Oriental mystic cults.[8]

Mark Graubard, writing in 1969 in *Natural History*, also speculated on why astrology was experiencing a resurgence:

Ours is an age in which romance, sentiment, patriotism, religion, and moral values have either been banished or are derided. To some, life seems to be an oppressive vacuum, frustrating and tormenting man's spiritual needs. This has apparently resulted in a need for faith and a desire to speculate about life's purpose and man's fate, as in affluent, decaying Rome. . . . Astrology, then, seems to satisfy the desire for science as well as the need for faith, for belief in powers that rule and manipulate. Moreover, the triumphs in the exploration of space and the new discoveries of astronomy increase man's appetite for renewed worship of unknown powers.[9]

Is there a relationship between astrology and loss of religious faith? Quoting Constella (Shirley Spencer), a well-known astrologer during the 1960s, *Time* declared "that many of astrology's new converts are refugees from religion: 'We're afraid to say no, no, no to the bearded man upstairs before we have a substitute.' "[10] And, for some people, astrology has become a religion. Howard Sheldon, astrological consultant, believes that young people relate to astrology because

unlike religion, it gives concrete answers. They simply didn't dig the stand-up, Sunday morning sermons . . .

It offers kids more security than they can find any place else. I have many young clients who've been through that guru thing, the Jesus movement and drugs before finally finding the Big answers in astrology.[11]

Is astrology still popular in America?

As many as one-third of Americans believe in astrology, that is, that the position of the stars and planets can affect peoples' lives (Harris 1998, Gallup 1996, and Southern Focus 1998). . . . Twelve percent said they read their horoscope every day or "quite often"; 32 percent answered "just occasionally."[12]

DOES ASTROLOGY WORK?

It is obvious that if astrology did not work, it would not have any followers. Many writers conclude that astrology works in the same way as good psychological advice:

The good astrologer senses the mood of his client, perceives his problems and finds the most positive way of fitting them into the context of the horoscope. . . . The client might have been better advised to consult a psychiatrist, marriage counselor, physician, lawyer or employment agency.[13]

The greatest problem faced in evaluating astrology is that it is so difficult to prove that it does not work:

There are so many variables and options to play with that the astrologer is always right. Break a leg when your astrologer told you the signs were good, and he can congratulate you on escaping what might have happened had the signs been bad. Conversely, if you go against the signs and nothing happens, the astrologer can insist that you were subconsciously careful because you were forewarned.[14]

Montgomery sees the same problem and makes an incisive observation:

> No matter how apparently "off" the portrait, this can be explained away as natal potential which has since been modified by environment or experience. Analytical philosophers rightly emphasize . . . that assertions compatible with any state of affairs whatever say nothing. To say something meaningful, one must at least indicate what could count against it; if no contradiction at all makes a difference to one's claims, then the claims really do not impart any information at all. This seems to be the exact situation with most astrological judgments.[15]

What about the times when astrologers are right? Does this not prove it to be a science? No. Two astrologers working with the same information have often produced conflicting horoscopes. Why? Because, as many astrologers admit, astrology "depends upon an almost mediumistic faculty."[16]

Koch tells the story of how astrology worked for a French psychology student who was writing his thesis at the Sorbonne. He advertised in the newspaper that he was an astrologer and would produce a personal horoscope for twenty francs. He received 400 responses. "He gave the same horoscope to all 400 customers, paying no heed to the signs of the Zodiac. His only consideration was the psychological aspect. . . . He received many letters of appreciation."[17]

Another example of the psychological explanation of how astrology works is reported by Geoffrey Dean. He found that "many people will rate a reading successful no matter what is said! He reversed the astrological readings of 22 subjects, substituting the opposite of what they were supposed to be. Nonetheless all said the readings applied to them."[18]

Astrology's success may be explained in some cases by spirit (demonic) influence. This is illustrated in the case of a minister who had his horoscope cast in an effort to debunk astrology. He was amazed to find that its predictions were being fulfilled. This went on for eight years. Koch reports:

> The thought came to him that he had sinned through the experiment, and he had placed himself under the influence of the powers of darkness. After his repentance he discovered to his surprise that his horoscope was now no longer correct. Through this experiment the minister clearly understood that demonic powers can be active in astrology.[19]

John Weldon asks, "Is there evidence for spiritistic influence in astrology?" He answers in the affirmative from his research and from his interviews, surveys, and attendance at the July 1988 American Federation of Astrologers Convention in Las Vegas:

> At the Conference I became aware of a great deal of spiritism. Most of the 300 different astrology books examined dealt with spiritistic and occult themes. Of the nine seminars I attended, in eight of them the professional astrology instructors admitted to having spirit guides or to being spiritists (that is, one who accepts the teachings of the spirits). . . .
> As for the astrologers I talked with, most of them were into other forms of the occult such as palmistry, numerology, psychic healing, crystal power, Tarot cards, and occult societies. . . . Most astrologers also accepted the idea that psychic abilities were necessary to "properly" interpret the horoscope.[20]

There is also some evidence that the heavenly bodies (at least the sun and the moon) do influence people. A team of psychiatric researchers from the medical school of the University of Miami concluded that "outbreaks of murder may be triggered by the moon tugging on 'biological tides' inside the human body."[21] But this and similar finds do not prove astrology's contentions.

ASTROLOGY'S PROBLEMS

A number of serious problems with astrology are pointed out by its critics. A few of these are presented here.

1. A comparison of astrological columns and articles written by different astrologers for a given day or other time period are often in hopeless contradiction.[22] (Many astrologers admit that daily horoscope columns are not reliable.)

2. Astrology has not kept up with the discovery of additional planets and the precession of the equinoxes. (Because of precession over the past two thousand years, the signs of the zodiac and their constellations no longer coincide.)[23]

3. Many scientists and scientific associations have denounced astrology as worthless from a scientific standpoint. Some very sharp criticisms have been made. George Sarton's statement is one example:

> Astrology was perhaps excusable in the social and spiritual disarray of Hellenistic and Roman days; it is unforgivable today. The professional astrologers of our times are fools or crooks or both, and they ought to be restrained, but who will do it? . . .
>
> Superstitions are like diseases, highly contagious diseases. We should be indulgent to Ptolemy, who had innocently accepted the prejudices endemic in his age and could not foresee their evil consequences, but the modern diffusion of astrological superstitions deserves no mercy, and the newspaper owners who do not hesitate to spread lies for the sake of money should be punished just as one punishes the purveyors of adulterated food.[24]

Montgomery quotes Paul Couderc of the Paris Observatory in his study to determine whether the sun's position in the zodiac bears any relationship to musical ability, as astrologers claim: "'The position of the Sun has absolutely no musical significance. . . . We conclude: the assets of scientific astrology are equal to zero, as is the case with com-mercialized astrology. This is perhaps unfortunate, but it is a fact.'"[25]

In an article subtitled "Scientific Tests Fail to Support Astrology," Paul Kurtz and Andrew Franknoi cite a number of studies that have challenged astrology's claims:

> When astronomers Roger Culver and Philip Ianna . . . exam-ined 3,011 specific predictions astrologers made over a five-year period, 90 percent turned out to be false! A sample of college students did slightly better by simple guesswork. . . . A test by staff members at the U.S. Geological Survey analyzed a total of 240 earthquake predictions of 27 astrologers and found their accuracy no better than would be expected by chance.
>
> . . . Geoffrey Dean, an Australian researcher, tested 45 as-trologers in Britain and the U.S. They were asked to exam-ine astrological charts of 240 individuals and merely predict whether they were introverted or extroverted. Based on psy-chological tests the subjects had taken separately, the results were a complete failure. Shawn Carlson, of the University of California, . . . reported his test of 30 leading astrologers in Europe and the United States. They were asked to match the personality profiles of 116 subjects with their horoscopes. . . . An astrologer was given each person's profile, which had been carefully prepared, and two profiles chosen at random together with that person's horoscope. They were asked to match the horoscope to the right profile. But astrologers were able to find the correct profile only as often as chance (guessing) would predict. Since 1980, at least five similar tests have been conducted and the results have invariably been negative.[26]

The *New Age Almanac* explains the new focus of many New Agers in their interpretation of astrology. They

ASTROLOGY AND THE BIBLICAL PERSPECTIVE

To embrace astrology is to hold a worldview at odds with the Judeo-Christian worldview, which understands God to be in control of history.

Since astrology is treated under the general category of divination in the Bible, there are comparatively few specific references to it. Biblically, astrology

> involved a twofold repudiation of God. In the first place it violated God's express command (Deut. 18:9–22), and in the second place, it was inevitably associated with idolatry. Although astrology does not appear to be mentioned explicitly in the list of forbidden divination practices of Deut. 18, the Moloch worship at the head of the list was intimately connected with astrology.[29]

John Davis has made five observations on Christians and modern astrology:

- Astrology leads to a false concept of the universe and its functions. . . .
- Astrology ultimately leads to idolatry and God's judgment . . . (cf. 2 Kings 17:16–17; 23:5).
- Astrology ultimately leads to psychological imbalance and frustration. It is a wretched form of fatalism.
- Worship of the stars is strictly forbidden in Scripture (Deut. 4:15–19; 17:2–5).
- Astrology and all of its attendant theories ignore the basic Biblical teaching about man's future. . . . Not all of the future is to be known by man. . . . God has already given us all we need to know about the future in the Holy Scriptures.[30]

Isaiah 47:13–15 provides the clearest reference to astrology in the le. The Babylonians (Chaldeans) are reproved for turning away from God to occult practices. Babylon and its astrologers are under God's sure judgment:

> You are wearied in the multitude of your counsels; let now the astrologers, the stargazers, and the monthly prognosticators stand up and save you from these things that shall come upon you. Behold, they shall be as stubble, the fire shall burn them; they shall not deliver themselves from the power of the flame; it shall not be a coal to be warmed by, nor a fire to sit before! . . . No one shall save you.

Do the Scriptures offer any support to astrology or astrologers? The answer is a firm no![31]

CONCLUSION

A choice must be made. Man may follow astrology or the God who created the sun, moon, and stars. The Bible is clear that the Creator is to be consulted and worshiped rather than his creation. The Christian does not need astrology to guide him; his future is in the hands of God.

SELECT BIBLIOGRAPHY

Ankerberg, John, and John Weldon. *Astrology: Do the Heavens Rule Our Destiny?* Eugene, Ore.: Harvest House, 1989. This is the best book from a Christian perspective.

_____. *The Facts on Astrology.* Eugene, Ore.: Harvest House, 1988. This is included in *Cult Watch* (Harvest House, 1991), 203–42.

Astrology and Astronomy. San Francisco: Astronomical Society of the Pacific, 1989. This is an information packet. The society's address is 390 Ashton Ave., San Francisco, CA 94112.

"Astrology: Fad and Phenomenon." *Time*, March 21, 1969, 47–48, 53–56.

Bass, Clarence B., and Thomas E. McComiskey. "Astrology." In *Baker Encyclopedia of the Bible*, edited by Walter A. Elwell. Grand Rapids: Baker, 1988.

Bjornstad, James, and Shildes Johnson. *Stars, Signs, and Salvation in the Age of Aquarius*. Minneapolis: Bethany, 1971.

Dean, Geoffrey, and Arthur Mather. "Sun Signs Columns: Response to an Invitation." *Skeptical Inquirer* (September/October 2000), 36–40. "The authors invited astrologers and interested scientists to submit ideas for testing sun sign columns. Their responses suggest that the negative results to date are unlikely to change" (36).

Fraknoi, Andrew. "Your Astrology Defense Kit." *Sky and Telescope* (August 1989), 146–50.

Godwin, John. *Occult America*. Garden City, N.Y.: Doubleday, 1972. Astrology is treated on 1–24.

Graubard, Mark. "Under the Spell of the Zodiac." *Natural History* (May 1969), 10–18.

Kole, Andre, and Terry Holley. *Astrology and Psychic Phenomena*. Grand Rapids: Zondervan, 1998.

Melton, J. Gordon, Jerome Clark, and Aidan A. Kelly. *New Age Almanac*. Chicago: Visible Ink Press, 1991. Chapter 6 includes a brief survey of the history of astrology, its New Age interpretation, and major periodicals.

Montgomery, John Warwick. *Principalities and Powers*. Minneapolis: Bethany, 1973.

Morey, Robert A. *Horoscopes and the Christian*. Minneapolis: Bethany, 1981.

Petersen, William J. *Those Curious New Cults in the 80s*. New Canaan, Conn.: Keats, 1982. Astrology is treated on 19–33.

Strohmer, Charles. *What Your Horoscope Doesn't Tell You*. Wheaton, Ill.: Tyndale, 1988. Strohmer was a former practitioner of astrology.

———. "Is There a Christian Zodiac, a Gospel in the Stars?" *Christian Research Journal*, 22, 4 (2000), 22–25, 40–44.

Walker, James. "Astrology: A Christian View," *Watchman Expositor* 10, 9 (1993), 3; Marcia Montenegro, "A Former Astrologer Looks at Astrology Today," "Astrology Today," and "Astrology: A Biblical Response," 4–8.

BAHA'I

No cult bears a gospel better suited to the temper of our times than the Baha'i," wrote Charles W. Ferguson.[1] What was true during the 1920s is even truer today. The ecumenical message of the Baha'i Faith has received a significant response in recent years, with membership in the United States tripling during the decade following 1963 and currently estimated to be more than 110,000.[2] A high percentage of converts to Baha'i in America have been between fifteen and thirty years of age and from minority groups. Worldwide membership of the cult is estimated to be more than 5 million. The largest Baha'i community in the world is in India, where there are 1.5 million followers.[3] Historian Arnold Toynbee has written that the Baha'i faith might be the religion of the future.

This chapter surveys Baha'i history, teachings, appeal, and outreach. After its attitude toward Christianity is reviewed, the Baha'i Faith is evaluated according to the Bible. A select bibliography concludes the chapter.

HISTORY

The Baha'i Faith came to America from Persia (Iran) in force about ninety years ago. The movement originated in 1844, when Mirza Ali Muhammad assumed the title of Bab (Persian for "Gate") and announced that he was the forerunner of the World Teacher who would appear to unite mankind and usher in a new era of peace. Many people were attracted to the Bab and his message. But orthodox Muslims and the government were alarmed by the growth of his following, and so they conspired to suppress the new movement. The Bab was arrested and in 1850 executed by a firing squad. During the persecution of the movement that followed, more than twenty thousand of his followers were killed, and many others were imprisoned.

In 1863 one of the Bab's disciples, Mirza Husayn-Ali, while an exile in Baghdad, proclaimed himself to be the promised World Teacher, and he took the name Baha'u'llah ("The Glory of God"), from which the name Baha'i is derived. Baha'u'llah remained an exile and prisoner until the time of his death in 1892. He designated as his successor his eldest son, Abbas Effendi, who assumed the name Abdul'l-Baha ("Servant of Baha"). After release from prison in 1908, Abdul'l-Baha made several missionary journeys and searched for a suitable location for the first Baha'i temple. In 1912 he spent eight months in America, during which time the cornerstone of the temple at Wilmette, Illinois, was laid.

When Abdul'l-Baha died in 1921, he left a will designating his eldest grandson, Shogi Effendi, as his successor. "Under thirty-six years of Shogi Effendi's direction the Baha'is throughout the world have adopted an administrative order that is an application of Baha'u'llah's teachings for a world order."[4] Shogi Effendi died in 1957 without leaving a will. He had no heir and had appointed no successor.

Six years later, the first Baha'i Universal House of Justice was elected. This nine-person board is held by Baha'is to be infallible, and it governs Baha'i affairs from world headquarters in Haifa, Israel.[5]

As the largest religious minority in Iran, with more than 300,000 members, and viewed as a heretical sect of Islam, Baha'is have suffered persecution since 1979, with many being imprisoned and executed. Thousands more have lost their jobs, homes, and possessions.[6]

Is BAHA'I HISTORY ACCURATE?

The official Baha'i account of the early history and teachings of the movement has been questioned by some who have investigated this period. William M. Miller, who served as a missionary in Iran for forty-three years, did extensive research on the Babi-Baha'i movement and its literature. He concluded that much of the current Baha'i literature does not give an accurate account of the history and teachings of the movement, according to the best available material.[7] For example, the claim that Baha'u'llah is the latest "Manifestation," or prophet of God, and that the Bab was his forerunner is historically suspect:

> The Bab claimed to be the greatest Manifestation who had come, but he would not be the last. After him yet another would come much greater than he. . . . Though he did not predict the exact time of the appearing of the next Manifestation, he assumed that it would not occur for many centuries. He specifically mentioned 1,511 and 2,001 years in the future as dates within which the Manifestations would appear (Bayan II, 17). And after that still other Manifestations would appear in the millenniums yet to come![8]

With this background, it is easy to understand why the public announcement of Mirza Husayn-Ali (about 1866) that he was the new Manifestation predicted by the Bab surprised the Babi community and was rejected by some. Baha'u'llah "adopted the Bab's doctrine of Manifestations, but he referred to the Bab not so much as a major manifestation but as a 'forerunner' of his. He indicated that the Bab had the same relation to him that John the Baptist had to Christ."[9] Miller's *The Baha'i Faith: Its History and Teachings* is an in-depth study of the history and theology of the Baha'i faith, and it fully documents the above and discusses other problems.[10]

THE ALLEGED UNITY OF BAHA'IS

One argument Baha'is use against Christianity is that it is divided, while the Baha'i Faith does not have any schisms. Baha'i writer David Hofman asserted that the Faith had "preserved its unity in the face of tests and opposition. Today there is no Baha'i sect." Again, he writes: "We have only to call to mind the existing faiths to realize that they are all divided into numerous sects. There are no Baha'i sects. There can never be."[11] This claim is not true. I have received literature from two Baha'i sects and have read of a third. The Free Baha'is denounced Shogi Effendi as the successor to Abdul'l-Baha. After the death of Shogi Effendi in 1957, the Orthodox Baha'i Faith was formed, claiming that the Baha'is "failed to recognize the first Guardian's [Shogi Effendi's] duly appointed successor," Charles Mason Remey.[12]

TEACHINGS

The Baha'i booklet *One God, One Religion, One Mankind* sets forth the main teachings of the Baha'i Faith:

> The Baha'i Faith revolves around three basic principles: the oneness of God, the oneness of religion, and the oneness of mankind. God, in His Essence, is unknowable; His Word is made known through His Chosen Messengers. Baha'u'llah's Teachings can be summarized in the following principles [bullets added]:
> - The independent search after truth, unfettered by superstition or tradition
> - The oneness of the entire human race, the pivotal principle and fundamental doctrine of the Faith
> - The basic unity of all religions
> - The condemnation of all forms of prejudice, whether religious, racial, class or national

- The harmony which must exist between religion and science
- The equality of men and women, the two wings on which the bird of human kind is able to soar
- The introduction of compulsory education
- The adoption of a universal auxiliary language
- The abolition of the extremes of wealth and poverty
- The institution of a world tribunal for the adjudication of disputes between nations
- The exaltation of work, performed in the spirit of service, to the rank of worship
- The glorification of justice as the ruling principle in human society, and of religion as a bulwark for the protection of all peoples and nations
- The establishment of a permanent and universal peace as the supreme goal of all mankind.

This Baha'i statement emphasizes "oneness" and "unity" in the religious, social, and political realms. The practical aspects of Baha'i are much like the aims of many modern clergy, sociologists, politicians, and other leaders.

Esslemont explains:

> In order to attain the Baha'i life *in all its fullness*, conscious and direct relations with Baha'u'llah are as necessary as is sunshine for the unfolding of the lily or rose. The Baha'i worships not the human personality of Baha'u'llah, but the Glory of God manifest through that personality. He reverences Christ and Muhammad and all God's former Messengers to mankind, but he recognizes Baha'u'llah as the Bearer of God's Message for the new age in which we live, as the Great Worldteacher Who has come to carry on and consummate the work of His predecessors.[13]

This is the crux: While speaking of unifying all religions, the Baha'is ask people to accept another prophet, Baha'u'llah, as the one who supersedes all the others. A study of Baha'i teachings reveals that most of them are antithetical to biblical Christianity.

APPEAL

James Moore summarizes the Baha'i appeal to converts as expressed by Salvatore A. Pelle, director of public information at Baha'i national headquarters:

> The inhumanity perpetrated in the name of Christianity, an outdated biblical revelation and a scientifically untenable doctrine of the incarnation cause today's youth to reject Christianity automatically. His "barrier breaking" religion, claims Pelle, will appeal to these spiritual rebels because the faith: 1) "fits the twentieth century" with a new revelation through Baha'u'llah which updates the Bible; 2) makes sense of the common element in the teachings of all religions by declaring that "all true religions come from the same Divine Source," and that "truth is continuous and relative, not final and absolute"; 3) refuses to define God, referring to Him as "Unknowable Essence"; 4) teaches as its fundamental doctrine the oneness of the entire race.[14]

Other features of the Baha'i faith that are attractive to converts include

- its concern for the social and political problems of mankind.
- its high standard of moral conduct.
- its lack of a professional clergy.
- its emphasis on the active involvement of every member.
- its aggressive missionary program.

OUTREACH

The Baha'i Faith is a missionary religion. Individual Baha'is accept the responsibility to promote their faith by holding meetings ("firesides") in their homes. Public gatherings are also sponsored. Hundreds of volunteer teachers, called "pioneers," leave their communities and set up new residences at home or abroad for the purpose of propagating Baha'i where it is not well known. Missionary work during the past eighty years has introduced Baha'i to hundreds of countries and smaller political and geographical units. It is claimed that the Baha'i Faith "has become the second fastest growing religion, after Christianity, and the most widespread denomination in the world."[15]

J. K. Van Baalen considered the beautiful temple in Wilmette, Illinois, as Baha'i's chief means of propaganda outreach in the United States.[16] Built at a cost of about three million dollars, it was formally dedicated in 1953. Other Baha'i temples have been built in Sydney, Australia; Kampala, Uganda; Frankfurt, Germany; Panama City, Panama; New Delhi, India; and Apia, Western Samoa. The only architectural requirement for each of the temples is that it have nine sides, surmounted by a dome. "Its nine entrances symbolize the unity of religion and the oneness of mankind."[17]

Extensive use has been made of the printed page, and Baha'i materials have been translated into hundreds of languages. All the evidence points toward an increasing encounter between Christianity and the Baha'i Faith.

BAHA'I, CHRISTIANITY, AND THE BIBLE

Can a Christian be a Baha'i? Miller gives the answer:

It has been supposed by some that a Christian is able to retain his faith and his membership in his church while he joins the

Baha'i movement and works for peace and brotherhood and justice for all. Some Christians have attempted to do this. However, Shoghi Effendi and other Baha'i leaders have made it clear that this is not possible. It should be clearly understood that when a Christian becomes a Baha'i he by so doing rejects the basic doctrines of the Bible, denies his Christian faith, and starts off in a different direction.[18]

As William J. Petersen so aptly puts it, "Baha'i collides head-on with Christianity; it isn't a pleasant merger."[19] Baha'i teachers do not emphasize the clash between Christianity and Baha'i; they would rather avoid the conflict. But interviews with them leave no doubt that Baha'i rejects the cardinal doctrines of historic, biblical Christianity.[20]

Baha'i author George Townshend identifies orthodox Christians as "false prophets," as those who have changed "the essential meaning of the Gospel" as taught by Christ.[21] What characterizes the beliefs of these Christian "false prophets"? They teach "that Jesus Christ was a unique incarnation of God such as had never before appeared in religious history and would never appear again,"[22] and that Christ's "teaching was absolute and final."[23] On the basis of Isaiah 9:6–7, they believe "that Christ was the Lord of Hosts of the Old Testament."[24] The "Gospel of Christ" they teach today "is wholly different from the Gospel which Christ preached in Galilee as recorded in the Bible."[25] And, "in spite of Christ's promise of further revelation of Truth," says Townshend, "the Christian Church regards His revelation as final, and itself as the sole trustee of true religion."[26] They say that "Christ's spiritual mission was . . . materialized, specifically in regard to such things as the miracles. . . . Even His own resurrection was made physical, missing the point entirely."[27] "To sum up, if Christians say 'our acts may be wrong,' they say truly. If they say 'however our Gospel is right' they are quite wrong. The false prophets have corrupted the Gospel as successfully as they have the deeds and lives of Christian people."[28]

Bible-believing Christians cannot accept Townshend's charge of being false prophets. They cannot accept the Baha'i invitation to join them. Nor can Christians accept the view that Jesus Christ is adequately represented in Baha'i simply because he is given a place in it. The Scriptures demand that he be given first place, to the exclusion of all others. According to Baha'u'llah, many passages of the Bible pertaining to Jesus Christ are not true today. They would include

> Jesus said to him, "I am the way, the truth, and the life. No one comes to the Father except through Me." (John 14:6)

> Nor is there salvation in any other, for there is no other name under heaven given among men by which we must be saved. (Acts 4:12)

> For no other foundation can anyone lay than that which is laid, which is Jesus Christ. (1 Cor. 3:11)

> For there is one God and one Mediator between God and men, the Man Christ Jesus, who gave Himself a ransom for all, to be testified in due time. (1 Tim. 2:5–6)

> Jesus Christ is the same yesterday, today, and forever. (Heb. 13:8)

The Baha'i faith also robs the Christian of the "blessed hope" of the second coming of Jesus Christ:

> If you are of the Christian Faith which had its origin approximately the year 1, your prophecy concerning the return of Christ in the glory of the Father has been fulfilled. His new name in this day is Baha'u'llah, which means "The Glory of God."[29]

This "fulfillment" does not agree with what Scripture says: "Looking for the blessed hope and glorious appearing of our great God and our Savior Jesus Christ" (Titus 2:13). At the ascension, the apostles were told by the angels that "this same Jesus, who is taken up from you into heaven, will so come in like manner as you saw Him go into heaven" (Acts 1:11).

Baha'i's teaching of "the oneness of religion" is not a biblical concept. While most religions have certain elements in common, Christianity cannot compromise its teachings to accommodate the doctrines set forth by Hinduism, Buddhism, Islam, or any other religion. None of them, including Baha'i, accepts the Bible's teaching concerning man's sin and the relationship of the work of Christ to man's redemption (Rom. 3:23; Isa. 64:6; John 1:29; 3:14–17), and "when one examines the doctrine of God's nature, as revealed by the so-called manifestations, there exists a mass of contradictory doctrine."[30]

CONCLUSION

Baha'i does not, nor can it, offer any present hope of sins forgiven and a sure standing before God. In fact, Baha'i views such a claim as presumptuous. John presents a different picture:

> And this is the testimony: that God has given us eternal life, and this life is in His Son. He who has the Son has life; he who does not have the Son of God does not have life. These things I have written to you who believe in the name of the Son of God, that you may know that you have eternal life, and that you may continue to believe in the name of the Son of God. (1 John 5:11–13)

SELECT BIBLIOGRAPHY

Ankerberg, John, and John Weldon. *Encyclopedia of Cults and New Religions*. Eugene, Ore.: Harvest House, 1999. Baha'i is treated on 5–44.

Bach, Marcus. *They Have Found a Faith*. New York: Bobbs-Merrill, 1946. Baha'i is treated on 189–221.

Beckwith, Francis J. *Baha'i*. Minneapolis: Bethany, 1985.

_____. "Baha'i-Christian Dialogue: Some Key Issues Considered." *Christian Research Journal* (winter/spring 1989), 15–19.

Bjorling, Joel. *The Baha'i Faith: A Historical Bibliography*. New York: Garland, 1985.

Boykin, John. *The Baha'i Faith*. Downers Grove, Ill.: InterVarsity Press, 1982. This is included as chapter 2 of *A Guide to Cults and New Religions*, ed. Ronald Enroth (Downers Grove, Ill.: InterVarsity Press, 1983).

Ferguson, Charles W. *The Confusion of Tongues*. Garden City, N.Y.: Doubleday, 1928. Baha'i is treated on 231–50.

Martin, Walter R. *The Kingdom of the Cults*. Rev. 1997 ed. Minneapolis: Bethany, 1997. Baha'i is treated on 321–31.

Melton, J. Gordon. *Biographical Dictionary of American Cults and Sect Leaders*. New York: Garland, 1986.

Miller, William M. *The Baha'i Faith: Its History and Teachings*. S. Pasadena, Calif.: William Carey Library, 1974. This book is also available in an abridgment by William N. Wysham entitled *What Is the Baha'i Faith?* (Grand Rapids: Eerdmans, 1977).

_____. "What Is the Baha'i World Faith?" *Incite* (December 1975), 22–28.

Moore, James. "A New Look at Baha'i." *His* (February 1971), 16–18.

Pardon, Robert. "The Baha'i Faith." *Watchman Fellowship Profile*, 1997.

Petersen, William J. *Those Curious New Cults in the 80s*. New Canaan, Conn.: Keats, 1982. Baha'i is treated on 190–201.

Tucker, Ruth A. *Another Gospel: Alternative Religions and the New Age Movement*. Grand Rapids: Zondervan, 1989. Baha'i is treated on 285–98.

Van Baalen, J. K. *The Chaos of Cults*. 4th rev. ed. Grand Rapids: Eerdmans, 1962. Baha'i is treated on 146–61.

Baha'i Materials

Materials may be obtained through local Baha'i centers or by writing to the Baha'i National Center, 1233 Central St., Evanston, IL 60201 (phone 847-869-9039). The official Baha'i website is www.bahai.org. *One Country* is the online newsletter of the Baha'i International Community (www.onecountry.org).

Esslemont, J. E. *Baha'u'llah and the New Era.* 4th rev. ed. Wilmette, Ill.: Baha'i Publishing Trust, 1976. The preface to the 1950 edition states that this is "a trustworthy introduction to the history and teachings of the Baha'i Faith."

ROSICRUCIANISM

E XPAND YOUR LEVEL OF CONSCIOUSNESS," reads the caption. The advertisement continues:

> Your consciousness has no limits—*if* you let it rise above its present bounds. *Inspiration* and *Intuition* are not just haphazard events. You are an infinite part of the *Universal Cosmic Intelligence*. You can draw, at *will*, upon this Intelligence for seemingly miraculous results. This Cosmic Intelligence flows through you. It is the very *vital force of life*. It is not supernatural; it is a natural phenomenon. Learn to reach for this higher level of your consciousness and avail yourself of its intuitive enlightenment.[1]

This statement, typical of many others that have been published over the years, epitomizes the appeal and goal of Rosicrucianism. The reader of the ad is invited to write for a free copy of *The Mastery of Life* (now *Mastery of Life*). This booklet presents the Rosicrucian philosophy, a brief treatment of the history of the order, the benefits of membership, and an invitation to unite with the Ancient Mystical Order Rosae Crucis, usually abbreviated to AMORC. Located in San Jose, California, this is the largest and most widely known of the Rosicrucian societies, with affiliated lodges and chapters in more than one hundred countries worldwide.

A rival California body, the Rosicrucian Fellowship, founded by Max Heindel (1865–1919), has its center in Oceanside. Heindel was a prolific writer whose "interest in astrology was responsible for making the Rosicrucian Fellowship an important factor in the revival of astrology in the twentieth century."[2] The oldest Rosicrucian order in the U.S., Fraternitas Rosae Crucis, established in 1858, did not experience solid growth until Reuben Swineburne Clymer became head of the order after the death of Edward H. Brown in 1922. Clymer established its headquarters in Quakertown, Pennsylvania. He was a voluminous writer "and his numerous books remain standard reading material for Rosicrucians."[3]

Another group that operates in the U.S. is Lectorium Rosicrucianum, with its American headquarters in Bakersfield, California, and its European headquarters in Haarlem, the Netherlands.[4] Several additional groups that identify with the Rosicrucian name are present in the United States.[5]

The Rosicrucian movement, like many other occult-oriented groups, has experienced rapid growth in recent years. In 1990 it was estimated that the Rosicrucian Order (AMORC) had a membership of about 250,000 worldwide.[6]

Charles Braden characterizes Rosicrucianism in this way:

> There are Rosicrucian societies, fraternities, orders, fellowships or lodges in most countries of the modern world. Some of them are very active; others are obscure and highly secret; some seem primarily religious in their emphasis, and some categorically deny that Rosicrucianism is a religion, holding rather that it is a philosophy, making use of the most modern scientific methods and techniques, as well as the methods of the occultist, the mystic and the seer, in the quest for truth.
>
> But, while Rosicrucianism is sectarian in character and the various branches are sometimes bitterly critical of each other, they do have common features, the central one being the purported possession of certain secret wisdom handed down from ancient times, through a secret brotherhood, an esoteric wisdom that can only be imparted to the initiated.[7]

What is the historical origin of Rosicrucianism? What are some of the basic Rosicrucian teachings? Why are people drawn to the movement? How is the order to be evaluated? After surveying these matters, this chapter concludes with a select bibliography. The Rosicrucian order primarily in view is AMORC of San Jose.

HISTORY

Harvey Spencer Lewis founded AMORC and served as its First Imperator for North and South America between 1915 and 1939. He claimed that Rosicrucianism began in ancient Egypt, a view that is also propagated in *The Mastery of Life:*

> What later evolved into Rosicrucianism—had its roots in the mystery traditions, philosophy, and myths of ancient Egypt from approximately 1500 B.C. However, the Rosicrucian movement is eclectic and uniquely draws upon the diverse mystical traditions of ancient Greece, China, India and Persia.[8]

It is also claimed that such movements as the Essenes and the early Christian church—and such individuals as Jesus, Plato, and Philo—were related to the Rosicrucian Order.[9] But non-Rosicrucian scholars are not convinced of this.

There is much controversy and obscurity surrounding the early history of the Rosicrucians. It is taught that Christian Rosenkreuz ("Rosy Cross") (1378–1484) was the founder. The story of his search for knowledge and true wisdom and of the founding of the order was published in 1614, in the famous *Fama Fraternitatis*. This document tells how Rosenkreuz traveled to Damascus, Damcar (Arabia?), Egypt, and Fez, where he came into possession of much secret wisdom. Then he journeyed to Spain, but being disappointed with his reception there, he returned to Germany, where he imparted his knowledge first to three disciples and then to four others, and the order was established. While many people hold to the historicity of Christian Rosenkreuz, it is generally held that he was not a real person but rather a legendary or symbolic character used for the mythical explanation of the order. Two other works appeared after the *Fama* that gave it further publicity: *Confessio Fraternitatis Rosae Crucis* (1615) and the *Chemical Wedding of Christian Rosenkreuz* (1616).[10]

The seventeenth century saw the spread of Rosicrucianism throughout Europe and to the United States. According to J. Gordon Melton, "Rosicrucianism almost completely disappeared in the eighteenth century, but in the nineteenth century it was a major component of the occult revival in the West. It emerged out of Masonry."[11]

The Rosicrucian Order (AMORC) was formally organized by H. Spencer Lewis in New York in 1915. In 1927 the headquarters of the movement were established in San Jose, and during the 1930s the buildings for the headquarters complex were constructed. When Lewis died in 1939, his son Ralph became his successor as Imperator until his death in 1987 at the age of eighty-two. The successor to Ralph Lewis, Gary L. Stewart, made the news in April 1990: "The leader of the Rosicrucian Order has been ousted as imperator and president of the mystic organization and is suspected of embezzling $3.5 million, a spokesman at world headquarters said this week."[12] The present Imperator, elected to replace Stewart, is Christian Bernard.

Many authors have suggested various meanings that might be associated with the rose and the cross which are used as an emblem by the Rosicrucians. H. Spencer Lewis writes that "a book might be written upon the Symbology or Mystical meaning of the Rose and the Cross." Then he explains:

> In our Work, the Cross represents many things esoterically; likewise the Rose. But esoterically, the Rose represents Secrecy and Evolution, while the Cross represents the Labor

and Burdens of Life and the karma which we must endure in our earthly existence.[13]

Rosicrucian writers do not comprehend the true meaning of the cross, which finds its significance not in man's evolutionary development but in God's provision of salvation through the death of Christ, "who Himself bore our sins in His own body on the tree, that we, having died to sins, might live for righteousness—by whose stripes you were healed" (1 Peter 2:24).

TEACHINGS

Rosicrucianism is a complicated system of thought, and it is difficult to extract a complete statement of beliefs. Walter R. Martin says that it

> is not only an eclectic theological system which mixes pagan mythology with Judaism, and Christianity with traces of Hinduism and Buddhism throughout, but it is a system of thinking which seeks to synthesize the basic truths of all religions and absorb them into a master system.
>
> In the literature of Rosicrucianism one will find enormous deposits of symbolism, anthropology, transmigration and even some spiritism.
>
> There is great similarity in some areas to the vocabulary of Theosophy and to the concept that man progresses through many reincarnations, each of which purges him of his preceding sins.[14]

While they take the position that they are not a religious organization, the Rosicrucians do a thorough job of contradicting every major teaching of orthodox Christianity. For example:
1. God is considered an impersonal being.
2. The Trinity "becomes a type of occult pantheism."

3. The unique deity of Christ is rejected along with the vicarious atonement.

4. Reincarnation is substituted for resurrection.

5. Man is viewed as evolving into a divine being.[15]

As a sample of the perversion of biblical Christianity set forth in Rosicrucian books, a few brief quotations will be cited from Lewis's *The Mystical Life of Jesus*. This book was advertised as the "Most Surprising Book Ever Printed" and as "The Greatest Story Never Told."[16]

1. Lewis writes that "Jesus was born of *Gentile* parents through whose veins flowed Aryan blood."[17]

2. He claims that Jesus' words from the cross "could not mean, 'My God, My God, why hast thou forsaken me?' but rather 'My Temple of Helois, My Brethren of Helois, why hast thou forsaken me?'"[18]

3. Jesus did not die on the cross, for "an examination of the body revealed that Jesus was *not dead*. The blood *flowing from the wounds* proved that his body was not lifeless."[19]

4. The ascension is rejected because "there is nothing in the original accounts of it to warrant the belief that Jesus arose physically or in His physical body in a cloud into the Heavens."[20]

5. And, finally, it is claimed that Rosicrucian archival records "clearly show that after Jesus retired to the monastery at Carmel He lived for many years, and carried on secret sessions with His Apostles."[21]

This book is filled with similar extrabiblical revelations, all in violent disagreement with what the Bible says. The book might more accurately be entitled *The Mythical Life of Jesus*.

In this same volume, a number of other books in the Rosicrucian library are advertised. Among these is *The Book of Jasher*, which is supposed to be the lost book mentioned in the Bible (Josh. 10:13; 2 Sam. 1:18). The advertisement carries the indignant questions:

BY WHAT right has man been denied the words of the prophets? Who dared expunge from the Holy Bible one of its inspired messages? For centuries man has labored under the illusion that there have been preserved for him the collected books of the great teachers and disciples—yet one has been withheld—*The Book of Jasher.*[22]

Bible scholar and translator Edgar J. Goodspeed included the *Book of Jasher* in *Modern Apocrypha* (retitled *Famous "Biblical" Hoaxes*). He exposed the rendition republished by the Rosicrucians as a literary fraud. It had already been so exposed in the eighteenth and nineteenth centuries. Goodspeed concludes, "The Book of Jasher, as they have published it, is no older than 1750."[23] How many other authoritative records in the Rosicrucian archives suffer from such a defect?

Appeal

Much of Rosicrucianism's appeal is to be found in its accent on the occult and the mysterious. Rosicrucian literature also promises answers to problems and the realization of one's full potential. One who is interested in uniting with AMORC is advised of the many benefits such membership can bring him, including an exciting program of home study, experiments and exercises to develop psychic and spiritual awareness, personal guidance, "personal association in a Rosicrucian assembly" with participation "in mystical convocations, lectures, meetings, conventions and other various activities," and subscriptions to *The Rosicrucian Digest*[24] and *The Rosicrucian Forum.*

Many people are attracted to the Order because of the statement that the Rosicrucians are "*not* a religion" or "religious organization." The emphasis on Rosicrucianism being a philosophy and not a religion allows many church members to join.[25]

Evaluation

Even a cursory investigation of Rosicrucian teachings makes it clear that it is anti-Christian, if the Bible is accepted as the standard. J. K. Van Baalen evaluates the Rosicrucian system as one that denies and perverts everything taught by Christ and concerning Christ. . . .

. . . The entire structure is built upon a false foundation, namely, another than the Christ of the Scriptures.

The crowning test of a religious or philosophical system of thought . . . must always be: How do its statements compare with what has been held to be in harmony with the Scripture by the entire Christian Church? When we do this, we reach the conclusion that the Apostle Paul would say of the followers of the Rose Cross that they are "enemies of the cross of Christ."[26]

After a study of Rosicrucian teachings, one can understand why Martin concludes that "everything Christian that it touches suffers violence at its hands."[27]

Joyce Blackwell, a former Rosicrucian, states that because Rosicrucians "said their teachings were an extension of the Bible," she didn't realize immediately after becoming a Christian that their doctrines "were actually anti-Christian." This contradiction between Rosicrucianism and the Bible became clear after studying the Scriptures. "After Bible class one night I said, 'There is a terrible discrepancy between the Rosicrucian teaching and what the Bible teaches.' "[28]

CONCLUSION

This brief survey has made it obvious that historic biblical Christianity and Rosicrucianism are incompatible. The Bible has a stern warning for those who follow a system apart from that revealed in Scripture: "There is a way that seems right to a man, but its end is the way of death" (Prov. 14:12).

SELECT BIBLIOGRAPHY

Blackwell, Joyce. "I Was a Rosicrucian." In We Found Our Way Out, edited by James R. Adair and Ted Miller, 27–34. Grand Rapids: Baker, 1964.

Braden, Charles S. "Rosicrucianism." *Encyclopaedia Britannica.* Chicago: Encyclopaedia Britannica, 1964.

Daraul, Arkon. *A History of Secret Societies.* New York: Pocket Books, 1961. The Rosicrucians are treated on 226–39.

Fogarty, Harry W. "Rosicrucians." In *The Encyclopedia of Religion.* New York: Macmillan, 1987.

Goodspeed, Edgar J. *Famous "Biblical" Hoaxes.* Grand Rapids: Baker, 1956. "The Book of Jasher" is treated on 81–87.

MacKenzie, Norman, ed. *Secret Societies.* New York: Collier, 1967. The Rosicrucians are treated on 109–27.

Martin, Walter R. *The Kingdom of the Cults.* Rev. ed. Minneapolis: Bethany, 1985. The Rosicrucians are treated on 507–12.

Mather, George A. and Larry A. Nichols, "Rosicrucianism." In *Dictionary of Cults, Sects, Religions and the Occult.* Grand Rapids: Zondervan, 1993.

Melton, J. Gordon. *Encyclopedic Handbook of Cults in America.* New York: Garland, 1986. The Rosicrucians are treated on 68–75.

Van Baalen, J. K. *The Chaos of Cults.* 4th rev. ed. Grand Rapids: Eerdmans, 1962. The discussion of Rosicrucianism, 104–27, focuses on the Rosicrucian Fellowship.

ROSICRUCIAN MATERIALS

Rosicrucian materials are readily available from The Rosicrucian Fellowship, Oceanside, California, and The Rosicrucians, AMORC, Rosicrucian Park, San Jose, California. Key Rosicrucian writers representing various orders include H. Spencer Lewis, Max Heindel, R. Swinburne Clymer, George Winslow Plummer, and J. Van Rijckenborgh. Their works are too numerous to list here.

The Rosicrucian Digest, the official magazine of the Rosicrucian Order, AMORC, is published quarterly. Another quarterly, *The Rosi-*

crucian Forum, is a private publication for Rosicrucian members. The official website of this group is www.rosicrucian.org.

The Rosicrucian Fellowship, Oceanside, California, publishes the *Rays from the Rose Cross* monthly magazine. The official website is www.rosicrucian.com.

13 | THE OCCULT AND THE
OUIJA BOARD

The occult (from the Latin: that which is hidden, covered, mysterious) holds a strong fascination for many people in the world. Some observers characterize what is taking place as an "occult explosion."[1] What is included in the occult, and how pervasive is it? William Watson explains:

> It is a term that covers wide-ranging practices including astrology, other forms of divination, Spiritualism, magic, witchcraft, Satanism, and Hindu/occult ancient wisdom groups such as ECKANKAR, Theosophy, Rosicrucianism, UFO cults, self-styled prophets, and the New Age movement. Outside the U.S. the occult takes the form of voodoo and macumba. . . .
>
> Occultic influence pervades society in subtle ways. Children's cartoons and toys, particularly those that are fantasy-oriented, are laden with occultic imagery. . . .
>
> Fantasy role-playing games offer children and young adults what amounts to a catechism of occultism. Gary North says, "These games are the most effective, most magnificently packaged, most profitably marketed, most thoroughly researched introduction to the occult in man's recorded history."[2]

A June 1990 Gallup poll showed a greater overall interest in the occult than there was in 1978, when another poll asked people the same questions.[3] This curiosity continues.

While millions are involved in occult practices, such participation is not supported by the Bible (Lev. 19:31; 20:6; Deut. 18:10–11; 2 Chron. 33:6; Isa. 8:19–20; 47:13–14). At Ephesus, the manifestation of the power of Jesus Christ (Acts 19:11–17) led new Christians to end their involvement with the occult (vv. 18–19):

> And many who had believed came confessing and telling their deeds. Also, many of those who had practiced magic brought their books together and burned them in the sight of all. And they counted up the value of them, and it totaled fifty thousand pieces of silver.

People who are attuned to biblical Christianity forsake the occult. At Ephesus a price was paid; the value of the materials destroyed represented a large sum of money.

One significant aspect of the occult in America, Europe, and other places in the world is the use of the Ouija board or a variation. I became interested in this device because of its frequent mention by young people and the questions they asked about it. Periodically pastors and youth workers wrote to me, asking for information about the board. My interest was further stimulated when my son gave a presentation on the occult at school. The teacher of the class thought it unusual that I would not let my son play with the board; after all, reasoned the teacher, "it is just a game." My study of Ouija board history and the cases of many users who encountered great difficulties through its use proved this common opinion wrong.

Information on the Ouija board is needed in this day when its popularity is still great. What is its history? What makes it work? Are there any dangers in its use? What should be the Christian's attitude toward it and similar devices? Books and articles for further study are listed in the select bibliography.

HISTORY OF THE BOARD

Writers state that devices similar to the Ouija board were known to the Egyptians and other ancient peoples. Psychical researcher Nandor Fodor states that an instrument like the Ouija board "was in use in the days of Pythagoras, about 540 B.C."[4] The fourth-century Byzantine historian, Ammianus Marcellinus, gave a detailed account of divination that employed a pendulum and the letters of the alphabet engraved on the rim of a round metal dish. A less sophisticated method of divination used by the Romans made use of a ring suspended by a hair or thread, in or within reach of a glass vessel. Answers to questions were obtained when the ring struck the glass in response to a predetermined code or when the correct letters of the alphabet were recited. Table tipping (in practice, more of a table rapping), while used in ancient times and during the Middle Ages, came into popular use during the nineteenth century. In addition to response through raps for yes and no, the letters of the alphabet were also recited and the table responded at the appropriate letters, and sentences could be spelled out.

In 1853 a French spiritualist invented the planchette, a small, heart-shaped table with three legs, one of which was a lead pencil. The operator's fingers were placed lightly on top of it, and when the instrument worked, it moved over the top of a piece of paper and wrote out messages. A cognate method of communication is automatic writing, where the subject sits with a pencil in hand and after a time writes automatically.

The Ouija board was born when the pencil of the planchette was replaced by two legs (modern Ouijas have three legs) and an alphabet board replaced the paper. If a patent establishes priority, the invention of the Ouija board should be credited to Elijah Bond, who filed for the patent on May 28, 1890. It was granted on February 10, 1891. It is unclear who its actual inventor was, but William Fuld of Baltimore and his sons have been historically connected with the board and its manufacture.[5]

With some minor variations, the Ouija board is a rectangular board about eighteen inches long and twelve inches wide. On it are printed the words *yes, no,* and *good-bye.* The message indicator is a small, plastic, heart-shaped table about six inches long. The three legs of the indicator are felt-tipped, so that they slide easily under the light, fingertip touch of one or two operators. Board sales increased during the First World War, and its popularity reached a peak in 1920. It again became popular in 1944 during the Second World War. The most recent interest in the occult also brought a surge in Ouija sales. The patents on the board were purchased in 1966 by Parker Brothers of Salem, Massachusetts. In 1967 the Ouija board became America's favorite board game, outselling Monopoly for the first and only time, with sales of 2.3 million. While sales did not continue at this level, the Ouija's popularity has continued, and sales are still substantial.[6]

As evidence of the continued popularity of the board, the December 1994 *Consumer Reports* published the results after questioning 17,000 students between 10 and 14 years of age. They were asked which games they played and which they liked best. Of 83 games played, the students liked Monopoly the best, and the Ouija board ranked second.

What Makes It Work?

Parker Brothers, which manufactures the Ouija board, offers no solution to what makes it work, stating that "how or why it works is a mystery."[7] Three explanations are usually given:

1. Imperceptible muscular movements cause the indicator to move, and the messages originate in the conscious or subconscious mind of the operator.

2. Much of the activity originates in the conscious or subconscious mind, but a smaller portion derives from contact with the spirits of the disincarnate dead or other intelligent entities.

3. Much originates in the conscious or subconscious mind of the operator, but a smaller portion comes from contact with evil spirits

(demons). This view of Ouija board phenomena is held by most Christians, who reject the Spiritualist interpretation because the Bible does not allow for the wandering about of disincarnate spirits (2 Cor. 5:8; Phil. 1:23; Luke 23:43; John 14:2). Some authors state that any attempt at present to deny the possible intrusion of the supernatural into Ouija board use is premature, for, as John Godwin points out, "the entire spectrum of automatism remains largely unexplored."[8]

For the following reasons, the Ouija board should be seen as a device that sometimes makes contact with the supernatural realm:

1. The content of the messages often goes beyond what can be reasonably explained as coming from the conscious or subconscious mind of the operator. Examples of such messages are presented in William F. Barrett's *On the Threshold of the Unseen* and in the experiences of Mrs. John H. Curran, which are related in Irving Litvag's *Singer in the Shadows*.[9]

2. The many cases of possession after a period of Ouija board use also support the claim that supernatural contact is made through the board. Psychics, parapsychologists, psychiatrists, medical doctors, and other professionals have had contacts with, and have received letters from, many people who have experienced possession (an invasion of their personalities).[10] One skeptical psychiatrist, Michael David, became a believer when he observed a frail fifteen-year-old girl who had been involved with Ouija boards "having a fit and virtually holding clear of the ground the four adults attempting to restrain her. 'She was coming out with incredible mouthsful of obscenity and abuse,' he recalls." It was obvious to David that the girl's problem was "severe demonic possession."[11] America's most well-known exorcism team, Ed Warren and Lorraine Warren, state that they have often been called to assist in Ouija-related cases of possession. In fact, says Ed Warren, "About seven out of ten of our cases are Ouija board related."[12]

3. The board has been subjected to tests that support supernatural intervention. After testing the board on various people, Barrett reported that it worked efficiently with the operators blindfolded, the board's alphabet rearranged, and its surface hidden from the sight of

those working it. It worked with such speed and accuracy under these conditions that Barrett concluded,

> Reviewing the results as a whole I am convinced of their supernormal character, and that we have here an exhibition of some intelligent, disincarnate agency, mingling with the personality of one or more of the sitters and guiding their muscular movements.[13]

In *On the Threshold of the Unseen,* Barrett refers to these same experiences and states, "Whatever may have been the source of the intelligence displayed, it was absolutely beyond the range of any normal human faculty."[14] Noted psychical researcher Hereward Carrington writes that "there are numerous cases on record when the board has continued to write after the hands of all the sitters have been removed."[15] Similar contemporary statements could be multiplied.

The fact remains that the Ouija board works. Most of its results are plainly the product of conscious and subconscious activity, but some of it is of supernatural character.

POTENTIAL DANGERS

There are potential dangers in the use of the Ouija board as a game or as an approach to psychic development. As the operator becomes more involved with the board, his fascination with it often leads him to dependence upon it and to the surrender of his will. After a time, the answers to the questions are anticipated in the mind before they are spelled out on the board. After this, the board may be discarded, and in its place the operator may hear a voice. Sometimes the voice (or voices) communicates almost continuously, and the messages are often profane and obscene. Beyond this, sensual feelings, sexual stimulation, and the use of the person's vocal cords for expression by the "possessing entity" (demon) may also take place.

G. Godfrey Raupert explains from his observations of an earlier period of Ouija popularity how occult entrapment often came about, and he warns of tragic results:

> Suggestions are made in the most subtle manner, in exalted language, appealing to the youthful imagination and to dangerous tendencies latent in all men; and when it is borne in mind that the invisible counselor who makes these suggestions is believed to be a kindly father or mother who could only desire the well-being of her child, and that the experimenter's power of discrimination is lost, one can imagine how far this kind of mischief can be carried.
>
> As the "psychic development" advances, the entire mental and moral nature of the experimenter becomes disordered; and he discovers to his cost that, while it was an easy thing for him to *open* the mental door by which the mind could be invaded, it is a difficult, if not an impossible thing, to *shut* that door and to expel the invader. For the impulse to communicate or to write now asserts itself imperatively and incessantly, at all hours of the day and in the midst of every kind of occupation, and, in the end, even at night, either suddenly awakening the victim or preventing him from securing any refreshing sleep. A pitiable condition of mental and moral collapse, often terminating in suicide or insanity, is frequently the ultimate result.[16]

More recently, well-known occult writer Martin Ebon has described entrapment as he has observed it. As in Raupert's account, involvement with the Ouija board begins "harmlessly enough"—"for kicks"—and concludes with possession "or hearing voices that control and command" the Ouija operator.[17]

Psychologists, psychiatrists, medical doctors, theologians, and many other informed persons have issued warnings of the dangers of Ouija board experimentation. While they do not always agree on the source of the danger (whether psychological, a disincarnate spirit or other entity, or a demon), they all agree that dangers do exist. If space permitted, dozens of statements could be cited.

Physician Carl Wickland, who became a Spiritualist, explains how he was drawn into psychical research:

> The serious problem of alienation and mental derangement attending ignorant psychic experiments was first brought to my attention by the cases of several persons whose seemingly harmless experiences with automatic writing and the Ouija board resulted in such wild insanity that commitment to asylums was necessitated. . . .
>
> Many other disastrous results which followed the use of the supposedly innocent Ouija board came to my notice and my observations led me into research in psychic phenomena for a possible explanation of these strange occurrences.[18]

Pastor H. Richard Neff concludes that for the most part the Ouija board works because of autosuggestion, but he also warns:

> A sufficient number of people have got into serious psychological difficulty through the use of a Ouija board to warn us that these instruments may not be "innocent toys." Most serious students of parapsychology strongly advise people not to use Ouija boards and such instruments.[19]

The *Guide Book for the Study of Psychical Research*, in the glossary under "Ouija Board," says:

> Many researchers have pointed out the inherent dangers of using the ouija board or of taking its "messages" seriously, because of the possibility of dredging up some very unpleasant and potentially disturbing attitudes and facts from one's subconscious. There have been numerous instances of persons

who have become very upset emotionally from the use of the ouija board.[20]

Veteran demonologist Ed Warren, after years of Ouija board-related cases, warns, "Ouija boards are just as dangerous as drugs. They're not to be played with."[21]

Stuart Checkley, dean of the Institute of Psychiatry at Maudsley Hospital, London, relates some of his experiences:

> I have seen patients whose involvement with relatively minor forms of the occult has caused them to suffer mental illness. I have seen someone who as the result of one experiment with an ouija board suffered frightening experiences outside his control, including automatic handwriting. He found himself writing frightening messages to himself.[22]

CONCLUSION

What should the Christian's attitude be toward the Ouija board? Obviously, he should not use it, because the Bible condemns involvement with the occult (Lev. 19:31; 20:6), many have had tragic experiences with it, and its messages are often false, obscene, or contrary to Bible truth.

Where the Christian is to go for his guidance, understanding, and wisdom is clear in the Scripture:

> And when they say to you, "Seek those who are mediums and wizards, who whisper and mutter," should not a people seek their God? (Isa. 8:19)

> If any of you lacks wisdom, let him ask of God, who gives to all liberally and without reproach, and it will be given to him. (James 1:5)

CULTS AND THE OCCULT

During a period of Ouija board popularity, Pastor I. M. Haldeman made the Christian position plain: "No more think of having a ouija board in your home or fooling with it . . . than you would invite the arch-enemy of God and man to dwell intimately with you."[23]

Contemporary British pastor Russell Parker, who has counseled and worked with many occult victims, writes:

> I consider the ouija board to be a dangerous occult door through which people have unwittingly opened themselves up to destructive powers. In so doing they have set themselves on a dangerous road which will only produce further spiritual deterioration.[24]

SELECT BIBLIOGRAPHY

Ankerberg, John, and John Weldon. *Encyclopedia of New Age Beliefs.* Eugene, Ore.: Harvest House, 1996. See "Divination Practices and Occult 'Games,'" 119–66.

Barrett, W. F. "On Some Experiments with the Ouija Board and Blindfolded Sitters." *Proceedings of the American Society for Psychical Research* (September 1914), 381–94.

———. *On the Threshold of the Unseen.* New York: Dutton, 1918. Chapter 14 is entitled "Proof of Super-Normal Messages: The Ouija Board."

Brittle, Gerald. *The Demonologist.* 1980. Reprint. New York: St. Martin's, 1991. Two significant Ouija board-related cases are discussed on 135–70 and 222–31.

Doorways to Danger. London: Evangelical Alliance, 1987.

Ebon, Martin, ed. *The Satan Trap: Dangers of the Occult.* New York: Doubleday, 1976.

Godwin, John. *Occult America.* Garden City, N.Y.: Doubleday, 1972.

Gruss, Edmond C. *The Ouija Board: A Doorway to the Occult.* Phillipsburg, N.J.: P&R, 1994.

_____. *La Tabla Ouija: Una Puerta a lo Oculto.* Santa Fe de Bogata, Columbia: Centros de Literatura Cristiana, 1997.

Litvag, Irving. *Singer in the Shadows: The Strange Story of Patience Worth.* New York: Macmillan, 1972. This relates one of the most unusual Ouija board experiences.

"Ouija, Ouija, Who's Got the Ouija?" *The Literary Digest* (July 3, 1920), 66 68. This article contains a brief history of the Ouija board.

Parker Brothers. *The Weird and Wonderful Ouija Talking Board Set.* Brochure sent in response to letters asking about the board.

Raupert, J. Godfrey. "The Truth About the Ouija Board." *The Ecclesiastical Review* (November 1918), 463–78. Written by a Catholic expert during a former period of Ouija popularity.

Truths That Transform radio broadcast, "The Ouija Board," aired March 27, 1995 (Action Sheet BV5). For more information call or write Truths That Transform, P.O. Box 33, Ft. Lauderdale, FL 33302; phone 1-800-229-WORD.

14

EDGAR CAYCE AND THE A.R.E.

Edgar Cayce (pronounced *Casey*) has been identified as America's "greatest mystic," "most famous clairvoyant," "most famous prophet," and, most recently, "the father of modern channeling" and "the father of the New Age Movement." Jeane Dixon said that "Cayce was clearly one of the most remarkable psychics who ever lived."[1] He became one of the most widely publicized psychics of the twentieth century. One of the unusual features of Cayce's fame is the fact that it reached its peak *after* his death in 1945.

Numerous questions may be asked concerning Edgar Cayce, his experiences, his psychic readings, the teachings derived from his sleeplike trances and how they compare with biblical Christianity, and the work of the Association for Research and Enlightenment, Inc. (A.R.E.). A brief survey of these matters is presented here. A select bibliography for further study is provided at the end of the chapter.

EDGAR CAYCE

Edgar Cayce was born on a farm near Hopkinsville, Kentucky, in 1877. His grandfather may have had psychic powers, for it was reported that among other things he was a successful water dowser and could "make a broom dance." Edgar explained that his father had an unusual attraction for snakes. They often would follow him home or wrap themselves around the brim of his hat when he left it in the field. "It got on his nerves so much that he gave up farming."[2]

As a child, Edgar was different from other boys in his behavior and interests. He became very fond of reading the Bible and enjoyed going to the Christian Church with his parents. Later he joined the church and was a Sunday school teacher. Edgar's son Hugh tells of the early signs of his father's psychic power:

> At the age of six or seven he told his parents that he was able to see and to talk to "visions," sometimes of relatives who had recently died. . . . Later, by sleeping with his head on his schoolbooks, he developed some form of photographic memory which helped him advance rapidly in the country school. The gift faded.[3]

By the age of fourteen Edgar had read the entire Bible several times, but he had difficulty in understanding it. He left school after completing the seventh grade and worked on a farm. After this he took a job in a shoe store, and later he became a salesman for a wholesale stationery company. At this time he developed a paralysis of his throat muscles, which defied medical diagnosis. The doctors could not find any physical explanation. Being unable to speak above a whisper for about a year, Cayce quit working as a salesman and became an apprentice photographer.

Attempts to cure his throat problem by hypnosis failed, but on March 31, 1901, Cayce's friend Al Layne helped him to reenter the trance state he had achieved as a child, and he was able to deal with his problem: "Speaking from an unconscious state, he recommended medication and manipulative therapy which successfully restored his voice and repaired his system."[4] This was Cayce's first reading. From this time until his death,

> it is estimated that he entered his sleep-like state at least 16,000 times during those years, although there is no way of

definitely knowing the total. The earliest reading in the files dates back to 1909, but regular records were not kept on a systematic basis until Cayce's lifelong secretary, Gladys Davis, joined him in September 1923.[5]

Up until 1923, Cayce's readings continued to be primarily "physical readings." His trance-derived information brought cures to hundreds, and newspapers picked up the story. In 1923 Cayce was contacted at his photography business in Selma, Alabama, by Arthur Lammers, a wealthy printer from Dayton, Ohio. His reason for visiting Cayce was different:

> He had other interests: philosophy, metaphysics, esoteric astrology, psychic phenomena. He asked questions Edgar did not understand. . . . He mentioned such things as the cabala, the mystery religions of Egypt and Greece, the medieval alchemists, the mystics of Tibet, yoga, Madame Blavatsky and theosophy, the Great White Brotherhood, the Etheric World. Edgar was dazed.[6]

Lammers wanted to see if Cayce's readings would confirm or deny his views. Lammers secured the first of the life readings (accounts of past earth lives), and his views on astrology and reincarnation were supported by the readings. At first, Cayce was disturbed when he was told what he had said while in a trance:

> But what you've been telling me today, and what the readings have been saying, is foreign to all I've believed and been taught, and all I have taught others, all my life. If ever the Devil was going to play a trick on me, this would be it.[7]

But instead of following this intuition, Cayce accepted Lammers's explanations on reincarnation and other matters and turned away from a literal interpretation of the Bible. Cayce's faith in the readings completed the transition. "Edgar Cayce had to reconcile reincarnation with his orthodox beliefs. He had to because he was confronted with the fact that the Readings didn't lie."[8]

At Lammers's invitation and with the promise of financial support, the Cayce family moved to Dayton. But after business reverses, Lammers's support ended. In 1925 the Cayces moved to Virginia Beach, Virginia, in accordance with what the readings had indicated. In 1928 the Cayce Hospital for Research and Enlightenment was dedicated. It was lost during the Depression; repurchased in 1956, it now serves as the headquarters of the A.R.E.[9]

Near the end of Cayce's life, the requests for help that came to him numbered some fifteen hundred a day. Although he was warned to cut down to two readings a day, he did seven or eight and burned himself out for "the Work." At the time of his death in 1945, the A.R.E. had fewer than seven hundred members. Edgar's son, Hugh Lynn Cayce, took over the organization when he returned after the war. After he had a heart attack in 1976, he became chairman of the board, and his son Charles Thomas Cayce was named president. Before his death in 1982, Hugh Lynn authored two books.[10]

The A.R.E. and the Edgar Cayce Foundation

In 1931 the Association for Research and Enlightenment, Inc., was founded in Virginia Beach, Virginia, replacing the Association of National Investigators, Inc. The announced purpose of the A.R.E. was "to preserve, study and present the Edgar Cayce readings." In 1975 the paid membership of the association was approaching 15,000. It reached 20,000 in 1980, and by 1989 it had grown to 100,000.[11] Members of the A.R.E. and their friends meet in hundreds of "Search for God" groups in the United States and other countries. Additional thousands became interested in Edgar Cayce through the dozens of books written about him and his readings. The books *There Is a River* and *Edgar Cayce—The Sleeping Prophet* were both high on best-seller lists. Others, like Hugh Cayce's *Venture Inward* and Noel Langley's *Edgar Cayce on Reincarnation*, went through a number of printings.[12]

Publications of the A.R.E. include the bimonthly *Venture Inward* and many other literature items. A.R.E. Press publishes many books based on the Edgar Cayce readings. One volume offered to new A.R.E. sponsoring members is *The Edgar Cayce Companion*, which quotes the readings on such subjects as karma, reincarnation, evolution of the soul, the Bible, diet, and health.

A new Library-Conference Center was dedicated in 1975. It houses the "Edgar Cayce readings, along with one of the most extensive metaphysical libraries in the world." The A.R.E. also holds workshops and conferences, runs summer youth camps, provides circulating files of the Cayce readings, offers courses through its Atlantic University, The Edgar Cayce Institute of Intuitive Studies, and the Cayce-Reilly School of Massotherapy.[13]

The Edgar Cayce Foundation was established in 1947. It acts as the custodian of the original copies of the Edgar Cayce readings, which are stored in a fireproof vault in the headquarters building. Duplicate copies of the readings are available for study in the A.R.E. library.

THE EDGAR CAYCE READINGS

The Edgar Cayce readings (a term used to describe the clairvoyant discourses Edgar Cayce gave while in a self-induced hypnotic state) consist of more than 49,000 pages of material that deals with a number of different topics. The readings have been cross-indexed on more than 200,000 file cards.

The readings break down into several categories: (1) 8,985 "physical readings" (concerned with the mind and body), (2) 2,500 "life readings" (dealing with past lives and with vocational, psychological, and interpersonal problems), (3) 667 readings on dream interpretation, and (4) 1,995 miscellaneous readings—in "almost as many categories as there are readings."[14] Of the approximately 1,600 people who had the 2,500 life readings, almost half had incarnations in the legendary Atlantis.[15]

EDGAR CAYCE AND CHRISTIAN DOCTRINE

Those who write about Edgar Cayce do not question his honesty, sincerity, motives, or humanitarian goals, but Bible-believing Christians reject his psychic readings because they are often diametrically opposed to orthodox Christianity. Acceptance of Cayce's psychic enlightenment requires a denial of the person and work of Jesus Christ as well as other Christian teachings. While A.R.E. officials state that the organization is "a study group and not a religion" (so I was told on my visit to Virginia Beach), the Cayce readings do present another "plan of salvation"—that is, "a different gospel" (Gal. 1:6–9). To the Christian, the core of Edgar Cayce is not his healings but his theology, in which reincarnation is the central theme. Several examples from Cayce's readings and from books based on them will illustrate their erroneous and heretical nature.

The readings teach that Jesus was Adam and that he learned he would be the Savior "when he fell in Eden." According to the readings, Jesus "possibly had some thirty incarnations during His development in becoming The Christ."[16]

The readings indicate that "much of the Bible can be interpreted either physically, mentally, or spiritually, and often on all levels simultaneously."[17] Such an approach makes a shambles of sound exegesis. The readings also state that the Gospel of John "was written by several; not the John who was the Beloved," and that "Luke was written by Lucius rather than Luke."[18] Lucius was Edgar Cayce in a previous incarnation, who at that time was a companion of Jesus Christ and the disciples.[19]

Gina Cerminara's *Many Mansions* ("The Edgar Cayce Story on

Reincarnation"), with an introduction and high recommendation by Hugh Lynn Cayce, clearly illustrates the basic incompatibility of biblical Christianity with the Cayce readings:

> For almost twenty centuries the moral sense of the Western world has been blunted by a theology which teaches the vicarious atonement of sin through Christ, the Son of God. . . . It can be felt then that perhaps the personality called Jesus was different from us only in that he was closer to the central light than we are.
>
> Moreover, Christ's giving of his life that men might be free is no unique event in history; the study of comparative religions reveals other saviors, among other peoples, who suffered martyrdom and death. In our own Western culture, many idealists have given their lives willingly for humanity's sake. . . . But no one feels that their effort redeems us from effort, or that their sacrifice absolves us of our own personal guilt.[20]

Cerminara goes on to state that to demand belief in the deity of Christ and his vicarious atonement for salvation is not Christian but the error of theologians and that

> it is a psychological crime because it places responsibility for redemption on something external to the self; it makes salvation dependent on belief in the divinity of another person rather than on self-transformation through belief in one's own intrinsic divinity.[21]

An article in the A.R.E. *Searchlight* presents the Cayce substitute for the biblical doctrine of redemption:

> Original sin is our reason for being incarnated; we are here to overcome our karma and win perfection which brings us into

eternal life with no more need to incarnate. This would be overcoming even as Jesus the Christ overcame.

There are over 100 quotations in the Bible on eternal life. Now this could mean that there is a plan of redemption from sin, through many lives, through Jesus Christ who showed the way through His various incarnations—growth to perfection. Otherwise, each brand-new soul (for each man born) would be taking on a sin he didn't commit. Otherwise only those who followed Jesus Christ could be redeemed. Would a wise and merciful Heavenly Father permit so many of His children to be unredeemed because of a circumstantial date in history or an accident of geography?[22]

In place of a basically Christian theology or philosophy, Cayce's readings present "a Christianized version of the mystery religions of ancient Egypt, Chaldea, Persia, India, and Greece."[23]

REINCARNATION AND THE BIBLE

Space does not permit an extensive treatment of reincarnation, which is refuted primarily by the biblical doctrine of the atonement.

Hebrews 1:3 strikes at the heart of reincarnation, which requires that each person purge his own sin through successive incarnations: "Who being the brightness of His glory and the express image of His person, and upholding all things by the word of His power, when He had by Himself purged our sins, sat down at the right hand of the Majesty on high." This is a brief yet comprehensive statement of the work of Christ at his first advent. It was Jesus Christ who purged or cleansed our sins, and in him sin's penalty was fully discharged. He "sat down," which indicates that his work was completed.

Hebrews 9:27–28 also refutes reincarnation: "And it is appointed for men to die once, but after this the judgment, so Christ was offered once to bear the sins of many. To those who eagerly wait for Him He will appear a second time, apart from sin, for salvation."

First John 1:7 presents the precious truth that "the blood of Jesus Christ His Son cleanses us from all sin." In John 10:28, Jesus tells us, "And I give them eternal life, and they shall never perish." And the apostle Paul writes that "the wages of sin is death, but the gift of God is eternal life in Christ Jesus our Lord" (Rom. 6:23). Scripture offers no support for the doctrine of reincarnation.[24]

Concluding Evaluation

While Edgar Cayce did not claim infallibility for his prophecies, Jess Stearn's *Edgar Cayce—The Sleeping Prophet*, first published in 1967, did add stature to Cayce's image as a prognosticator. But Robert Somerlott was not too impressed with either Cayce's prophecies or Stearn's techniques:

> Although physicians may dismiss Cayce's psychic healing, it is supported by extensive testimony. His ESP, less well substantiated, remains interesting and worth further investigation. But in the field of precognition Cayce's record is a catastrophe, and one stands in awe of Stearn's achievement: seldom has a man been able to make so much out of so little. To verify the rambling, vaguely stated forecasts is to make bricks without straw and the results are the same—the prophecies hold up when glanced at, crumble when touched.[25]

> It would be a tedious waste of time to go through more of the prophecies and their purported fulfillment. . . . There are so many predictions and most of them are of such a general nature that one can be found—or stretched—to fit almost any event.[26]

Although the A.R.E. denies that Edgar Cayce was a Spiritualist, occult expert Kurt Koch classified him along with Harry Edwards as a spiritualistic healer.[27] It is interesting that after reading the introduction to early Spiritualist Andrew Jackson Davis's *Principles of Nature*, Cayce remarked, "This sounds so much like me it gives me the creeps."[28] There were many similarities: the diagnosis of disease, healing, prophecy, and other features that are all well known in Spiritualism.

It is also significant that Edgar Cayce was well aware of the fact that the readings were often contrary to what he had learned, believed, and taught, based upon the Bible alone. John Warwick Montgomery concludes that in Edgar Cayce is to be found "a classic case of a 'seer' being in reality *blind*: the blind leading the blind."[29]

SELECT BIBLIOGRAPHY

Bjornstad, James. *Twentieth-Century Prophecy: Jeane Dixon, Edgar Cayce*. Minneapolis: Bethany, 1969. See 75–151 for a Christian analysis of Cayce.

Chandler, Russell. "New Age Ventures into Cayce's Realm." *Los Angeles Times*, February 25, 1989, II-6–7.

Godwin, John. *Occult America*. New York: Doubleday, 1972. See chapter 5, "The Heritage of Edgar Cayce."

Guiley, Rosemary E. "Cayce, Edgar (1877–1945)." In *Encyclopedia of Mystical and Paranormal Experience*. San Francisco: HarperCollins, 1991.

Klimo, Jon. *Channeling*. Los Angeles: Tarcher, 1987. Klimo is sympathetic to channeling.

Melton, J. Gordon, Jerome Clark, and Aidan A. Kelly, eds. *New Age Almanac*. Chicago: Visible Ink Press, 1991. This work contains material on the A.R.E. Clinic and on Edgar, Hugh Lynn, and Charles Thomas Cayce (41–45, 174–75).

Petersen, William J. *Those Curious New Cults in the 80s*. New Canaan, Conn: Keats, 1982. Chapter 5, "Edgar Cayce and the A.R.E.," is written from a Christian perspective.

Somerlott, Robert. *"Here, Mr. Splitfoot": An Informal Exploration into Modern Occultism.* New York: Viking, 1971. Edgar Cayce is discussed on 265–72.

Swihart, Phillip J. *Reincarnation: Edgar Cayce and the Bible.* Downers Grove, Ill.: InterVarsity Press, 1975.

Whitworth, Lou. "Edgar Cayce: The Sleeping (False) Prophet," www.probe.org (1996).

Wright, J. Stafford. *Man in the Process of Time.* Grand Rapids: Eerdmans, 1956. Chapter 13, "The Evidence for Reincarnation," is written from a Christian perspective. See the other treatments of reincarnation listed in note 24.

PUBLICATIONS RECOMMENDED BY THE A.R.E.

The books and booklets in support of Edgar Cayce and on his readings are too numerous to list. These include Edgar Cayce on dreams, prophecy, psychic experience, karma and reincarnation, ESP, astrology, Atlantis, religion, diet and health, healing, the Dead Sea Scrolls, Jesus, and the Bible. Some books recommended for study by the A.R.E. are *There Is a River* (Sugrue), *A Seer Out of Season: The Life of Edgar Cayce* (Bro), *Edgar Cayce—The Sleeping Prophet* (Stearn), *Many Mansions* and *The World Within* (Cerminara), *Venture Inward* (H. L. Cayce), *A Search for God* (books 1 and 2), *Edgar Cayce on Religion and Psychic Experience* (Bro), and *Edgar Cayce: An American Prophet* (Kirkpatrick). *The Complete Edgar Cayce Readings* are on one CD-ROM.

The A.R.E., Inc. website is www.edgarcayce.org.

15 | SUN MYUNG MOON AND THE UNIFICATION CHURCH

Before Sun Myung Moon's Day of Hope tour in 1972, few Americans had ever heard of the Korean evangelist or the Holy Spirit Association for the Unification of World Christianity, commonly called the Unification Church. Moon claimed that he was speaking in America because God had commissioned him to do so on January 1, 1972. On this tour, Moon spoke in seven major American cities, but what brought him into the national limelight were the full-page ads placed in newspapers in October 1973, calling on Americans to unite in support of President Richard M. Nixon. Moon's "Answer to Watergate" message called on Americans to "forgive, love," and "unite." The 1973 and 1974 Day of Hope speaking tours took Moon to sixty-one cities. His speech at Madison Square Garden on September 18, 1974, attended by more than 25,000 persons, marked the culmination of three years of speaking to the American people.[1]

It is difficult to accurately determine the membership of the Unification Church, as claims by representatives do not always agree with other estimates. For example, in 1985 the Unification Church claimed a U.S. membership of 40,000 to 45,000 and a following of 300,000 in Japan. But one outside observer estimated U.S. membership at only 3,500, and another at 10,000 (in 1989); a former editor of the Japanese church newspaper said that membership in Japan was only 8,000. In 1985 the church also claimed a worldwide membership of 3 million in more than 120 countries,[2] but in 1999, another source placed it at only 2 million.[3] A survey of the newspapers and magazines that have treated the activities of Moon's Unification Church over the years indicates that beyond the gaining of converts the movement has provoked much controversy, speculation, and suspicion, as well as some strong opposition.

Who is Sun Myung Moon? What are the teachings of Moon and his Unification Church? Are these teachings biblical? Only a brief examination of these questions is given here, but sources of further information are listed in the select bibliography.

SUN MYUNG MOON AND THE ORIGIN OF THE UNIFICATION CHURCH

Sun Myung Moon (originally Yung Myung Moon) was born in North Korea in 1920. His parents were members of the Presbyterian Church, the largest Protestant denomination in Korea. He attended high school in Seoul. Moon relates how he often withdrew for prayer, and he claims that on Easter morning in 1936 Jesus Christ appeared to him and told him " 'to carry out my unfinished task.' Then a voice from heaven said, 'You will be the completer of man's salvation by being the second coming of Christ.' "[4] He did not begin his preaching ministry at that time but studied and prepared himself for his mission. He went to Japan and studied electrical engineering at Waseda University in Tokyo. In 1944 he returned to Korea, and in 1946 he founded the Broad Sea Church. He was excommunicated from the Presbyterian Church for his heretical teachings. For six months, Moon attached himself to a community in South Korea called the Israel Monastery, "learning what was to become the basis of his own theology, the 'Divine Principle.' "[5] After his return to North Korea, he was arrested by the communists and imprisoned for several years. Unification Church accounts indicate that Moon's years in prison were a time of great suffering and that his arrest and incarceration were because of his Christian stand and his anticommunist activities. But "it is also widely believed in Korea that the immediate cause of his arrest was adultery. Moon had divorced his first wife to whom he was legally married and was twice remarried."[6]

After he was freed by United Nations forces late in 1950, Moon returned to South Korea with some of his disciples and settled in Pusan. In 1954 he founded the Holy Spirit Association for the Unification of World Christianity—in reality a radical departure from biblical Christianity. In the years that followed, Moon built a network of industries and a personal fortune often estimated at $15 million. Because of his anticommunist stance, he enjoyed a privileged relationship with President Park's regime. On June 7, 1975, more than a million people gathered in Seoul to hear him speak against communism at the World Rally for Korean Freedom.

In 1959 Young Oon Kim was sent to the United States as the Unification Church's first missionary. She established Unification centers and prepared an English adaptation of *Divine Principle* entitled *The Divine Principle and Its Application.* Since 1972 the Unification Church has acquired millions of dollars worth of property, much of it in the state of New York (Tarrytown, Barrytown, Irvington, and Greenburg), as well as in Oklahoma, California, Louisiana, and Washington. The church owns the *Washington Times*, which has not shown a profit since it began, although more than $800 million has been invested in it since 1982. The church also publishes a weekly news magazine, *Insight*, and in 1989 had "at least 335 closely affiliated companies worldwide, 280 in the U.S."[7] The church now has centers in all fifty states, where members are busy soliciting converts and money. Through the Collegiate Association for the Research of Principles (or CARP—which has even appropriated the Christian fish symbol), the Unificationists have been able to recruit a number of college students on campuses across America.

The *New York Times* of May 30, 1992, announced that the University of Bridgeport in Connecticut had closed a deal that ceded control of the institution to the Professors World Peace Academy, an affiliate of the Unification Church. The bailout of the financially strapped university amounted to $50 million.[8]

On May 15, 2000, the church's News World Communications announced the acquisition of UPI (United Press International) wire service.[9]

In 1975 one writer stated that the Unification Church was "probably the most active new Christian movement in the United States" and that its impact was being felt not only on the East and West Coasts but also in the traditionally conservative Midwest.[10] Its efficient organization, financial strength, anticommunist stance, youth orientation, missionary spirit, and dedicated membership would seem to indicate that the Unification Church is a cult with which Christians must be prepared to contend.

THE TEACHINGS OF MOON AND THE UNIFICATION CHURCH

A study of such Unification Church publications as *Divine Principle* and *Divine Principle and Its Application,* along with *Unification Theology and Christian Thought,* by Young Oon Kim, professor of systematic theology and world religions at Unification Theological Seminary, will quickly convince the Christian reader that this church represents a radical departure from "the faith" (Jude 3–4). How has the Unification Church and its theology been characterized? Dean Peerman states that it is "a strange amalgam of Oriental family worship, Eastern religious teachings, spiritism, and dubious interpretations of history and Christianity."[11]

Robert S. Ellwood Jr. has said that the movement

has all the marks of a Far Eastern new religion of the Japanese type. It has . . . strong traces of the traditional shamanism of the Korean countryside as well as of missionary Christianity, it places no small emphasis on clairvoyance, clairaudience, healing, and spiritualistic phenomena. Believers feel spiritual fire and electricity, and communicate mediumistically with spirits, Jesus and God.[12]

A *Time* writer concluded that

in essence, Moon's theology makes wide use of Biblical personae and events, but is no more than nominally Christian. Added ingredients are an odd mix: occultism, electrical engineering, Taoist dualism, pop sociology and opaque metaphysical jargon.[13]

J. Gordon Melton sees Unification Church theology not as a heresy but rather as

a new form of religion. Like such other new forms as Theosophy or Spiritualism, it uses Christian symbols, but in a manner quite foreign to the Christian faith. We cannot argue with the Moonies as we do with liberals, conservatives, Methodists, Baptists, or radicals. Rather, we must confront them as we do Hindus or Buddhists, or, more pertinently, the Baha'is.[14]

Moon's Unification Church theology is one of denial or perversion of all the major doctrines of historic, biblical Christianity. Ten examples are given here, together with scriptural refutations.

1. He teaches that his "New Truth" supersedes the Bible. "It may be displeasing to religious believers, especially to Christians, to learn that a new expression of truth must appear. They believe that the Bible, which they now have, is perfect and absolute in itself."[15] "The New Testament Words of Jesus and the Holy Spirit will lose their light. . . . To lose their light means that the period of their mission has elapsed with the coming of the new age."[16] "Until our mission with the Christian Church is over, we must quote the Bible and use it to

explain the Divine Principle. After we receive the inheritance of the Christian Church we will be free to teach without the Bible."[17] (Refutation: Isa. 40:8; Matt. 24:35; Mark 13:31; 2 Tim. 3:16–17; 1 Peter 1:23–25.)

2. He denies the virgin birth of Jesus Christ. "Jesus was born of a father and a mother, just as anyone else is, but in this case the Spirit of God was working also."[18] "Modern theologians deny completely any supernatural birth for Jesus. They say Jesus had two parents. Conservatives say that he was born of the Holy Spirit without a human father. In our explanation we can reconcile these two extremely different positions."[19] (Refutation: Matt. 1:18–20, 25; Luke 1:34–35.)

3. He denies the deity of Jesus Christ. Although Moon speaks of Jesus as "God" and as "deity," he does not use these words with orthodox meaning. Jesus, he says, "can by no means be God Himself."[20] John 8:58, he asserts, "does not signify that Jesus was God Himself. Jesus, on earth, was a man no different from us except for the fact that he was without original sin."[21] "But after Jesus' crucifixion, Christianity made him into God. This is why a gap between God and man has never been bridged."[22] (Refutation: John 1:1; 20:28; Titus 2:13; Heb. 1:6–12; 2 Peter 1:1.)

4. He denies that the death of Christ on the cross was God's will. "We, therefore, must realize that Jesus did not come to die on the cross."[23] "We can see that Jesus' crucifixion was the result of the ignorance and disbelief of the Jewish people and was not God's predestination to fulfill the whole purpose of Jesus' coming as the Messiah."[24] Jesus' ministry is viewed as a partial failure because it provided only spiritual salvation, not physical salvation also. (Refutation: Mark 10:45; Luke 24:25–26; John 17:4; 1 Cor. 15:3; Col. 1:20–22; Heb. 9:26; 10:14.)

5. He denies the bodily resurrection of Jesus Christ. Moon was asked, "Was Jesus' physical body resurrected?" He answered, "No. Jesus no longer needed the physical body."[25] (Refutation: Luke 24:39; Acts 2:27–32; 13:33–37; Rom. 8:11.)

6. He denies the second coming of Christ as taught in Acts

1:9–11. "Although many Christians up to the present have believed that Jesus would come on the clouds, there are no grounds to deny the possibility of the Lord being born in the flesh on the earth at the Second Advent."[26] (Refutation: Acts 1:11; 1 Thess. 4:15–17; Rev. 1:7.)

7. He perverts the biblical account of the fall of man. "Man fell because of fornication. . . . Both man and angel [Satan] fell because of fornication."[27] As a result of this "illicit blood relationship," Adam and Eve "could not multiply the good lineage of God, but rather multiplied the evil lineage of Satan."[28] (Refutation: Gen. 2:16–17; 3:1–12.)

8. He teaches the abolition of hell and the universal reconciliation of all, including Satan. "The ultimate purpose of God's providence of restoration is to save all mankind. Therefore, it is God's intention to abolish Hell completely, after the lapse of the period necessary for the full payment of all indemnity."[29] "Even evil spirits . . . will take part in the fulfillment of God's will."[30] "Will he [Satan] be restored completely?" Moon's answer: "Of course. But it will take almost an eternity for it to happen. He has a great deal of indemnity to pay."[31] (Refutation: Matt. 25:41, 46; 2 Thess. 1:7–10; Heb. 9:27; Rev. 20:10.)

9. He claims to have had contact with the spirit world and is involved with Spiritualism. In *Unknown but Known,* the medium Arthur Ford included an account of a séance at which Moon was present. The communication through "Fletcher," Ford's control, confirmed Moon's mission.[32] Unification Church members are told that "even without contacting the spirit world, our Leader can control mediums. When a medium reports to him, he knows which part of the message is correct and which part is incorrect and what advice he would give to the medium."[33] Young Oon Kim states that "some members came to this group through direct guidance of the spirit world. The Blessed Mother Mary, Gautama Buddha, and Confucius are among those in the spirit world who are directing certain of their followers to this group."[34] (Refutation: Lev. 19:31; 20:6, 27; Deut. 18:10–12; Isa. 8:19–20.)

10. He teaches that he is the Messiah, the Lord of the Second Advent. When he began his ministry to America, it was difficult to establish definitely that Moon considered himself to be the new Messiah. Jane D. Mook, in agreement with other writers, states that "in the early days of the movement, he admitted that he did."[35] Wi Jo Kang notes that all the members of the movement who answered his questions "also confessed that they truly believe that Rev. Mr. Moon is the Messiah."[36]

Reporter John Dart further confirms that Moon is recognized as the Messiah by his loyal followers. In a confidential Unification Church training manual, Moon is referred to as "Father," "Master," and "Messiah."[37] In my examination of this manual, I found Moon referred to as "Messiah" many times. It is also stated that he is "sinless," that he has been given the "authority here on earth by God to forgive sin," that "every word that he utters is a word that comes from the mouth of God," and that he is greater than Jesus.[38] (It is interesting that Ken Sudo, who issued the manual, said that the Unification Church had not authorized it and that he "wouldn't stand behind it . . . not any of it.")[39]

After serving thirteen months in a Danbury, Connecticut, prison for tax evasion, Moon spoke to his followers on August 29, 1985:

> My victory at Danbury also has meant my own resurrection, both physically and spiritually. *I am now in the position of Lord of the Second Advent to the world.* . . . Much confusion and chaos prevailed before I entered prison. *But with my emergence as the victorious Lord of the Second Advent for the world,* a new order has come into being.[40]

With this pronouncement, Moon without question claims to be the second coming of Christ, the Messiah—in Unification Church language, the "Lord of the Second Advent." (Refutation: Matt. 24:23–27.)[41]

CONCLUSION

In ending this brief treatment, I am reminded of two passages of Scripture. The first is Mark 13:5–6, which finds its fulfillment in men like Moon: "And Jesus, answering them, began to say: 'Take heed that no one deceives you. For many will come in My name, saying, "I am He," and will deceive many.'" The other passage is 1 Timothy 4:1, which is especially appropriate because of Moon's admitted contacts with Spiritualism: "Now the Spirit expressly says, that in latter times some will depart from the faith, giving heed to deceiving spirits and doctrines of demons."

SELECT BIBLIOGRAPHY

Ankerberg, John, and John Weldon. *Encyclopedia of Cults and New Religions.* Eugene, Ore.: Harvest House, 1999. The Unification Church is treated on 449–500.

Austin, Charles M. "Sun Myung Moon." *Christian Herald* (December 1974), 14–16, 19–20.

Berry, Harold J. *Unification Church.* Lincoln, Neb.: Back to the Bible, 1987.

Beverly, James A. "The Unification Church." In *Evangelizing the Cults,* edited by Ronald Enroth, 73–82. Ann Arbor, Mich.: Servant, 1990.

Bjornstad, James. *The Moon Is Not the Son.* Minneapolis: Bethany, 1976.

Ellwood, Robert S., Jr. *Religious and Spiritual Groups in Modern America.* Englewood Cliffs, N.J.: Prentice-Hall, 1973. The Unification Church is treated on 291–95.

Ferraro, Susan. "Trouble in Tarrytown." *New York Sunday News,* July 20, 1975, 14–16.

Judis, John B. "Rev. Moon's Rising Political Influence." *U.S. News and World Report,* March 27, 1989, 27–29, 31.

Kang, Wi Jo. "The Influence of the Unification Church in the United States of America." *Missiology, An International Review* (July 1975): 357–68.

Levitt, Zola. *The Spirit of Sun Myung Moon.* Irvine, Calif.: Harvest House, 1976.

Melton, J. Gordon. *Encyclopedic Handbook of Cults in America.* New York: Garland, 1986. The Unification Church is treated on 193–99.

Mook, Jane Day. "New Growth on Burnt-Over Ground III: The Unification Church." *A.D.* (May 1975), 32–36.

Tucker, Ruth A. *Another Gospel: Alternative Religions and the New Age Movement.* Grand Rapids: Zondervan, 1989. The Unification Church is treated on 245–66, 396–97.

Waldrep, Bob. "'The Son Doesn't Fall Far From the Moon'"; "Moonshine for the Soul"; "Unification Church Influence in America." *Watchman Expositor* 13, 5 (1996), 3–10, 21–22.

Yamamoto, J. Isamu. *The Moon Doctrine.* Downers Grove, Ill.: InterVarsity Press, 1976.

———. *The Puppet Master.* Downers Grove, Ill.: InterVarsity Press, 1977.

———. *Unification Church.* Grand Rapids: Zondervan, 1995.

Books by Ex-Members; Other Sources

Edwards, Christopher. *Crazy for God.* Englewood Cliffs, N.J.: Prentice-Hall, 1979.

Elkins, Chris. *Heavenly Deception.* Wheaton, Ill.: Tyndale, 1980.

Hassan, Steven. *Combatting Cult Mind Control.* Rochester, Vt.: Park Street Press, 1988.

Hong, Nansook. *In the Shadow of the Moons: My Life in the Reverend Sun Myung Moon's Family.* Boston: Little Brown, 1998.

Kemperman, Steve. *Lord of the Second Advent.* Ventura, Calif.: Regal, 1981.

Underwood, Barbara, and Betty Underwood. *Hostage to Heaven.* New York: Potter, 1979.

Apologetics Index (www.gospelcom.net/apologeticsindex), under (U) "About the Unification Church," provides access to a library of information on the subject, including books, book reviews, articles, newspaper reports, testimonies of ex-members, and websites.

A number of short treatments and reports on the Unification Church have appeared in *Time, Newsweek, Christian Century,* and *Christianity Today.*

For a study of Unification Church theology, *Divine Principle* and *Divine Principle and Its Application* are essential. *Unification Theology and Christian Thought,* by Young Oon Kim, gives a more academic approach. A good summary of some of the main ideas of Unification theology is presented in Moon's Madison Square Garden speech, "The New Future of Christianity," which was published as an advertisement in major newspapers, such as the *Los Angeles Times,* on December 24, 1974.

In the study document "A Critique of the Theology of the Unification Church As Set Forth in 'Divine Principle'" (*Occasional Bulletin* [July 1977], 18–23), prepared by the Commission on Faith and Order of the National Council of Churches, the following conclusions are stated (23):

A.   The Unification Church is not a Christian Church.
1. Its doctrine of the nature of the Triune God is erroneous.
2. Its Christology is incompatible with Christian teaching and belief.
3. Its teaching on salvation and the means of grace is inadequate and faulty.

B.   The claims of the Unification Church to Christian identity cannot be recognized.
1. The role and authority of Scripture are compromised in the teachings of the Unification Church.

2. Revelations are invoked as divine and normative in *Divine Principle* which contradict basic elements of Christian faith.

3. A "new, ultimate, final truth" is presented to complete and supplant all previously recognized religious teachings, including those of Christianity.

THE NEW AGE
MOVEMENT

The interested student of religion could not miss the proliferation of books and articles on the New Age movement (NAM) since the mid-1980s. Ruth Tucker identifies the NAM as "the most popular and widely publicized new religion in recent years . . . a difficult-to-define variety of mystical, spiritualistic, and occultic groups that above all else are not *new*."[1] The *New Age Almanac* observes that "an attempt to understand the New Age Movement easily can be frustrated by the movement's diversity." It "has no single leader, no central organization, no firm agenda, and no group of official spokespersons."[2] Award-winning journalist Russell Chandler says that writing his book on the NAM was the most challenging writing project in his more than twenty years as a writer on religion.[3] The NAM presents a major challenge to Christianity as "New Age influence touches virtually every area of life, and thousands of New Age activists seek to transform society through New Age precepts."[4]

Many excellent and extensive treatments of the New Age movement have been written by evangelical scholars; some of these are listed in the select bibliography. These should be consulted for detailed coverage. The presentation here must be limited to several key questions: What is the New Age movement? What movements and individuals are its predecessors? When and how did it become well known? What are the basic assumptions of New Age philosophy, and how do these compare with the Bible? In what ways is New Age teaching a counterfeit? The chapter concludes with some information on witnessing to New Agers and with a testimony and a challenge from Randall Baer. A select bibliography lists a number of publications for further study.

WHAT IS THE NEW AGE MOVEMENT?

When Elliot Miller speaks on the New Age movement, one question frequently asked by his audience is, "What is the New Age movement?" Miller writes that "definitively answering this seemingly direct and simple question is actually so complicated and involved" he devoted a chapter of *A Crash Course on the New Age Movement* to explaining it.[5]

During March 1985, a conference sponsored by Evangelical Ministries to New Religions was held in Denver. In attendance were many of the leading researchers on new cults and the NAM. A "Statement on the New Age Movement" was distributed at the end of the conference. The introductory paragraph explains:

> The New Age movement is a spiritual, social, and political movement to transform individuals and society through mystical enlightenment, hoping to bring about a utopian era, a "New Age" of harmony and progress. While it has no central headquarters or agencies, it includes loosely affiliated individuals, activist groups, businesses, professional groups, and spiritual leaders and their followers. It produces countless books, magazines, and tapes reflecting a shared worldview and vision. How that worldview is expressed, what implications are drawn, and what applications are made differ from group to group.[6]

Russell Chandler sees New Age as "a hybrid mix of spiritual, social, and political forces, and it encompasses sociology, theology, the physical sciences, medicine, anthropology, history, the human potentials movement, sports, and science fiction." It "is not a sect or cult, per se."[7]

PREDECESSORS OF THE NEW AGE MOVEMENT

Robert J. L. Burrows has surveyed the predecessors of the New Age movement, beginning with the historical ancestors of the nineteenth century. These are Transcendentalism, Spiritualism, New Thought (which may be viewed as a stepchild of Christian Science), Theosophy, psychoanalysis (Sigmund Freud and Carl Jung), and Oriental traditions (examples are Swami Vivekananda and Paramahansa Yogananda).[8] Of these, the Theosophical Society (1875) and Helena Petrovna Blavatsky were very influential. Madame Blavatsky "stands out as the fountainhead of modern occult thought, and was either the originator and/or popularizer of many of the ideas and terms which have a century later been assembled within the New Age Movement."[9] Other precursors of the NAM include Emanuel Swedenborg (1688–1772) and Franz Anton Mesmer (1734–1815).[10]

THE FORMATIVE DECADE

Burrows views the 1960s as "the formative decade" for the NAM. "Zen Buddhism was the inspirational focus of the fifties' beats, the final movement of major significance before the sixties' explosion. To the disenchanted Westerner, Zen had much appeal."[11] The 1960s and early 1970s saw gurus coming from the East (Maharishi Mahesh Yogi—TM; Yogi Bhajan—Kundalini Yoga; Swami Muktananda; Guru Maharaj Ji—Divine Light Mission; and many others).[12] The repeal of the Asian immigration exclusion laws in 1965 resulted in tens of thousands of Asian immigrants coming to America, joined by religious teachers. And as J. Gordon Melton explains:

Many of these teachers came not to work within the new Asian-American communities but to spread their teaching among Westerners. *The last days of the 1960s saw the launching of a major missionary thrust by the Eastern religions toward the West.*[13]

In the 1970s various schools of Tibetan Buddhism were founded in America, which also contributed to "the counterculture drift Eastward."[14] In 1968 Carlos Castaneda published *The Teachings of Don Juan: A Yaqui Way of Knowledge,* his first of four books that deal with South American sorcery. Castanada's books were significant because they communicated "the new consciousness worldview" to a wide audience, as they became bestsellers and were widely read by college students.[15]

Finally, as preparation for the NAM, Burrows mentions humanistic and transpersonal psychology with Abraham Maslow, Fritz Perls, Carl Rogers, and Rollo May as key figures:

What they offered was a psychology that glorified the self. It pronounced people's impulses essentially good, affirmed the unfathomable depths of human potential, and held out personal growth as an individual's highest goal. The affinities between the new psychology and mysticism did not go unnoticed, even by its founding fathers. Moving from vast to infinite potential and from personal growth to spiritual transformation required a virtually imperceptible shift.[16]

According to Burroughs, Maslow

affirmed that humanity had a transcendent dimension that needed to be satisfied before self-actualization was complete . . . that dimension of the individual that intersected with the larger and more numinous realities of the cosmos. Maslow's self-actualized man was truly a self-satisfied man, a man fulfilled, who was full of himself.[17]

Douglas R. Groothuis explains:

Maslow's pathbreaking efforts cleared the way for an exodus from the old psychological view of humanity toward a new human that is essentially good and has within himself unlimited potential for growth. . . . Human experience is thus the center and source of meaning and is valuable apart from any dependence on or subservience to a higher power.[18]

The new transpersonal or cosmic humanist says, "There is no Deity but humanity." God is pulled into the human breast. Scientific prowess and rationality as the crowning human achievements are outstripped by psychic abilities and unlimited potential.[19]

The NAM obviously has borrowed much from its many predecessors, and it "has combined the teachings and practices of those traditions in novel and innumerable ways."[20]

A GROWING INFLUENCE

The *New Age Almanac* states that the New Age movement can be dated from about 1971. "By that year, Eastern religion and transpersonal psychology (the key new elements needed to create the distinctive New Age synthesis) had achieved a level of popularity, and metaphysical leaders could begin to articulate the New Age vision."[21] As Elliot Miller observes, "Until the latter 1980s the majority of Americans were unfamiliar with the New Age movement," although they might have had contact with various expressions of it, such as astrology, TM and reincarnation.[22] This lack of New Age name recognition would change late in 1986 and during 1987, says Miller, with

"Shirley MacLaine's bold use of the media for New Age proselytation," the August 1987 Harmonic Convergence event, and great interest in such New Age practices as "channeling" and "the occult use of crystals."[23] With all that was taking place, and with many celebrities being involved, the media became interested, and "one article or program on the movement after another began to appear, including a cover story in *Time* magazine (Dec. 7, 1987)."[24]

BASIC ASSUMPTIONS OF NEW AGE PHILOSOPHY CONTRASTED WITH BIBLICAL CHRISTIANITY

A number of Christian authors have summarized the basic assumptions of the NAM worldview.[25] In a statement prepared by Evangelical Ministries to New Religions, a list of basic assumptions of New Age philosophy is given, and they are contrasted with biblical Christianity. The statement is reproduced below, with appropriate Scripture references added in parentheses.

1. **New Age:** God is an impersonal undifferentiated Oneness, not separate from creation.
   Bible: God is a personal, transcendent Creator, fundamentally distinct from creation. (Gen. 2:7; Deut. 4:39; Ps. 11:4; 103:19; John 4:24; Acts 7:48–50; 14:15–17; 17:24–25)[26]
2. **New Age:** Humanity, like all creation, is an extension of this divine Oneness, shares its essential being. Humanity is divine.
   Bible: Although created in God's image, humanity is not an extension of God and does not share God's being. Humanity is not God. (Isa. 45:18; 55:8–9; 46:9; Jer. 17:5–10; Rev. 4:11)
3. **New Age:** Humanity's crises stem from a fragmented vision blind to this essential Oneness and to humanity's innate divinity.
   Bible: Humanity's crises stem from alienation from God brought about by sinful rebellion. (Isa. 53; John 3:19–20; Rom. 3:10–18; 5:12–21)

4. **New Age:** Humanity needs to be transformed—each individual actualizing his/her divine nature, becoming aware of the One.

   Bible: Humanity needs to be transformed through the renewing work of the Holy Spirit, made possible by the death and resurrection of Jesus Christ, which reconciles us to God. (John 3:3–8; 1 Cor. 6:9–11; Col. 1:20–22; Titus 3:3–6)

5. **New Age:** Transformation is brought about through a myriad of techniques which can be applied to mind, body, and spirit. Examples of such techniques, used variously by New Age groups, include meditation, yoga, chanting, creative visualization, hypnosis, and submission to a guru.

   Bible: Humanity does not acquire God's forgiveness through the application of any technique. It is a free gift to be humbly received by faith. (John 3:14–16; 5:24; Rom. 3:21–30; 5:1; Eph. 2:8–9; Phil. 3:7–9; Titus 3:4–7)

6. **New Age:** Personal transformation is the basis for global transformation and the spiritual evolution of humankind, characterized by mass enlightenment and social unity. This unity will transcend the individual and social self-centeredness which has created the present crises in environment, world hunger, international relations, racism, etc.

   Bible: Although personal rebirth through Jesus Christ will result in some transformation of social institutions, permanent global transformation will not occur until after the physical return of Jesus Christ in judgment. (Isa. 65:17; Acts 3:20–21; Rom. 8:18–22; 1 Cor. 15:22–28; Titus 2:11–13; Rev. 21:1–8)[27]

THE NEW AGE MOVEMENT AS A COUNTERFEIT

The idea of religious counterfeits is not foreign to biblical writers. As Groothuis reminds us:

Scripture repeatedly speaks of spiritual counterfeits, warning of counterfeit Christs (Mt 24:5; Acts 5:36–37), counterfeit prophets (Deut 13:1–4; Mt 7:15; 24:11), counterfeit miracles (Ex 7:8–13), counterfeit angels (2 Cor 11:14), counterfeit gods (Gal 4:8), counterfeit good works (Mt 7:15–23), counterfeit godliness (2 Tim 3:5), counterfeit converts (1 John 2:19; 2 Cor 11:26), counterfeit spirits (1 John 4:1–3), counterfeit doctrine (1 Tim 4:1–3) and counterfeit gospels (Gal 1:6–10).[28]

While evangelical New Age analyst Groothuis recognizes the diversity within the movement, he concludes that "several of its unifying ideas can be distilled into a basic world view," which he summarizes in nine doctrines. Each of these constitutes a counterfeit teaching, viewed from the biblical perspective:

1. Evolutionary Optimism: A Counterfeit Kingdom
   [Christians look for the return of Christ to bring radical change—not evolution to a New World Order.]
2. Monism: A Counterfeit Cosmos
   [All is not One (monism). God created diversity and plurality. Persons will face the judgment of God as individuals.]
3. Pantheism: A Counterfeit God and Humanity
   [God is personal. Man is not deity.]
4. Transformation of Consciousness: Counterfeit Conversion
   [True conversion is not the realization of one's divinity through some New Age technique.]
5. Create Your Own Reality: Counterfeit Morality
   [Biblical morality is grounded in the moral character of a personal God, his commandments, and his will.]
6. Unlimited Human Potential: Counterfeit Miracles
   [Man is limited by original sin, depravity, and being finite—he is not God.]
7. Spirit Contact: Counterfeit Revelations

[If entities are contacted by various means, these are demons who have consistently denied every major doctrine of biblical Christianity.]

8. Masters from Above: Counterfeit Angels
   [Claimed UFO and extraterrestrial sightings and contacts, if true, would also be interpreted as demonic—see Alnor's *UFOs in the New Age* in the bibliography.]

9. Religious Syncretism: Counterfeit Religion
   New Age spirituality is a rather eclectic grab bag of Eastern mysticism, Western occultism, neopaganism and human potential psychology. . . .

   Christians reject syncretism on at least three counts. First, it disregards the historical differences between religions. Second, it distorts Christianity by making it fit onto a pantheistic Procrustean bed. Third, it demotes Jesus Christ to merely one of many masters enshrined in the pantheistic pantheon.[29]

WITNESSING TO NEW AGERS

A number of books on the NAM contain a chapter or more on witnessing to New Agers. Former New Age leader Randall Baer suggests that one should distinguish three basic categories of New Age followers. These are

1. Occasional dabblers—those who might occasionally contact a psychic, have a horoscope cast, use a Ouija board, or have other occult involvements.

2. Regular experimenters—those who involve themselves in the New Age menu of offerings, such as regular attendance at New Age events.

3. Hard-core New Age participants—"Persons who have a self-identity and lifestyle founded upon the principles of New Age philosophy and activities."[30]

Baer, from his experience of fifteen years in the movement and of helping others to leave, writes:

> I wholeheartedly agree that prayer, patience, endurance, kindness, and love are powerful elements in Christian intercession on behalf of New Agers. It may take a long time, with much prayer, before the conviction of the Holy Spirit pierces the delusions. Kindness, longsuffering compassion, and unconditional love for such people, even as they sin and blaspheme, is fertile soil from which much good may blossom.[31]

He suggests that, when appropriate, the Christian should share materials that contrast the Christian faith with New Age philosophy. He especially recommends Groothuis's *Unmasking the New Age* and Ankerberg and Weldon's *The Facts on the New Age Movement*.[32] Several other books with suggestions for witnessing to those involved with the NAM are Walter Martin's *The New Age Cult* (chap. 8, "Christian Confrontation with New Agers"); *Evangelizing the Cults*, edited by Ronald Enroth (chap. 3, by Gordon Lewis, "The New Age"); Douglas Groothuis, *Confronting the New Age* (chaps. 3–5: "Developing a Strategy," "The Bible and Reincarnation," and "Comparing Gods"); and Ron Rhodes's *New Age Movement* (Part 3: "Witnessing Tips"). All these books are listed in the bibliography.

A PERSONAL TESTIMONY AND A CHALLENGE

In "An Open Letter to the New Agers," in *Inside the New Age Nightmare*, Baer entreats them to accept Christ, writing:

> I testify to you, in love and compassion, that what I found when I accepted Jesus as my Lord and personal Savior opened my eyes to seeing truth in a totally different way, a much grander way than anything I ever knew in the New Age. What

I have experienced as a Christian *far* surpasses even the most incredible, mind-blowing mystical experiences I had as a New Ager.[33]

Randall had a heart for New Agers and was concerned for their salvation. He addressed the Christian community:

> Part of my testimony is that there is a desperate need for more Christian outreach programs taken to New Agers themselves.
>
> I earnestly pray that the Lord will call out and raise up a veritable army of Christian evangelists to go forth into New Age "wilderness areas" to shine the Light of Jesus Christ's atoning sacrifice and gift of salvation to the spiritually hungry, thirsty, and deluded New Age masses.[34]

Baer was "killed in a tragic auto accident on May 5, 1989, the very day his book was published."[35] Will Christians respond to his challenge to evangelize the New Age "wilderness areas"?

Select Bibliography

Albrecht, Mark C. *Reincarnation: A Christian Critique of a New Age Doctrine*. Downers Grove, Ill.: InterVarsity Press, 1982.

Alnor, William M. *UFOs in the New Age*. Grand Rapids: Baker, 1992.

Ankerberg, John, and John Weldon. *The Facts on the New Age Movement*. Eugene, Ore.: Harvest House, 1988.

_____. *Encyclopedia of New Age Beliefs*. Eugene, Ore.: Harvest House, 1996.

Baer, Randall N. *Inside the New Age Nightmare*. Lafayette, La.: Huntington, 1989.

Barker, Jason. "Are We Living in a New Age?" *Watchman Expositor* 16, 4 (1999), 4–6. See also 7–9.

Branch, Craig. "Public Education or Pagan Indoctrination? A Report on New Age Influence in the Schools." *Christian Research Journal* (fall 1995), 32–40.

Burrows, Robert J. L. "The Coming of the New Age." In *The New Age Rage*, edited by Karen Hoyt and J. I. Yamamoto. Old Tappan, N.J.: Revell, 1987.

Chandler, Russell. *Understanding the New Age*. Dallas: Word, 1991.

Clark, David K., and Norman L. Geisler. *Apologetics in the New Age: A Christian Critique of Pantheism*. Grand Rapids: Baker, 1990.

Groothuis, Douglas R. *Confronting the New Age*. Downers Grove, Ill.: InterVarsity Press, 1988.

_____. *Revealing the New Age Jesus*. Downers Grove, Ill.: InterVarsity Press, 1990.

_____. *Unmasking the New Age*. Downers Grove, Ill.: InterVarsity Press, 1986.

Jones, Peter. *The Gnostic Empire Strikes Back: An Old Heresy for the New Age*. Nutley, N.J.: P&R, 1992.

_____. *Spirit Wars: Pagan Revival in Christian America*. Mukilteo, Wash.: Winepress, 1997.

Kjos, Berit. *Your Child and the New Age*. Wheaton, Ill.: Victor, 1990.

Lewis, Gordon. "The New Age." In *Evangelizing the Cults*, edited by Ronald Enroth. Ann Arbor, Mich.: Servant, 1990.

Lind, Mary Ann. *From Nirvana to the New Age*. Old Tappan, N.J.: Revell, 1991.

Mangalwadi, Vishal. *When the New Age Gets Old*. Downers Grove, Ill.: InterVarsity Press, 1992.

Martin, Walter R. *The New Age Cult*. Minneapolis: Bethany, 1989.

_____. *The Kingdom of the Cults*. Rev. 1997 ed. Minneapolis: Bethany, 1997. The New Age movement is treated on 333–49.

Matrisciana, Caryl. *Gods of the New Age*. Eugene, Ore.: Harvest House, 1985.

Melton, J. Gordon. *Encyclopedic Handbook of Cults in America*. New York: Garland, 1986.

Miller, Elliot. *A Crash Course on the New Age Movement*. Grand Rapids: Baker, 1989.

Reisser, Paul C., Teri Reisser, and John Weldon. *The Holistic Healers*. 1983. Expanded and updated in *New Age Medicine* (Downers Grove, Ill.: InterVarsity Press, 1987).

Rhodes, Ron. *The Counterfeit Christ of the New Age Movement*. Grand Rapids: Baker, 1990.

_____. *New Age Movement*. Grand Rapids: Zondervan, 1995.

Smith, F. LaGard. *Out on a Broken Limb*. Eugene, Ore.: Harvest House, 1986.

Tucker, Ruth A. *Another Gospel: Alternative Religions and the New Age Movement*. Grand Rapids: Zondervan, 1989. Chapter 15.

Weldon, John, and Clifford Wilson. *Occult Shock and Psychic Forces*. San Diego: Master Books, 1980.

THE CHRISTIAN IN AN AGE OF CONFUSION

One cannot ignore the popularity and influence of the many cults, old and new, the occult, and the New Age movement. Religions imported from the East and cults of many kinds are flourishing. One can venture almost anywhere in America and find evidence of, and even sometimes an obsession with, cultism and the occult. From all appearances, the trend will continue and perhaps even accelerate. We find ourselves in a new religious atmosphere, but unfortunately it is often characterized by religious deception and the rejection of biblical Christianity.

In this age of religious and occult confusion, many people have discontinued the search for ultimate truth, considering it a hopeless quest. A number of others have concluded that religious truth cannot be found easily, and they have become confirmed truth seekers—"always learning and never able to come to the knowledge [recognition] of the truth" (2 Tim. 3:7). Some of these seekers have resisted the truth, and others have not recognized their need and the redemption provided by Jesus Christ.

Bible-believing Christians cannot accept the popular statement that "all religions lead to the same place." Instead, they accept the Bible's promise that one can know the truth, for ultimate truth is not a system—an "it"—but a person, Jesus Christ ("I am . . . the truth," John 14:6). Truth to the Christian is also conformity to the revealed will of God as set forth in the Bible. "To the law and to the testimony!

If they do not speak according to this word, it is because there is no light in them [or, "they have no dawn," NASB, i.e., no future hope] (Isa. 8:20). "Every human opinion, religion, or philosophy is valid only as it agrees with God's Word—the only absolute yardstick of spiritual truth."[1]

Paul's admonition to Timothy (2 Tim. 4:2–4) and the predicted apostasy that will reach its culmination in the present age is essential reading for the Christian:

> Preach the word! Be ready in season and out of season. Convince, rebuke, exhort, with all longsuffering and teaching. For the time will come when they will not endure sound doctrine, but according to their own desires, because they have itching ears, they will heap up for themselves teachers; and they will turn their ears away from the truth, and be turned aside to fables.

The believer in Christ is to "preach the word," that is, to herald the gospel message of redemption in Jesus Christ. Why must the Christian be diligent in preaching, convincing, rebuking, and exhorting? Because the time when "they will not endure sound doctrine" is at hand. "Sound doctrine" is that doctrine which promotes spiritual health. Instead, many men and women crave and acquire teachers who preach and teach that which suits their perverted appetites. Such people are often more interested in something different, sensational, fascinating, or philosophical than in the truth. As a result, in turning away from the truth they "turned aside to fables" (cf. 1 Tim. 1:4; 4:7; Titus 1:14). This description well characterizes the situation of many in the cults and the occult.

TESTING RELIGIOUS TEACHINGS

In addition to exposing doctrinal error through teaching and preaching "the whole counsel of God" (Acts 20:27), it is helpful for the Christian to have a series of questions by which to examine and test the teachings of any individual or group. The following list could be expanded, but these questions will assist the Christian to discern truth and error. Some will apply to certain individuals or groups and not to others.

1. What is their attitude toward the person of Jesus Christ: do they hold to his incarnation; do they accept his deity?

2. Do they believe in a personal God and accept the Trinity?

3. Do they believe in the bodily resurrection of Christ?

4. Do they alter the Bible by adding to or subtracting from it? Do they follow the Bible for doctrinal authority? Do they study the Bible as a whole?

5. Do they base their doctrines on the plain and direct statements of the Bible? Is their doctrinal foundation that of types, parables, figures of speech, prophecy, etc.?

6. Are their main doctrinal points based on the Old Testament? On the New Testament? Do they place their current organization in the events of Revelation after the time of the third chapter?

7. Do they exalt human leaders? Are these leaders and/or the organizations they represent deemed essential for the understanding of the Bible or for salvation?

8. Do they see man as a helpless sinner?

9. Do they approach God and salvation on the basis of works or on the basis of grace?

10. Do they believe in the conscious punishment of the lost?

11. Do they believe in the judgment to come? Do they believe in a second chance?

These questions are only suggestions as to what might be asked. Others should be added and Scriptures should be compiled for each. The Christian should also discuss what the adherents of any group mean by the terms they use. (For a discussion of the problem of semantics, see chap. 2 of Walter Martin's *The Kingdom of the Cults*.)

In dealing with the followers of a cult or other non-Christian group, two questions are vital: (1) What is the basis of their personal relationship to God? (2) To what extent do they have assurance of salvation as a present possession? First John 5:10–13 presents the heart of the gospel message and the standard for these two vital questions:

> He who believes in the Son of God has the witness in himself; he who does not believe God has made Him a liar, because he has not believed the testimony that God has given of His Son. And this is the testimony: that God has given us eternal life, and this life is in His Son. He who has the Son has life; he who does not have the Son of God does not have life. These things I have written to you who believe in the name of the Son of God, that you may know that you have eternal life, and that you may continue to believe in the name of the Son of God.

REACHING THE LOST IN CULT AND OCCULT CONFUSION

Many Christians are pessimistic concerning the fruitfulness of time spent in attempting to reach persons involved in the cults, the occult, and other religions. Are such attempts worth the effort? Can these people be reached? The answer to both of these questions is yes.

There are a number of books that give or contain the personal testimonies of converts from non-Christian groups. *We Found Our Way Out*, edited by James Adair and Ted Miller (Baker, 1964), gives the testimonies of persons who were delivered from a number of the cults as well as from such diverse backgrounds as Satanism and communism. Six former members tell their stories of deliverance from the Jehovah's Witnesses, Christian Science, New Age, and witchcraft involvements in *Why We Left a Cult*, by Latayne Scott (Baker, 1993). *I Talked with Spirits*, by Victor Ernest (Tyndale, 1970), and *The Challenging Counterfeit*, by Raphael Gasson (Logos, 1966), both include accounts of conversion from Spiritualism. *Mormonism—Shadow or Reality?* (Utah Lighthouse Ministry, 1987) is only one of dozens of excellent works written by Jerald Tanner and Sandra Tanner, converts from Mormonism. Some testimonies of conversion from Mormonism include *Beyond Mormonism: An Elder's Story*, by James Spencer (Revell, 1984); *Mormon Chronicles*, by Tom Hall (Promise, 1991); Leslie Reynolds, in the preface to *Mormons in Transition* (Baker, 1998); and *Ex-Mormons: Why We Left*, by Latayne Scott (Baker, 1990), which presents the experiences of eight who left. Roberta Blankenship wrote about her experiences in *Escape from Witchcraft* (Zondervan, 1972), as did Doreen Irvine in *From Witchcraft to Christ* (Concordia, 1973). *Death of a Guru* (Holman, 1977) is an autobiography of Rabindranath R. Maharaj, a convert from Hinduism.

My book *We Left Jehovah's Witnesses* (P&R, 1974) presents the experiences and testimonies of six couples. Another testimony of deliverance from the Jehovah's Witnesses is presented in *Pilgrimage Through the Watchtower*, by Kevin Quick (Baker, 1989). "Cult Explosion" (New Liberty Enterprises, 1979) is a powerful film (and video) that gives the testimonies of converts from a number of the cults. Deborah Davis (the daughter of Children of God founder Moses David Berg), with the assistance of her husband, wrote *The Children of God: The Inside Story* (Zondervan, 1984). *Children of Darkness*, by Ruth Gordon (Tyndale, 1988), is another account of escape from the COG. Caryl Matrisciana wrote of her deliverance from drugs and Eastern mysticism in *Gods of the New Age* (Harvest House, 1985). Former New Age leader Randall Baer wrote of his experience and conversion in *Inside the New Age Nightmare* (Huntington House, 1989). And in *The Religion That Kills: Christian Science: Abuse, Neglect, and Mind Control* (Huntington House, 2000), Linda S. Kramer concludes with her account of coming to Christ after thirty years as a dedicated Christian Scientist ("My Story: A Journey to Freedom"). The stories of deliverance from cults and the occult could be multiplied many times. Some accounts are referred to elsewhere in this book, and many are published in the periodicals of the various outreach ministries.

A number of the countercult ministries have produced testimonies on cassette and videotape and in their printed materials. Materials for witnessing to members of specific groups are also available (see the bibliographies and additional information in each chapter and the Appendix: Some Christian Countercult Resource Organizations). Books such as *Evangelizing the Cults* (Servant Publications, 1990) and *Hard Case Witnessing* (Chosen, 1991) will assist the Christian to be effective in witnessing.[2]

Is it worth the time and effort to attempt to reach cultists and those involved in other religious error? Again, yes it is! I was led to Christ from the Jehovah's Witnesses as a result of the faithful testimony of my teenage friends. They were not well trained in the Scriptures, since they had only recently accepted Christ, but they did know him as a living reality in their lives. Thank God for those who share their Christian faith in this age of religious and occult confusion.

APPENDIX:
SOME CHRISTIAN
COUNTERCULT RESOURCE
ORGANIZATIONS

The organizations included here, which deal with a number of the cults, isms, and the occult, represent only a small selection of the hundreds that are available. The websites listed often include recommendations or provide links to many other sources of information. The entries under each listing are not intended to be complete, so the particulars of each ministry should be determined by contact with that organization. Two additional listings provide further information to search for and order books online.

Apologetics Index
Website www.apologeticsindex.com

"Apologetics Index . . . provides research and resources on religious cults, sects, new religious movements, alternative religions, apologetics, anticult and countercult organizations, doctrines, religious practices and world views."

Topics in the index are arranged alphabetically, and the index "contains links to Christian, non-Christian and secular information on cults, sects, new and/or alternative religious movements, apologetics ministries, apologetics-related articles, countercult resources, etc."

Apologia

P.O. Box 63422
Colorado Springs, CO 80962
Phone 719-277-0069
Fax 719-277-0069
Website www.apologia.org

"Apologia's mission is primarily educational, to equip the body of Christ for spiritual discernment. . . . Apologia's areas of specialization include:

- Non-Christian religions, sects, and cults
- Occult movements, phenomena, and behavior
- Aberrant Christian teachings, movements and practices. . . ."

See Apologia's website for information on *Apologia Report* and other features of this ministry.

Christian Apologetics & Research Ministry (CARM)

Website www.carm.org
"Its purpose is to equip Christians with good information on Doctrine, various religious groups (Mormonism, Jehovah's Witnesses, etc.), Evolution, New Age, and related subjects."

Christian Research Institute (CRI) International

P.O. Box 7000
Rancho Santa Margarita
CA 92688-7000 USA
Phone 888-7000-CRI 949-858-6100
Fax 949-858-6111
Website www.equip.org

CRI Canada
56051 Airways P.O.
Calgary, Alberta T2E 8K5
Phone 800-665-5851

CRI publishes the *Christian Research Journal* quarterly. Its online CRI Resource Center can be searched for materials that are available dealing with apologetics, Christian doctrine, various cults, etc., which can be ordered online.

Cult Awareness & Information Center Australia
Website www.caic.org.au
This site provides extensive material on cults and isms and the occult. Some files from other sites are also linked to theirs.

Evangelical Ministries to New Religions (EMNR)
402 Office Park Drive C-20
Birmingham, AL 35223
Phone 205-871-2858
Website www.emnr.org

One helpful feature of the EMNR website is its Members Links, which lists the websites maintained by its members. The ministry of each individual or organization is briefly explained. The EMNR website also includes a list of available resources: books, cassette tapes, and videos.

Personal Freedom Outreach
P.O. Box 26062
Saint Louis, MO 63136-0062
Phone 314-921-9800
Website www.pfo.org.

PFO publishes *The Quarterly Journal* and *The Quarterly Journal Index*, which is available for every year of its publication, beginning in 1981. PFO also has a *Resource Material Price List* of tracts, books, booklets, audiotapes, and videotapes.

Probe Ministries
1900 Firman Drive, Suite 100
Richardson, TX 75081

In addition to a catalog, the CBD website makes it possible to locate and order a number of books that deal with the cults and the occult. The entire inventory can be checked by author, title, or subject and ordered online at a discount. Contact with CBD and orders can also be made by phone.

Catalog orders 978-977-5000

Customer service 978-977-5050

Barnes and Noble

Website www.bn.com

Books, new and used, on various cults and the occult can be searched by title, author, or subject and purchased online.

NOTES

Chapter 1: An Introduction to Cults

1 Charles R. Swindoll, *Growing Strong in the Seasons of Life* (Portland, Ore.: Multnomah, 1983), 147–48.

2 Gordon R. Lewis, *Confronting the Cults* (Philadelphia: P&R, 1966), 1.

3 Walter R. Martin, *Martin Speaks Out on the Cults* (Ventura, Calif.: Regal, 1983), 17.

4 Lewis, *Confronting the Cults*, 4.

5 John H. Gerstner, *The Theology of the Major Sects* (Grand Rapids: Baker, 1960), 9.

6 Anthony A. Hoekema, *The Four Major Cults* (Grand Rapids: Eerdmans, 1963), 377–78.

7 Ibid., 378–403.

8 Walter R. Martin, *The Kingdom of the Cults*, rev. 1997 ed. (Minneapolis: Bethany, 1997), 517.

9 Lewis, *Confronting the Cults*, 124–25; Gerstner, *Theology of the Major Sects*, 10; Hoekema, *Four Major Cults*, 388–403.

10 J. K. Van Baalen, *The Chaos of Cults*, 4th rev. ed. (Grand Rapids: Eerdmans, 1962), 250.

11 Josh McDowell and Don Stewart, *The Deceivers* (San Bernardino, Calif.: Here's Life, 1992), 298–99.

12 Dale Ratzlaff, *The Cultic Doctrine of Seventh-day Adventists* (Sedona, Ariz.: Life Assurance Ministries, 1996), 303.

13 *Los Angeles Times*, December 1, 1978, A-1. See John Ankerberg and John Weldon, *Encyclopedia of Cults and New Religions* (Eugene, Ore.: Harvest House, 1999), xv–xvi.

14 Keith E. Tolbert, "What Is a Cult?" *ARC Update* (July–September 1988), 10.

15 Ibid. Tolbert summarizes the three perspectives with the following outline:
   Sociological definition of a cult:
      a Descriptive lifestyle

b No value judgment added
Philosophical/religious definition:
    a Describe the belief system
    b Value judgment added
Media definition:
    a Describe lifestyle
    b Value judgment added

Tolbert explains, "The media has taken one aspect from the sociological definition and one aspect from the philosophical/religious definition and mixed the two" (11).

16 Craig Branch, "Cult or Cultic?" *Watchman Expositor* 10, 4 (1993), 21.
17 Ibid.
18 Brooks Alexander, "What Is a Cult?" *Spiritual Counterfeits Project Newsletter* (January–February 1979), 2–3.
19 Ibid., 3.
20 Dave Breese, *Know the Marks of Cults* (Wheaton, Ill.: Victor, 1975).
21 Martin, *Martin Speaks Out*, 22.

CHAPTER 2: JEHOVAH'S WITNESSES

1 Kenneth Wooden, *The Children of Jonestown* (New York: McGraw-Hill, 1981), 171; Tim Reiterman, "Parallel Roads Led to Jonestown, Waco," *Los Angeles Times*, April 23, 1993, A-24.
2 Reiterman, "Parallel Roads," A-24.
3 Rodney Clapp, "The Jehovah's Witnesses Are a 'Killer Cult,' Says a Defector," *Christianity Today*, November 20, 1981, 70.
4 Ibid.
5 David A. Reed, "More Dead Than Waco," *Comments from the Friends* (summer 1993), 2.
6 Russell Chandler, " 'Rather Die Than Take Blood'—Witnesses," *Los Angeles Times*, August 20, 1977, I–26.
7 Reed, "More Dead Than Waco," 3.
8 Ibid. Baptisms for 1999 and 2000 were 323,439 and 288,907.
9 *Christian Century*, February 13, 1957, 197.
10 *Watchtower*, January 1, 2001, 21.
11 M. James Penton, *Apocalypse Delayed: The Story of Jehovah's Witnesses* (Toronto: University of Toronto Press, 1985), 80.
12 Paul R. Blizard, "Frederick William Franz 1893–1992: Personal Reflections on His Life by a Former Third Generation Jehovah's Witness," *The Quarterly Journal* (April–June 1993), 10.

13 Ibid.

14 Further details of the history of the Jehovah's Witnesses are found in the books by Franz, Penton, Rogerson, Gruss, Schnell, Martin, and Hoekema listed in the bibliography. The Watchtower Society's account of its history is found in *Jehovah's Witnesses in the Divine Purpose* (1959) and *Jehovah's Witnesses—Proclaimers of God's Kingdom* (1993).

15 *Watchtower*, January 15, 2001, 31. "Jehovah's Witnesses Change Corporate Profile," *Christian Research Journal* 23, 3 (2001), 6–9.

16 Anthony A. Hoekema, *The Four Major Cults* (Grand Rapids: Eerdmans, 1963), 238–39; see also Robert H. Countess, *The Jehovah's Witnesses' New Testament*, 2d ed. (Phillipsburg, N.J.: P&R, 1987).

17 "So, does Jehovah have a prophet to help them, to warn them of dangers and *to declare things to come?* . . . These questions can be answered in the affirmative. *Who is this prophet?* . . . This 'prophet' was not one man, but was a body of men and women. It was the small group of footstep followers of Jesus Christ, known at that time as International Bible Students. *Today they are known as Jehovah's Christian witnesses.* . . .

"Of course, it is easy to say that this group acts as a 'prophet' of God. It is another thing to prove it. The only way that this can be done is to review the record. What does it show?" (" 'They Shall Know That a Prophet Was Among Them,' " (*Watchtower* [April 1, 1972], 197; italics added). What did the record of more than one hundred years show? Prophetic speculation and failure!

"True, there have been those in times past who predicted an 'end to the world,' even announcing a specific date. . . . Yet nothing happened. The 'end' did not come. They were guilty of false prophesying. Why? What was missing?

"Missing was the full measure of evidence required in fulfillment of Bible prophecy. Missing from such people were God's truths and the evidence that he was guiding and using them" ("A Time to Lift Up Your Head," *Awake!* [October 8, 1968], 23).

Would this statement not also apply to the Watchtower Society? Surely the Society cannot escape the judgment of its own words.

18 Edmond C. Gruss, *The Jehovah's Witnesses and Prophetic Speculation* (Nutley, N.J.: P&R, 1976) and *Jehovah's Witnesses: Their Claims, Doctrinal Changes and Prophetic Speculation* (Fairfax, Va.: Xulon Press, 2001).

19 "Why So Many False Alarms?" *Awake!* March 22, 1993, 3–4.

20 Cassette tape of F. W. Franz, transcribed in Gruss, *Jehovah's Witnesses*, 96ff.

21 Leonard and Marjorie Chretien, *Witnesses of Jehovah* (Eugene, Ore.: Harvest House, 1988), 209–10.

Chapter 3: The Latter-day Saints (Mormons)

1 Rick Branch, "Media + Missionaries = Membership," *Watchman Expositor* 7, 9 (1990), 10. See Ron Rhodes, the *Culting of America* (Eugene, Ore.: Harvest House, 1994), 104–8.

2 *Joseph Smith's Testimony,* 5–6.

3 *A Uniform System for Teaching Investigators* (Salt Lake City: The Church of Jesus Christ of Latter-day Saints, 1961), 18.

4 Bruce R. McConkie, *Mormon Doctrine,* 2d ed. (Salt Lake City: Bookcraft, 1966), 44, 131.

5 *The Seer* 2 (January 1854), 205–6.

6 James R. Spencer, "Tell Me Again . . . You Are My Brother?" *Through the Maze* 6 (1993), 1.

7 Ibid.

8 Ibid.

9 Robert M. Bowman Jr., "How Mormons Are Defending Mormon Doctrine," *Christian Research Journal* (fall 1989), 26.

10 Ibid.

11 Ibid.

12 Ibid.

13 Ibid. For additional documentation, see John R. Farkas, *Does the Mormon Church Attack Orthodox Christianity?* (St. Louis: Personal Freedom Outreach, 1988).

14 James E. Talmage, *The Great Apostasy* (n.p., n.d.), preface. Italics added.

15 *Joseph Smith's Testimony,* 5.

16 *History of the Church,* 2d ed., 7 vols. (Salt Lake City: Deseret, 1978), 1:xl. Italics added.

17 *The Falling Away and the Restoration of the Gospel of Jesus Christ Foretold* (Salt Lake City: Missionary Dept. LDS, 1973).

18 Talmage, *Great Apostasy,* 23–28.

19 Heber C. Snell, "The Bible in the Church," *Dialogue: A Journal of Mormon Thought* 2, 1 (spring 1967), 62.

20 Edmond C. Gruss, "Examining a Mormon Claim: Was There a Universal Apostasy?" *The Discerner* (April–June 1986), 2–9.

21 *The Falling Away and the Restoration.*

22 Hans-George Link, *The New International Dictionary of New Testament Theology,* 3 vols. (Grand Rapids: Zondervan, 1978), 3:148.

23 Wesley P. Walters, "Joseph Smith's First Vision Story Revisited," *The Journal of Pastoral Practice* 4 (1980): 92.

24 Wesley P. Walters, "New Light on Mormon Origins from the Palmyra (N.Y.) Revival," *Journal of the Evangelical Theological Society* 10 (fall 1967): 227–44;

New Light on Mormon Origins (La Mesa, Calif.: Utah Christian Tract Society, 1967).

25 "The Question of the Palmyra Revival," *Dialogue* (spring 1969): 59–100.

26 Milton V. Backman, Jr., "Awakenings in the Burned-over District: New Light on the Historical Setting of the First Vision," *BYU Studies* 9 (spring 1969): 301–20; *Joseph Smith's First Vision*, rev. ed. (Salt Lake City: Bookcraft, 1980).

27 Walters, "Smith's First Vision Story Revisited," 109.

28 *The Religious Bodies of America*, 4th ed. (St. Louis: Concordia, 1961), 462.

29 Ibid., 458.

30 For changes in *Doctrine and Covenants*, see Jerald Tanner and Sandra Tanner, *Mormonism—Shadow or Reality?* 5th ed. (Salt Lake City: Utah Lighthouse Ministry, 1987), 14–31B.

31 C. C. Riddle, *Lectures on Jesus Christ*, 3. On February 22, 1980, Ezra Taft Benson, president of the Quorum of Twelve, gave a devotional at Brigham Young University (recorded on cassette tape). In summarizing the "14 fundamentals in following the prophet," number 2 was, "The living prophet is more vital to us than the standard works." He then illustrated the point:

"Brigham Young took the stand and he took the Bible, the *Book of Mormon* and the book of *Doctrine and Covenants* and laid them down; and he said, 'There is the written Word of God concerning the work of God from the beginning of the world almost to our day. When compared with the living oracles those books are nothing to me. Those books do not convey the Word of God direct to us as do the words of the prophet or a man bearing the holy priesthood in our day and generation. I would rather have the living oracles than all the writings in the books.'"

32 William E. Berrett, *Teachings of the Book of Mormon* (Salt Lake City: Deseret Sunday School Union Board, 1950), 5.

33 Joseph Fielding Smith, *Doctrines of Salvation*, comp. Bruce R. McConkie (Salt Lake City: Bookcraft, 1956), 3:191.

34 Joseph Fielding Smith, comp., *Teachings of the Prophet Joseph Smith* (Salt Lake City: Bookcraft, 1938), 345–46.

35 Brigham Young, *Journal of Discourses* (Liverpool: Latter-day Saints Book Depot, 1855), 1:51. Joseph Fielding Smith, *Doctrines of Salvation*, comp. Bruce R. McConkie (Salt Lake City: Bookcraft, 1954), 1:19: "They ['Reorganites'] tell us the *Book of Mormon* states that Jesus was begotten of the Holy Ghost. I challenge the statement. The *Book of Mormon* teaches no such thing! Neither does the Bible."

36 Orson Hyde, *Journal of Discourses* (Liverpool: Latter-day Saints Book Depot, 1855), 2:81–82, 210; Young, *Journal of Discourses* (Liverpool: Latter-day Saints Book Depot, 1867), 11:328; Jedediah M. Grant, 1:346: "A belief in the doctrine

of a plurality of wives caused the persecution of Jesus and his followers." Orson Pratt, *The Seer* (November 1853), 172: "The great Messiah who was the founder of the Christian religion, was a Polygamist."

37 McConkie, *Mormon Doctrine,* 92. See the detailed discussion of blood atonement in Tanner and Tanner, *Mormonism—Shadow or Reality?* 398–404B.

38 Smith, *Doctrines of Salvation,* 1:114.

39 See Hal Hougey, *Latter-Day Saints—Where Do You Get Your Authority?* (Concord, Calif.: Pacific, n.d.).

40 Gordon R. Lewis, *The Bible, the Christian, and the Latter-day Saints* (Nutley, N.J.: P&R, 1966), 19. For documentation on false prophecies see James D. Bales, *The Testing of Joseph Smith, Jr.—Was He a Prophet?* (Concord, Calif.: Pacific, n.d.); Tanner and Tanner, *Mormonism—Shadow or Reality?* 186–95H.

41 Marvin W. Cowan, *Mormon Claims Answered,* rev. ed. (n.p., 1989), 101.

42 Used with the permission of Sandra Tanner.

43 "Scaling the Language Barrier" is the title of the second chapter of Walter R. Martin, *The Kingdom of the Cults,* rev. 1997 ed. (Minneapolis: Bethany, 1997). For a further discussion of the semantic problem see the chapter "Terminology" by Jerald Tanner and Sandra Tanner in *The Counterfeit Gospel of Mormonism,* 185–231.

44 Used by permission of Sandra Tanner. For other suggestions for witnessing to Mormons, see James R. Spencer, *Have You Witnessed to a Mormon Lately?* (Old Tappan, N.J.: Chosen, 1986); Wesley P. Walters, "Mormonism," in *Evangelizing the Cults,* ed. Ronald Enroth (Ann Arbor, Mich.: Servant, 1990), 83–100.

45 Used, with revisions, by permission of Mormonism Research Ministry, P. O. Box 20705, El Cajon, CA 92021.

Chapter 4: Christian Science

1 Art. 8, sec. 28 (89th ed.).

2 Affirmed by independent Christian Scientist Mrs. Ann Beals of *The Bookmark* (January 5, 2001).

3 Mary Baker Eddy, *Retrospection and Introspection* (Boston: Trustees Under the Will of Mary Baker G. Eddy, 1920), 13–15.

4 Walter R. Martin and Norman H. Klann, *The Christian Science Myth,* rev. ed. (Grand Rapids: Zondervan, 1955), 18–19.

5 Edwin F. Dakin, *Mrs. Eddy: The Biography of a Virginal Mind* (New York: Scribner's, 1929), 166–68.

6 Raymond J. Cunningham, "The Impact of Christian Science on the American Churches, 1880–1910," *American Historical Review* (April 1967), 886.

7 *Science and Health with Key to the Scriptures* (Boston: First Church of Christ, Scientist, 1971), 107.

8 Dakin, *Mrs. Eddy*, 60–62.

9 *Christian Science Journal* (January 1901), cited in Martin and Klann, *Christian Science Myth*, 55.

10 Art. 35, sec. 1; see also sec. 3 (89th ed.).

11 Bob Baker, "Christian Science in Bad Health," *Los Angeles Times*, June 2, 1992, A-18.

12 Ibid.

13 Charles S. Braden, *These Also Believe* (New York: Macmillan, 1949), 215. See Braden's calculations on 216–19 for a more complete assessment and total.

14 Baker, "Christian Science in Bad Health," A-18. Membership in the United Kingdom has also declined: 15,000 in 1980, 13,500 in 1985, 12,000 in 1987, and "it is estimated that this figure will almost be halved by A.D. 2000" (Eryl Davis, *Truth Under Attack* [Darlington, England: Evangelical Press, 1990], 95).

15 Thomas B. Rosenstiel, "High Tech Heresy at the Monitor?" *Los Angeles Times*, February 20, 1989, I–26.

16 Ibid.

17 Richard N. Ostling, "Tumult in the Reading Rooms," *Time*, October 14, 1991, 57.

18 James L. Franklin, "Christian Science Church Plans to Close TV Channel, Cut Staff," [Woodland Hills, Calif.] *Daily News*, June 6, 1992, 14.

19 Ibid.

20 Franklin, "What Ails Christian Science?" 54.

21 Peter Steinfels, "Christian Science Church Tested by Internal Dilemmas," *Daily News*, March 14, 1992, 16.

22 Russell Chandler, "Church Beats California Institutions to Bequest," *Los Angeles Times*, October 2, 1991, A-3, A-14.

23 Ostling, "Tumult in the Reading Rooms," 57.

24 Chandler, "Church Beats California Institutions," A-3.

25 Ibid., A-3, A-14.

26 Franklin, "What Ails Christian Science?" 54; Meg Sullivan, "Ruling Gives Art Museum Millions from Sisters' Trust," *Daily News*, December 16, 1993, 8.

27 Baker, "Christian Science in Bad Health," A-18. For further information see Caroline Fraser and Rita Swan in the bibliography.

28 Martin and Klann, *Christian Science Myth*, 132.

29 Ibid., chap. 9.

30 Ibid., 143–49.

31 George Wittmer, *Christian Science in the Light of the Bible* (St. Louis: Concordia, 1949), 23.

32 William J. Whalen, *Separated Brethren*, rev. ed. (Milwaukee: Bruce, 1961), 191.

33 Carolyn Poole, "Christian Science: Cult for the Cultured," *Moody Monthly* (October 1981), 29. See the editorial in *The Bookmark* (P.O. Box 801143, Santa Clarita, CA 91380), where many specific examples of censorship are cited (fall/winter 2000, 9).

34 Nancy Kind, *New Beginnings* (Lancaster, Calif.: Christian Way, n.d.), 2.

35 P. G. Chappell, "Church of Christ, Scientist," in *Evangelical Dictionary of Theology*, ed. Walter A. Elwell (Grand Rapids: Baker, 1986), 243. Italics added.

36 *Science and Health*, 497.

37 Anthony A. Hoekema, *The Four Major Cults* (Grand Rapids: Eerdmans, 1963), 182; see also 183–86.

38 Ibid., 189–90.

39 Ibid., 200.

40 Ibid., 207.

41 Ibid., 209.

42 Ibid., 212.

43 Ibid., 221.

44 Ibid.

45 See Appendix A, "Christian Science and the Bible," in Linda S. Kramer, *The Religion That Kills* (Lafayette, La.: Huntington House, 2000), 211–46.

46 Gaius G. Atkins, *Modern Religious Cults and Movements* (London: George Allen and Unwin, 1930), 164–65. Atkins distinguishes a correct approach to Scripture from Mrs. Eddy's erroneous one (164–66):

> Mrs. Eddy naturally sought the authority for her philosophy between the covers of the Scriptures. Beyond debate her teachings have carried much farther than they otherwise would, in that she claims for them a Scriptural basis, and they must be examined in that light. Now there are certain sound and universally recognized rules governing the scholarly approach to the Old and New Testaments. Words must be taken in their plain sense; they must be understood in their relation to context. A book is to be studied also in the light of its history; the time and place and purpose of its composition, as far as these are known, must be considered; no changes [may be] made in the text save through critical emendation, nor any translations [be] offered not supported by accepted texts, nor any liberties be taken with grammatical constructions. By such plain tests as these Mrs. Eddy's use of the Scriptures will not bear examination. She violates all recognized canons of Biblical interpretation on almost every page.
>
> Her method is wholly allegorical and the results achieved are conditioned only by the ingenuity of the commentator. . . .
>
> She has insight, imagination, boundless allegorical resource, but the whole Bible beneath her touch becomes a plastic material to be subdued

to her peculiar purpose by omissions, read-in meanings and the substantial and constant disregard of plain meanings. . . .

Everything means something else [see the Glossary in *Science and Health* for examples].

Chapter 5: Unity School of Christianity

1 Walter R. Martin, *Unity* (Grand Rapids: Zondervan, 1957), preface.
2 James D. Freeman, *The Household of Faith* (Lee's Summit, Mo.: Unity, 1951), 42.
3 Ibid., 39.
4 Quoted in ibid., 44.
5 Ibid., 49.
6 Ibid., 22–24.
7 Quoted in ibid., 55.
8 *Unity: 100 Years of Faith and Vision* (Unity Village, Mo.: Unity Books, 1988), 55.
9 Quoted in Freeman, *Household of Faith*, 42.
10 Quoted in Marcus Bach, *They Have Found a Faith* (New York: Bobbs-Merrill, 1946), 223.
11 Quoted in Freeman, *Household of Faith*, 170.
12 *Unity: 100 Years*, 167–69.
13 Ibid., 26.
14 Ibid., 26–29, 49, 62–63; James A. Decker, ed., *Unity's Seventy Years of Faith and Works* (Lee's Summit, Mo.: Unity, 1959), 93.
15 Letter from Unity's public relations director, Lavena Davis, March 29, 1993.
16 Charles. W. Ferguson, *The Confusion of Tongues* (Garden City, N.Y.: Double-day, 1928), 217.
17 J. K. Van Baalen, *The Chaos of Cults*, 4th rev. ed. (Grand Rapids: Eerdmans, 1962), 134. See the discussion on 133–37.
18 F. E. Mayer, *The Religious Bodies of America*, 4th rev. ed. (St. Louis: Concordia, 1961), 545, summarizing Marcus Bach.
19 Gordon R. Lewis, *Confronting the Cults* (Philadelphia: P&R, 1966), 156; emphasis and format of quotation, mine.
20 *Unity's Statement of Faith*, art. 22.
21 J. Oswald Sanders, *Heresies Ancient and Modern* (London: Marshall, Morgan and Scott, 1948), 61.
22 Martin, *Unity*, 31.
23 Russ Wise, "Unity School of Christianity" (Richardson, Tex.: Probe Ministries www.prob.org/docs/unity, 1995), 7.

24 Ruth A. Tucker, *Another Gospel* (Grand Rapids: Zondervan, 1989), 189–90.

25 Ibid., 190.

26 Kurt Van Gorden, in "The Unity School of Christianity," in *Evangelizing the Cults*, ed. Ron Enroth (Ann Arbor, Mich.: Servant, 1990), 148, explains:

> Many Christians have misunderstood the Unity concept of God. They usually equate Unity with pantheism, meaning that God is the material world. Unity is actually panentheism, where God is part of the world in the way that the mind or soul is a part of the body. Panentheism has been well refuted by Dr. Norman Geisler in his book *Christian Apologetics*. . . .
>
> The importance of this distinction cannot be overlooked. If you or I were to suggest to a Unity member that Unity is pantheistic, he or she will turn a deaf ear toward all that we say. The Unity member feels that if you are so "unenlightened" as to have mistaken his or her beliefs as pantheistic, then what new truth could you share with him or her?

CHAPTER 6: WORLDWIDE CHURCH OF GOD: FROM ARMSTRONGISM TO THE N.A.E.

1 Leslie K. Tarr, "Herbert W. Armstrong: Does He Really Have the 'Plain Truth'?" *Moody Monthly* (September 1972), 24.

2 Roger Campbell, "Herbert W. Armstrong: Mr. Confusion," *The King's Business* (February 1962), 24.

3 *The Plain Truth* (February 1973), 1.

4 Harry Lowe, *Radio Church of God: How Its Teachings Differ from Those of Seventh-day Adventists* (Mountain View, Calif.: Pacific Press), 18–19.

5 *The Autobiography of Herbert W. Armstrong*, vol. 1 (Pasadena: Ambassador College Press, 1967), 503.

6 Herman L. Hoeh, *A True History of the True Church* (Pasadena, Calif.: Ambassador College Press, 1959), 26.

7 *The Plain Truth* (July 1965), 30.

8 "Transformed by Christ: A Brief History of the Worldwide Church of God," www.wcg.org/lit/AboutUs/history (1998), 2.

9 Marion McNair, *Armstrongism: Religion or Rip-Off?* (Orlando: Pacific Charters, 1977), 203.

10 Joseph Tkach Jr., *Transformed by Truth* (Sisters, Ore.: Multnomah, 1997), 174.

11 Tkach lists eight new organizational splinter groups that formed from 1972 through 1974 (ibid., 209).

12 Bert Mann, "Armstrong Son Establishes His Own Church," *Los Angeles Times*, July 30, 1978, I–3.

13 Tkach, *Transformed by Truth*, 175.

14 Ibid., 88.

15 Ibid., 89.

16 Ibid., 98; Joseph Hopkins, "Herbert W. Armstrong," *Christianity Today*, December 17, 1971, 8; Larry Nichols and George Mather, *Discovering the Plain Truth* (Downers Grove, Ill.: InterVarsity Press, 1998), 61, 69.

17 Tkach, *Transformed by Truth*, 92.

18 Jon Trott, "The Saga of a 'Cult' Gone Good," *Cornerstone* 26, 111 (1997), 42.

19 *The Plain Truth* (July-August 1955), 4.

20 *The Plain Truth* (April 1963), 10.

21 Tkach, *Transformed by Truth*, 92–93.

22 Ibid., 94.

23 Ibid., 95.

24 Ibid., 96.

25 Ibid., 99.

26 Ibid., 119.

27 Ibid., 121–22.

28 Ibid., 98. For more extensive discussions of the doctrinal changes in the WCG see Nichols and Mather, *Discovering the Plain Truth*, appendix 1, and Tkach, *Transformed by Truth*. For answers to Armstrong's theology, see the above and the books by Anderson, Benware, Hopkins, and Sumner in the bibliography.

29 Tkach, *Transformed by Truth*, 155.

30 Ibid., 157.

31 McNair, *Armstrongism*, 169–70, 209–10.

32 *The Plain Truth* (June 1976), 22.

33 McNair, *Armstrongism*, 165–66, 169–70.

34 Tkach, *Transformed by Truth*, 113–118, 131, 134.

35 Ibid., 71.

36 "A Brief List of Doctrines of the Worldwide Church of God," www.wcg.org/lit/AboutUs/brieflist (1998), 3.

37 Phillip Arnn, "Tkach Clarifies 'Sabbath' and 'True Church' Doctrines," *Watchman Expositor* 12, 1 (1995), 19.

38 Ruth Tucker, "From the Fringe to the Fold: How the Worldwide Church of God Discovered the Plain Truth of the Gospel," *Christianity Today*, July 15, 1996, 27.

39 Tkach, *Transformed by Truth*, 200; Mark A. Kellner, "Worldwide Church of God Joins NAE," *Christianity Today*, June 16, 1997, 66.

40 Joseph Tkach Jr., "A Church Reborn," *Christian Research Journal* (winter 1996), 53.

41 Tkach, *Transformed by Truth*, 209–11.

42 Tkach, "Transformed by Christ," 6.

43 Tkach, *Transformed*, 216.

44 Tim Martin, "The Philadelphia Church of God," *Watchman Fellowship Profile*, 2000, 2.

45 Massimo Introvigne, "Schism in the Global Church of God," CESNUR www.cesnur.org/testi/Living (n.d.), 1; Mark A. Kellner, "Splinter Groups Dismiss Leaders," *Christianity Today*, March 2, 1998, 74.

46 Kellner, "Splinter Groups Dismiss Leaders," 74.

CHAPTER 7: SPIRITUALISM (SPIRITISM)

1 For a helpful discussion, see John Ankerberg and John Weldon, *The Facts on Spirit Guides* (Eugene, Ore.: Harvest House, 1988); Elliott Miller, *A Crash Course on the New Age Movement* (Grand Rapids: Baker, 1989), chaps. 8 and 9.

2 J. Stafford Wright, *Man in the Process of Time* (Grand Rapids: Eerdmans, 1956), 101.

3 B. F. Austin, *The A.B.C. of Spiritualism* (Indianapolis: Summit Publications, n.d.), questions 3, 5. Originally published in 1920, this work is currently distributed by the National Spiritualist Association of Churches (N.S.A.C.).

4 Marily Awtry, *History of National Spiritualist Association of Churches* (Cassadaga, Fla.: N.S.A.C., 1983), i; Ann Braude, *Radical Spirits* (Boston: Beacon, 1989), 165–73.

5 Braude, *Radical Spirits*, 173–75.

6 Awtry, *History*, 4–6. The association was originally called the National Spiritualist Association of the United States of America. It changed its name in 1920 to the National Spiritualist Association, and in 1953 it adopted its present name, the National Spiritualist Association of Churches.

7 J. Gordon Melton, *Encyclopedic Handbook of Cults in America* (New York: Garland, 1986), 84: Those who established the Progressive Spiritualist Church "wished to replace the Declaration of Principles with a Confession of Faith based upon the authority of the Bible." Those who left to form the National Spiritual Alliance and the General Assembly of Spiritualists both accepted reincarnation, which was rejected and viewed as subversive by the N.S.A.C. Efforts to segregate blacks and to "curtail their participation in the national conventions" led to the formation of the National Colored Spiritualist Association of Churches in 1925.

8 See the bibliography for further details.

9 Melton, *Encyclopedic Handbook of Cults*, 83. The Declaration of Principles of the N.S.A.C.:

> 1. We believe in Infinite Intelligence. 2. We believe that the phenomena of Nature, both physical and spiritual, are the expression of Infinite Intelligence. 3. We affirm that a correct understanding of such expression and living in accordance therewith, constitute true religion. 4. We affirm that the existence and personal identity of the individual continue after the change called death. 5. We affirm that communication with the so-called dead is a fact, scientifically proven by the phenomena of Spiritualism. 6. We believe that the highest morality is contained in the Golden Rule: "Whatsoever ye would that others should do unto you do ye also unto them." 7. We affirm the moral responsibility of the individual, and that he makes his own happiness or unhappiness as he obeys or disobeys Nature's physical and spiritual laws. 8. We affirm that the doorway to reformation is never closed against any human soul here or hereafter. 9. We affirm that the precepts of Prophecy and Healing contained in the Bible are Divine attributes proven through Mediumship.

10 Edwin B. Morse, *The "Why's" of Spiritualism* (Summit, N.J.: Stow Memorial Foundation, n.d.), 9. Originally published in 1933, this work is currently distributed by the N.S.A.C.

11 John Kraus, "An Apology," *The National Spiritualist* (March 1961), 16.

12 Wright, *Man in the Process of Time*, 109–10.

13 Austin, *The A.B.C. of Spiritualism*, question 45.

14 Ibid., questions 28, 34, 43.

15 For a discussion of the reality and origin of demons, see Merrill F. Unger, *Demons in the World Today* (Wheaton: Tyndale, 1971) and *Biblical Demonology* (Wheaton: Scripture Press, 1952).

16 F. E. Mayer, *The Religious Bodies of America*, 4th rev. ed. (St. Louis: Concordia, 1961), 565.

17 Melton, *Encyclopedic Handbook of Cults*, 83.

18 Raphael Gasson, *The Challenging Counterfeit* (Plainfield, N.J.: Logos, 1966), 1.

19 Ibid., 92.

20 Victor H. Ernest, *I Talked with Spirits* (Wheaton, Ill.: Tyndale, 1970), 59.

21 Ibid., 32.

22 Austin, *The A.B.C. of Spiritualism*, question 23.

23 Ibid., question 22.

24 Unger, *Biblical Demonology*, 144.

25 J. Stafford Wright, *Christianity and the Occult* (Chicago: Moody, 1971), 112.

26 Gasson, *Challenging Counterfeit*, 19.

Chapter 8: Seventh-day Adventism

1 Ruth A. Tucker, *Another Gospel* (Grand Rapids: Zondervan, 1989), 93.

2 Ibid.

3 See the books by Canright, Hunt, Slattery, and Cleveland in the bibliography and Greive's testimony in this chapter.

4 Anthony A. Hoekema, *The Four Major Cults* (Grand Rapids: Eerdmans, 1963), 403.

5 Walter R. Martin, *The Truth About Seventh-day Adventism* (Grand Rapids: Zondervan, 1960), 7. While this book is out of print, Martin's evaluation of the SDA Church is available in *Kingdom of the Cults*, rev. ed. (Minneapolis: Bethany, 1985), 409–500; Appendix C, 1997 ed.

6 Walter R. Martin, "Seventh-day Adventism," *Christianity Today*, December 19, 1960, 14.

7 Norman F. Douty, *Another Look at Seventh-day Adventism* (Grand Rapids: Baker, 1962), 188.

8 *Seventh-day Adventists Answer Questions on Doctrine*, 8.

9 Ibid.

10 John H. Gerstner, *The Theology of the Major Sects* (Grand Rapids: Baker, 1960), 10.

11 *Christianity Today*, February 8, 1980, 64; Adventist News Network 2000 (December 27) www.adventist.org/news and www.adventist.org/factsandfigures.

12 A. S. Maxwell, *Your Friends the Adventists* (Mountain View, Calif.: Pacific Press, 1967), 85.

13 Martin, *Truth About Seventh-day Adventism*, 29–30.

14 "There is a sanctuary in heaven, the true tabernacle which the Lord set up and not man. In it Christ ministers on our behalf, making available to believers the benefits of His atoning sacrifice offered once for all on the cross. He was inaugurated as our great High Priest and began His intercessory ministry at the time of His ascension. In 1844, at the end of the prophetic period of 2300 days, He entered the second and last phase of His atoning ministry. It is a work of investigative judgment which is part of the ultimate disposition of all sin, typified by the cleansing of the ancient Hebrew sanctuary on the Day of Atonement. In that typical service the sanctuary was cleansed with the blood of animal sacrifices, but the heavenly things are purified with the perfect sacrifice of the blood of Jesus. The investigative judgment reveals to heavenly intelligences who among the dead are asleep in Christ and therefore, in Him, are deemed worthy to have part in the first resurrection. It also makes manifest who among the living are abiding in Christ, keeping the commandments of God and the faith of Jesus, and in Him, therefore, are ready for translation into His everlasting king-

dom. This judgment vindicates the justice of God in saving those who believe in Jesus. It declares that those who have remained loyal to God shall receive the kingdom. The completion of this ministry of Christ will mark the close of human probation before the Second Advent." (Fundamental Beliefs, 23, quoted in *Seventh-day Adventists Believe . . . A Biblical Exposition of 27 Fundamental Doctrines* [Hagerstown, Md.: Review and Herald, 1988], 312).

In 1983 prominent Seventh-day Adventist theologian Desmond Ford had his ordination "annulled." Ford "denied that the year 1844 had any biblical significance and offered eighty 'implicit' Seventh-day Adventist teachings on the doctrine of Investigative Judgment that could not be supported by Scripture" (Tucker, *Another Gospel*, 110).

15 Hoekema, *Four Major Cults*, 98.

16 Ibid., 97.

17 See *Defending the Faith*, vol. 2 (1985). This contains transcripts of a series prepared for television by the John Ankerberg Show, P. O. Box 8977, Chattanooga, TN 37411. Five programs entitled "Seventh-Day Adventism: Who's Telling the Truth?" feature Walter Martin and William Johnsson, the editor of *Adventist Review*, with host John Ankerberg. The entire transcript makes interesting reading. Martin makes the point that while *QOD* was being affirmed, hundreds of ex-Adventist ministers and others were saying, "We believe *Questions on Doctrine*. We cited *Questions on Doctrine*. We presented our views in the light of *Questions on Doctrine* and we were disfellowshipped; we were removed from the church" (242). In the last program, Ankerberg asked Martin, "What would have to change, Walter, for you to call them a cult? And we might go on to the next step, do you think it's heading in that direction?" After presenting examples of what he saw taking place, Martin stated, "I fear that if they continue to progress at this rate, that the classification of cult can't possibly miss being re-applied to Seventh-day Adventism" (266).

18 Reprinted by permission from *The King's Business* (July 1958), 18–19.

19 Kenneth R. Samples, "The Recent Truth About Seventh-day Adventism," *Christianity Today*, February 5, 1990, 18. Desmond Ford, an excommunicated SDA theologian, in a letter to the editor commends Samples's article for being "perceptive, accurate, and sympathetic" (*Christianity Today* [March 19, 1990], 6).

20 Joan Craven, "The Wall of Adventism," *Christianity Today*, October 19, 1984, 20.

21 Samples, "Recent Truth About Seventh-day Adventism," 18–19.

22 Ibid., 19.

23 Ibid., 19–20.

24 Kenneth R. Samples, "From Controversy to Crisis: An Updated Assessment of Seventh-day Adventism," *Christian Research Journal* (summer 1988), 12–13 (used by permission of the Christian Research Institute):

The major doctrinal issues which united this group [evangelical Adventists] were

1) **Righteousness by faith:** This group accepted the reformation understanding of righteousness by faith (according to which righteousness by faith includes justification only, and is a judicial act of God whereby he declares sinners to be just on the basis of Christ's own righteousness). Our standing before God rests in the imputed righteousness of Christ, which we receive through faith alone. Sanctification is the accompanying fruit and not the root of salvation.

2) **The human nature of Christ:** Jesus Christ possessed a sinless human nature with no inclination or propensities toward sin. In that sense, Christ's human nature was like that of Adam's before the Fall. Though Christ certainly suffered the limitations of a real man, by nature he was impeccable (i.e., incapable of sin). Jesus was primarily our substitute.

3) **The events of 1844:** Jesus Christ entered into the most holy place (heaven itself) at his ascension; the sanctuary doctrine and the investigative judgment (traditional literalism and perfectionism) have no basis in Scripture.

4) **Assurance of salvation:** Our standing and assurance before God rest solely in Christ's imputed righteousness; sinless perfection is not possible this side of heaven. Trusting Christ gives a person assurance.

5) **Authority of Ellen G. White:** Ellen White was a genuine Christian who possessed a gift of prophecy. However, neither she nor her writings are infallible, and they should not be used as a doctrinal authority.

The following positions were taken by traditional Adventism in response to the doctrinal debates:

1) **Righteousness by faith:** Righteousness by faith includes both justification and sanctification. Our standing before God rests both in the imputed and imparted righteousness of Christ (God's work for me and in me). Justification is for sins committed in the past only.

2) **The human nature of Christ:** Jesus Christ possessed a human nature that not only was weakened by sin but had propensities toward sin itself. His nature was like that of Adam after the Fall. Because of his success in overcoming sin, Jesus is primarily our example.

3) **The events of 1844:** Jesus entered into the second compartment of the heavenly sanctuary for the first time on October 22, 1844, and began an investigative judgment. This judgment is the fulfillment of the second phase of Christ's atoning work.

4) **Assurance of salvation:** Our standing before God rests in both the imputed and imparted righteousness of Christ; assurance of salvation be-

fore the judgment is presumptuous. As Jesus, our example, showed us, perfect commandment keeping is possible.

5) **The authority of Ellen G. White:** The spirit of prophecy was manifest in the ministry of Ellen White as a sign of the remnant church. Her writings are inspired counsel from the Lord and authoritative in doctrinal matters.

. . . Not every Adventist would fit neatly into one of these two groups. Neither of these groups were totally unified in their doctrinal beliefs. . . . Though small, there was and is a segment in Adventism which could be described as being theologically liberal.

A letter in *Christian Research Journal* (fall 1988), 4, from the associate secretary of the General Conference of Seventh-day Adventists, J. David Newman, states that Samples's article "is a remarkably accurate portrayal of what is happening within Adventism today."

25 Samples, "Recent Truth About Seventh-day Adventism," 21.
26 Ibid.
27 Ibid.
28 Ibid.
29 Samples, "From Controversy to Crisis," 14.
30 Ibid.
31 Samples, "Recent Truth About Seventh-day Adventism," 21.
32 Samples, "From Controversy to Crisis," 14.
33 *The Truth About Seventh-day Adventist "Truth"* (Glendale, Ariz.: Life Assurance Ministries, 2000), 37.

Chapter 9: Occult Obsession and the New Cults

1 John Godwin, *Occult America* (Garden City, N.Y.: Doubleday, 1972), 1.
2 J. Gordon Melton, Jerome Clark, and Aidan A. Kelly, *New Age Almanac* (Chicago: Visible Ink Press, 1991), 272.
3 John Weldon, "A Sampling of the New Religions," *International Review of Mission* (October 1978), 407.
4 Vernon C. Grounds, "Understanding the Neo-mystical Movement," *Christian Heritage* (January 1973), 5.
5 Joseph Newman, ed., *The Religious Awakening of America* (Washington, D.C.: U.S. News, 1972), 11.
6 Peter Rowley, *New Gods in America* (New York: McKay, 1971), 3–4.
7 George A. Mather and Larry A. Nichols, *Dictionary of Cults, Sects, Religions and the Occult* (Grand Rapids: Zondervan, 1993), vii.

8 T. K. Wallace, "What's Behind the Occultism Craze," *Family Weekly*, February 28, 1971, 4.

9 Russ Parker, *Battling the Occult* (Downers Grove, Ill.: InterVarsity Press, 1990), 53–60.

10 For a number of examples as they relate especially to the young, see Berit Kjos, *Your Child and the New Age* (Wheaton, Ill.: Victor, 1990); Neil T. Anderson and Steve Russo, *The Seduction of Our Children* (Eugene, Ore.: Harvest House, 1991); Bob Passantino and Gretchen Passantino, *When the Devil Dares Your Kids* (Ann Arbor, Mich.: Servant, 1991).

11 For a discussion and evaluation of the Harry Potter books from a Christian perspective see Gene Edward Veith, "Good Fantasy and Bad Fantasy," *Christian Research Journal* 23, 1 (2001):12–22; James Bjornstad, "Potter Mania: What's It All About?" *The Quarterly Journal* (October-December 2000), 1, 16–19; David L. Brown, "The Problem with Harry Potter" (2000), Logos Communication Consortium, Inc., P.O. Box 173, Oak Creek, WI 53154; Richard Abanes, *Harry Potter and the Bible* (Camp Hill, Pa.: Horizon Books, 2001).

12 Wallace, "What's Behind the Occultism Craze," 4.

13 *Llewellyn's New Worlds of Mind and Spirit* (March/April, May/June 1993).

14 Oswald Guinness, "The Eastern Look of the Modern West," *His* (February 1972), 2–3.

15 Ibid., 5.

16 Oswald Guinness, "The East No Exit," *His* (March 1972), 31.

17 A treatment of each of these (except Unity) is included in J. Gordon Melton, *Encyclopedic Handbook of Cults in America* (New York: Garland, 1986).

18 Ibid.

19 *Los Angeles Times*, December 1, 1978, 1.

20 Christian Apologetics: Research and Information Service, P.O. Box 1659, Milwaukee, WI 53201.

21 Mather and Nichols, *Dictionary of Cults*, ix.

CHAPTER 10: ASTROLOGY

1 J. Gordon Melton, Jerome Clark, and Aiden A. Kelley, *New Age Almanac* (Chicago: Invisible Ink Press, 1991), 277.

2 William J. Petersen, *Those Curious New Cults in the 80s* (New Canaan, Conn.: Keats, 1982), 20.

3 Kurt Koch, *Between Christ and Satan* (Grand Rapids: Kregel, 1962), 12.

4 Petersen, *Those Curious New Cults*, 20.

5 John Ankerberg and John Weldon, *The Facts on Astrology* (Eugene, Ore.: Harvest House, 1988), 8.

6 John Warwick Montgomery, *Principalities and Powers* (Minneapolis: Bethany, 1973), 108.

7 See James Bjornstad and Shildes Johnson, *Stars, Signs, and Salvation in the Age of Aquarius* (Minneapolis: Bethany, 1971), 11–35, on the nature and history of astrology.

8 Bernard Kaplan, "Astrology Gaining New Acceptance in Europe," *Los Angeles Times*, November 18, 1971. Astrologers have often cited Michael Gauquelin's research in support of their views. But as John Ankerberg and John Weldon point out in *Astrology: Do the Heavens Rule Our Destiny?* (Eugene, Ore.: Harvest House, 1989), 87, "Gauquelin has fully discredited traditional astrology. In essence . . . citing Gauquelin as a defender of astrology is like citing Karl Marx as a defender of capitalism." For more on Gauquelin, see 87–95.

9 Mark Graubard, "Under the Spell of the Zodiac," *Natural History* (May 1969), 18.

10 "Astrology: Fad and Phenomena," *Time*, March 21, 1969, 56.

11 Gail Cottman, "New Youth Look in Astrology Boom," *Los Angeles Times*, March 12, 1972, E-2.

12 "Science Indicators 2000: Belief in the Paranormal or Pseudoscience," *Skeptical Inquirer* (January/February 2001), 13.

13 "Astrology: Fad and Phenomena," 56.

14 Ibid.

15 Montgomery, *Principalities and Powers*, 116.

16 Colin Wilson, *The Occult—A History* (New York: Random House, 1971), 251.

17 Koch, *Between Christ and Satan*, 16–17.

18 Paul Kurtz and Andew Fraknoi, "Belief in the Stars Is Not a Good Sign: Scientific Tests Fail to Support Astrology," in *Astrology and Astronomy* (San Francisco: Astronomical Society of the Pacific, 1989).

19 Koch, *Between Christ and Satan*, 18.

20 John Weldon, "Astrology: An Inside Look, Part II," *News and Views* (November 1988), 1–2. Two chapters in *Astrology: Do the Heavens Rule Our Destiny?* discuss astrology's spiritist connection: "Astrology and Spiritism" (201–23) and "Spiritism and Chart Interpretation" (225–55).

21 *Los Angeles Times*, May 5, 1972, A-12.

22 Petersen, *Those Curious New Cults*, 26; Montgomery, *Principalities and Powers*, 114–15.

23 The precession of the equinoxes and its impact on astrology are explained in more detail in Robert A. Morey, *Horoscopes and the Christian* (Minneapolis: Bethany, 1981), 38–39; "Precession (Astronomy)," *Van Nostrand's Scientific Encyclopedia*, 7th ed. (New York: Van Nostrand, 1989), 2303–4.

24 George Sarton, *Ancient Science and Modern Civilization* (New York: Harper, 1959), 61–62.

25 Montgomery, *Principalities and Powers*, 114.

26 Kurtz and Fraknoi, "Belief in the Stars."

27 Melton, *New Age Almanac*, 276–77.

28 Petersen, *Those Curious New Cults*, 29, reformatted for emphasis.

29 F. Kingsley Elder, "Astrology," in *The Encyclopedia of Christianity* (Wilmington, Del.: National Foundation for Christian Education, 1964), 451.

30 John Davis, "Astrology and Your Future," *Brethren Missionary Herald*, July 22, 1972, 15, reformatted for emphasis.

31 See chapter 2 of *Stars, Signs, and Salvation in the Age of Aquarius*, by Bjornstad and Johnson, and chapter 9 of *Astrology: Do the Heavens Rule Our Destiny?* by Ankerberg and Weldon, for further discussion.

CHAPTER 11: BAHA'I

1 Charles W. Ferguson, *The Confusion of Tongues* (Garden City, N.Y.: Doubleday, 1928), 231.

2 *The American Baha'i* (April 1973), 1; Tammerlin Drummond, "Baha'is Celebrate Unity, Diversity of Their Faith," *Los Angeles Times*, May 23, 1992, B-12.

3 Heidi Kezmoh, "Working for the Unity of Mankind," *Newhall* [Calif.] *Signal*, December 14, 1991, 22; Nancy Ryan, "Baha'is' Temple Symbolizes Unity of World Religions," [Woodland Hills, Calif.] *Daily News*, August 8, 1987.

4 *The American Baha'i* (April 1973), 3.

5 John Boykin, "The Baha'i Faith," in *A Guide to Cults and New Religions*, ed. Ronald Enroth (Downers Grove, Ill.: InterVarsity Press, 1983), 27.

6 Dozens of articles have appeared in newspapers since 1979 detailing the suffering of the Baha'i community in Iran, with such headlines as: "Iran's Persecution of Baha'i Unchecked: 10 Women Reported Hanged After Refusing to Renounce Faith"; "U.S. Assails Iran's 'Alarming' Persecution of Baha'is: 198 Sect Members Executed Since 1979, State Department Says"; "Man Hopes to Help Persecuted Friends: Baha'i Faith Members 'Killed' Under Orders." The persecution continues to the present (see the online newsletter of the Baha'i International Community, *One Country*, www.onecountry.org).

7 William M. Miller, "What Is the Baha'i World Faith?" *Incite* (December 1975), 23.

8 Ibid.

9 Ibid., 24.

10 *What Is the Baha'i Faith?* is an abridgment of Miller's book by William N. Wysham (Grand Rapids: Eerdmans, 1977).

11 David Hofman, *The Renewal of Civilization*, rev. ed. (London: George Ronald, 1972), 34, 123.

12 Francis J. Beckwith, *Baha'i* (Minneapolis: Bethany, 1985), 7–8; Francis J. Beckwith, "Baha'i-Christian Dialogue: Some Key Issues Considered," *Christian Research Journal* (winter/spring, 1989), 19; *The Orthodox Baha'i Faith* (Roswell, N.M.: Mother Baha'i Council of the U.S., 1981), 3–4; Herman Zimmer, *A Fraudulent Testament Devalues the Bahai Religion into Political Shoghism* (Stuttgart, Germany: Free Bahais, 1973).

13 J. E. Esslemont, *Baha'u'llah and the New Era*, 4th rev. ed. (Wilmette, Ill.: Baha'i Publishing Trust, 1976), 84.

14 James Moore, "A New Look at Baha'i," *His* (February 1971), 17.

15 Kezmoh, "Working for the Unity of Mankind," 22.

16 J. K. Van Baalen, *The Chaos of Cults*, 4th rev. ed. (Grand Rapids: Eerdmans, 1962), 150.

17 *One God, One Religion, One Mankind* (Wilmette, Ill.: Baha'i, n.d.).

18 Miller, "What Is the Baha'i World Faith?" 28.

19 William J. Petersen, *Those Curious New Cults in the 80s* (New Caanan, Conn.: Keats, 1982), 198.

20 Walter R. Martin, *The Kingdom of the Cults*, rev. 1997 ed. (Minneapolis: Bethany, 1997), 331. See Martin's interview with a Baha'i teacher on 325–27.

21 George Townshend, *Christ and Baha'u'llah*, rev. ed. (Oxford: George Ronald, 1966), 25.

22 Ibid.

23 Ibid., 26.

24 Ibid., 27.

25 Ibid., 28.

26 Ibid.

27 Ibid., 29.

28 Ibid., 30.

29 "The Baha'i Faith Unites All Races, All Religions," *Los Angeles Times*, October 22, 1971.

30 Beckwith, *Baha'i*, 16. After looking at what the past manifestations (as identified by Baha'is) taught about the nature of God, Beckwith summarizes (18):

> There appears to be a confusion about God's nature among the alleged manifestations. . . . God cannot be impersonal, personal, transcendent, polytheistic, pantheistic, monotheistic, able to beget, not able to beget, relevant, and irrelevant all at the same time. If it is true that God is all those things, then we are driven to agnosticism. Such an illogical God can never be known based on contradictory information given to us by His alleged manifestations. Irreconcilable data gives us no knowledge of God whatsoever.

Chapter 12: Rosicrucianism

1 *Fate* (November 1992), 23.

2 J. Gordon Melton, Jerome Clark, and Aidan A. Kelly, *New Age Almanac* (Chicago: Visible Ink Press, 1991), 290–91.

3 J. Gordon Melton, *Encyclopedic Handbook of Cults in America* (New York: Garland, 1986), 70.

4 Ibid., 74–75.

5 Ibid., 68–75.

6 "Rosicrucian Leader Stole $3.5 Million, Sect Alleges," *Los Angeles Times*, April 21, 1990, F-15.

7 Charles Braden, "Rosicrucianism," *Encyclopaedia Britannica* (Chicago: Encyclopaedia Britannica, 1964), 558.

8 *The Mastery of Life*, 31st ed., 15. The current edition (2000), titled *Mastery of Life*, is much shorter than the edition cited.

9 H. Spencer Lewis, *Rosicrucian Questions and Answers with Complete History of the Rosicrucian Order*, 14th ed. (San Jose: Rosicrucian Press, 1979), 75–88.

10 See Norman MacKenzie, ed., *Secret Societies* (New York: Pocket Books, 1967), 109–27, for further details of Rosicrucian history.

11 Melton, *Encyclopedic Handbook of Cults in America*, 69.

12 "Rosicrucian Leader Stole $3.5 Million," *Los Angeles Times*, F-15.

13 H. Spencer Lewis, *Rosicrucian Manual*, 10th ed. (San Jose: Rosicrucian Press, 1947), 42.

14 Walter R. Martin, *The Kingdom of the Cults*, rev. ed. (Minneapolis: Bethany, 1985), 507.

15 Ibid., 509–12.

16 H. Spencer Lewis, *The Mystical Life of Jesus*, 22d ed. (San Jose, Calif.: Rosicrucian Press, 1974).

17 Ibid., 53.

18 Ibid., 263.

19 Ibid., 265.

20 Ibid., 283.

21 Ibid., 289.

22 Ibid., listings after 320.

23 Edgar J. Goodspeed, *Famous "Biblical" Hoaxes* (Grand Rapids: Baker, 1956), 87.

24 *Mastery of Life*, 19–27.

25 Ibid., 28, and numerous Rosicrucian ads.

26 J. K. Van Baalen, *The Chaos of Cults*, 4th rev. ed. (Grand Rapids: Eerdmans, 1962), 121–22.

27 Martin, *Kingdom of the Cults*, 508.

28 Joyce Blackwell, "I Was a Rosicrucian," in *We Found Our Way Out*, ed. James R. Adair and Ted Miller (Grand Rapids: Baker, 1964), 31–32.

CHAPTER 13: THE OCCULT AND THE OUIJA BOARD

1 Russ Parker, *Battling the Occult* (Downers Grove, Ill.: InterVarsity Press, 1990), 9–19.

2 William Watson, *A Concise Dictionary of Cults and Religions* (Chicago: Moody, 1991), 170–71.

3 Josh McDowell and Don Stewart, *The Occult* (San Bernardino, Calif.: Here's Life, 1992), 17.

4 Nandor Fador, "Ouija Board," in *Encyclopedia of Psychic Science* (New Hyde Park, N.Y.: University Books, 1966), 270.

5 Edmond C. Gruss, *The Ouija Board* (Chicago: Moody, 1986), 5.

6 Ibid., 5–6; Edmond C. Gruss, *The Ouija Board: Doorway to the Occult* (Chicago: Moody, 1975), 21, 35; letter from Parker Brothers' consumer relations advisor Evelyn Cusco, May 5, 1992.

7 *The Weird and Wonderful Ouija Talking Board Set*, 2. "Ouija" and "Mystifying Oracle" are registered trademarks of Parker Brothers of General Mills Fun Group, Inc.

8 John Godwin, *Occult America* (Garden City, N.Y.: Doubleday, 1972), 273.

9 William R. Barrett, *On the Threshold of the Unseen* (New York: Dutton, 1918), 176–89; Irving Litvag, *Singer in the Shadows* (New York: Macmillan, 1972).

10 Gruss, *Ouija Board: Doorway*, 17, 168–73 (on the Ouija board connection with the case behind *The Exorcist*); Gerald Brittle, *The Demonologist* (1980; reprint, New York: St. Martin's, 1991), 135–70, 222–31. Stoker Hunt, *Ouija: The Most Dangerous Game* (New York: Barnes and Noble, 1985), 67–68.

11 *Doorways to Danger* (London: Evangelical Alliance, 1987), 3.

12 Telephone conversation with Ed Warren, October 17, 1992; Hunt, *Ouija*, 71.

13 William Barrett, "On Some Experiments with the Ouija Board and Blindfolded Sitters," *Proceedings of the American Society for Psychical Research* (September 1914), 381–94.

14 Barrett, *On the Threshold*, 181.

15 Hereward Carrington, *The Problems of Psychical Research* (New York: Dodd, Mead, 1921), 249.

16 G. Godfrey Raupert, "The Truth About the Ouija Board," *The Ecclesiastical Review* (November 1918), 474–75.

17 Martin Ebon, ed., *The Satan Trap: Dangers of the Occult* (New York: Doubleday, 1976), ix.

NOTES

18 Carl Wickland, *Thirty Years Among the Dead* (1924; reprint, Toronto: Coles, 1980), 28–29.
19 H. Richard Neff, *Psychic Phenomena and Religion* (Philadelphia: Westminster, 1971), 131.
20 Robert H. Ashby, *The Guide Book for the Study of Psychical Research* (New York: Weiser, 1972), 182.
21 Ed Warren and Lorraine Warren, with Robert D. Chase, *Graveyard* (New York: St. Martin's, 1992), 137.
22 *Doorways to Danger*, 2.
23 M. Haldeman, *Can the Dead Communicate with the Living?* (New York: Revell, 1920), 116.
24 Letter from Russell Parker, November 8, 1992.

CHAPTER 14: EDGAR CAYCE AND THE A.R.E.

1 Jon Klimo, *Channeling* (Los Angeles: Tarcher, 1987), 23. Dixon's quote is on the cover of Gina Cerminara's *Many Mansions* (see note 20).
2 Thomas Sugrue, *There Is a River* (1945; reprint, New York: Dell, 1967), 14.
3 Mary Ellen Carter and William A. McGarey, *Edgar Cayce on Healing* (New York: Paperback Library, 1972), 8–9.
4 Ibid., 9.
5 *A.R.E. Introductory Brochure*, 6. *Give Your Life New Meaning* brochure and A.R.E. website.
6 Sugrue, *There Is a River*, 200.
7 Ibid., 210.
8 Albert E. Turner, "Is Reincarnation in the Bible?" *The Searchlight* (December 1958), 2.
9 *A.R.E. Organization Benefits*.
10 J. Gordon Melton, Jerome Clark, and Aidan A. Kelly, *New Age Almanac* (Chicago: Visible Ink Press, 1991), 45.
11 Russell Chandler, "New Age Ventures into Cayce's Realm," *Los Angeles Times*, February 25, 1989, II–6.
12 Melton, *New Age Almanac*, 45. The positive response to a series of books based on the Edgar Cayce readings, published with the Paperback Library imprint, "placed Hugh Lynn in charge of a rapidly expanding association and a growing publication program which was being pursued by the foundation" (ibid).
13 Ibid., 174–75; *A.R.E. Organization Benefits*.
14 *Give Your Life New Meaning* brochure and A.R.E. website.
15 Edgar Evans Cayce, *Edgar Cayce on Atlantis* (New York: Warner, 1968), 27.

16 Jeffrey Furst, *Edgar Cayce's Story of Jesus* (1968; reprint, New York: Berkley, 1970), 23 (reading 2067–7), 76–77.

17 Ibid., 79.

18 Ibid., 83.

19 Ibid., 310–37.

20 Gina Cerminara, *Many Mansions* (1950; reprint, New York: New American Library, 1967), 63.

21 Ibid.

22 Turner, "Is Reincarnation in the Bible?" 4.

23 Sugrue, *There Is a River*, 305.

24 For a Christian response to reincarnation see: Mark Albrecht, *Reincarnation: A Christian Appraisal* (Downers Grove, Ill.: InterVarsity Press, 1982); Maurice S. Rawlings, *Life Wish* (Nashville: Thomas Nelson, 1981); Norman L. Geisler and J. Yutaka Amano, *The Reincarnation Sensation* (Wheaton, Ill.: Tyndale, 1986).

25 Robert Somerlott, *"Here, Mr. Splitfoot": An Informal Exploration into Modern Occultism* (New York: Viking, 1971), 266 67.

26 Ibid., 269.

27 Kurt Koch, *Demonology, Past and Present* (Grand Rapids: Kregel, 1973), 124.

28 Sugrue, *There Is a River*, 288.

29 John Warwick Montgomery, *Principalities and Powers* (Minneapolis: Bethany, 1973), 126.

CHAPTER 15: SUN MYUNG MOON AND THE UNIFICATION CHURCH

1 Many of the publications listed in the bibliography briefly cover Unification Church history.

2 Art Toalson, "The Unification Church Aims a Major Public Relations Effort at Christian Leaders," *Christianity Today*, April 19, 1985, 51.

3 Paul Carden, "Crisis of the Cults," *World Pulse* (September 17, 1999), 6.

4 Jane D. Mook, "New Growth on Burnt-Over Ground III: The Unification Church," *A.D.* (May 1974), 33.

5 Ibid.

6 Wi Jo Kang, "The Influence of the Unification Church in the United States of America," *Missiology, An International Review* (July 1975), 360. The accusations of immorality are briefly discussed in Ruth A. Tucker, *Another Gospel* (Grand Rapids: Zondervan, 1989), 249–50.

7 Paul Farhi, "Moon Pledges Washington Times Support," *Washington Post*, July 22, 1991, G-1; John B. Judis, "Rev. Moon's Rising Political Influence," *U.S. News and World Report*, March 27, 1989, 29.

8 "Bridgeport U. Closes Deal to Cede Control," *New York Times*, May 30, 1992, A-25.

9 *Watchman Expositor* 17, 2 (2000), 23.

10 Kang, "The Influence of the Unification Church," 359.

11 Dean Peerman, "Korean Moonshine," *Christian Century*, December 4, 1974, 1139.

12 Robert S. Ellwood, *Religious and Spiritual Groups in Modern America* (Englewood Cliffs, N.J.: Prentice-Hall, 1973), 292.

13 "Moon Landing in Manhattan," *Time*, September 30, 1974, 69.

14 J. Gordon Melton, "What Is Moon Up to?" *Christianity Today*, April 7, 1978, 49.

15 *Divine Principle*, 2d ed. (Washington, D.C.: Holy Spirit Association, 1973), 9. *Divine Principle* is the key doctrinal authority of the Unification church, hereinafter cited as *DP*.

16 *DP*, 118.

17 *The Master Speaks*, 7:1. *The Master Speaks* (hereinafter abbreviated MS) consists of questions and answers transcribed from tapes taken when Moon visited the U.S. in March and April 1965.

18 MS, 7:4.

19 MS, 7:5.

20 *DP*, 210–11.

21 *DP*, 212.

22 *Christianity in Crisis* (Washington, D.C.: Holy Spirit Association, 1974), 12–13.

23 *DP*, 143.

24 *DP*, 145.

25 MS, 4(2):9.

26 *DP*, 500–01.

27 *DP*, 72–73.

28 *DP*, 75.

29 *DP*, 190.

30 *DP*, 191.

31 MS, 6:4.

32 Arthur Ford, *Unknown but Known* (New York: New American Library, 1968), 119–20.

33 MS, 4(2):10.

34 Young Oon Kim, *Divine Principle and Its Application* (Washington, D.C.: Holy Spirit Association, 1968), x.

35 Mook, "New Growth on Burnt-Over Ground III," 34.

36 Kang, "The Influence of the Unification Church," 368.

37 John Dart, "Cult's Goal: 'Power to Rev. Moon,'" *Los Angeles Times*, January 1976, I–3.

38 *120 Day Training Manual* (photocopy), 2, 41, 64, 96, 101–2, 114, 160, 392, etc.
39 John Maust, "The Moonies Cross Wits with Cult-watching Critics," *Christianity Today*, July 20, 1979, 39.
40 Moon's "Causa Seminar Speech," August 29, 1985, 7–8 (italics added), quoted by James A. Beverly, "The Unification Church," in *Evangelizing the Cults*, ed. Ronald Enroth (Ann Arbor, Mich.: Servant, 1990), 73. For a survey of key church beliefs and for suggestions for responding to Unification theology and evangelizing church members, this book is helpful.
41 For a detailed examination of Unification Church theology see John Ankerberg and John Weldon, *Encyclopedia of Cults and New Religions* (Eugene, Ore.: Harvest House, 1999), 472–82.

CHAPTER 16: THE NEW AGE MOVEMENT

1 Ruth A. Tucker, *Another Gospel* (Grand Rapids: Zondervan, 1989), 319
2 J. Gordon Melton, Jerome Clark, and Aidan A. Kelly, *New Age Almanac* (Chicago: Visible Ink Press, 1991), ix.
3 Russell Chandler, *Understanding the New Age* (Dallas: Word, 1991), 4.
4 Ibid., 5.
5 Elliot Miller, *A Crash Course on the New Age Movement* (Grand Rapids: Baker, 1989), 183.
6 Prepared by Evangelical Ministries to New Religions, P.O. Box 10000, Denver, CO 80210.
7 Chandler, *Understanding the New Age*, 5.
8 Robert J. L. Burrows, "The Coming of the New Age," in *The New Age Rage*, ed. Karen Hoyt and J. I. Yamamoto (Old Tappan, N.J.: Revell, 1987), 21–27.
9 Melton, Clark, and Kelly, *New Age Almanac*, 16. See 6–8, 16–18 for more details.
10 Ibid., 4–5.
11 Burrows, "Coming of the New Age," 27.
12 Ibid., 28.
13 J. Gordon Melton, *Encyclopedic Handbook of Cults in America* (New York: Garland, 1986), 110.
14 Burrows, "Coming of the New Age," 28; Melton, *Encyclopedic Handbook of Cults*, 200–203.
15 Burrows, "Coming of the New Age," 29; James W. Sire, *The Universe Next Door* (Downers Grove, Ill.: InterVarsity Press, 1976), 183–84.
16 Burrows, "Coming of the New Age," 29–30.
17 Ibid., 30. See chapter 6, "Transpersonal Psychology: Psychology and Salvation Meet."

18 Douglas R. Groothuis, *Unmasking the New Age* (Downers Grove, Ill.: InterVarsity Press, 1986), 77–78.

19 Ibid., 81.

20 Burrows, "Coming of the New Age," 31.

21 Melton, Clark, and Kelly, *New Age Almanac*, 3.

22 Miller, *Crash Course on the New Age Movement*, 18.

23 Ibid., 19.

24 Ibid.

25 Burroughs, "Coming of the New Age," 247–55; Groothuis, *Unmasking the New Age*, 167.

26 See Walter H. Elwell, ed., *Topical Analysis of the Bible* (Grand Rapids: Baker, 1991), 1–68, for Scripture references on "The Personal God."

27 Evangelical Ministries to New Religions, P.O. Box 10000, Denver, CO 80210, March 1985, 1–2.

28 Douglas Groothuis, *Confronting the New Age* (Grand Rapids: Baker, 1988), 19–20.

29 Ibid., 20–31. The comments in brackets are made by the present writer, not by Groothuis.

30 Randall Baer, *Inside the New Age Nightmare* (Lafayette, La.: Huntington, 1989), 172–74.

31 Ibid., 174–75.

32 Ibid., 178.

33 Ibid., 186.

34 Ibid., 180–81.

35 Letter from Randall Baer's wife, Victoria, May 12, 1992.

CHAPTER 17: THE CHRISTIAN IN AN AGE OF CONFUSION

1 Gleason L. Archer, *The Wycliffe Bible Commentary*, ed. Charles F. Pfeiffer and Everett F. Harrison (Chicago: Moody, 1962), 619.

2 John Ankerberg and John Weldon's *Encyclopedia of Cults and New Religions* (Eugene, Ore.: Harvest House, 1999) contains a Doctrinal Appendix (661–727) that provides helpful "information on major doctrinal themes. It offers quick comparisons and contrasts to any group's teachings on important subjects" (661).

corrupt organisations and their practices (see Chapter Three) is also introduced. Primarily, though, these discussions allow the book to build a more nuanced and comprehensive discussion of state crime and state immorality/deviance.